World-famous as a writer, D... analyst, economist and social thinker. She was born in Sinyang (Henan), China, in 1917, and was educated in Beijing and at Brussels University. She then worked as a midwife in Sichuan province during the Japanese invasion. Her first book, *Destination Chunking*, was published in 1942. In 1944 she entered London University to complete her medical studies, graduating LRCP, MRCS, MBBS in 1948. She subsequently worked as a doctor in Hong Kong until 1952, the publication year of her first major success, *A Many-Splendoured Thing*. Dr Han then moved to Malaysia, where she practised medicine until the mid 1960s and wrote several highly acclaimed novels. The publication of her autobiographies established her as one of a handful of definitive authorities on contemporary China, in demand as a lecturer at leading international universities. She has also lectured on litera-ture, perhaps most notably in her course in Singapore on contempor-ary Asian literature attended by many well-known Asian scholars, poets and writers. She has been married for many years to Colonel Vincent Ruthnaswamy, and lives in Switzerland between trips to China and lecturing engagements all over the world.

Aamer Hussein

Aamer Hussein, who edited and introduces this volume, was born in Karachi, Pakistan, in 1955, and has a degree from London Univer-sity in South Asian studies. He has worked as a researcher, script editor, translator and consultant for films and television but now concentrates on writing fiction and literary criticism. He is inter-ested in the relationship between history and literature in Asian writing, and it was in the context of his research in contemporary literature that he realized the seminal importance of Dr Han's work. He has since interviewed her and written about her work in depth and has chaired lectures given by her in London.

Also by Han Suyin

Autobiography:

The Crippled Tree (London, 1965)

A Mortal Flower (London, 1967)

Birdless Summer (London, 1968)

My House Has Two Doors (London, 1980; published in two volumes in paperback, the second volume entitled *Phoenix Harvest*)

A Share of Loving (London, 1987)

Fleur de Soleil: Histoire de ma vie (Paris, 1988)

Novels:

Destination Chungking (London, 1942)

A Many-Splendoured Thing (London, 1952)

... And the Rain My Drink (London, 1956)

The Mountain Is Young (London, 1958)

Cast But One Shadow and *Winter Love* (London, 1961)

The Four Faces (London, 1963)

Till Morning Comes (London, 1982)

The Enchantress (London, 1985)

Biography:

The Morning Deluge: Mao Tsetung and the Chinese Revolution 1893–1953 (London, 1972)

Wind in the Tower: Mao Tsetung and the Chinese Revolution 1949–1975 (London, 1976)

General Non-fiction:

China in the Year 2001 (London, 1967)

Asia Today (Montreal, 1969)

Lhasa, the Open City (London, 1977)

Han Suyin's China (Oxford, 1987)

TIGERS AND BUTTERFLIES

Selected Writings on Politics, Culture and Society

by Han Suyin

Edited and with an introduction by
Aamer Hussein

Earthscan LONDON

This collection first published in Great Britain 1990
by Earthscan Publications Ltd
3 Endsleigh Street, London WC1H 0DD

British Library Cataloguing in Publication Data
Han, Suyin, *1917-*
   Tigers and butterflies: selected writings on politics,
   culture and society.
   1. Society
   2. Title
   301

ISBN 1-85383-069-0

Production by David Williams Associates (01-521 4130)
Typeset by DP Photosetting, Aylesbury, Bucks
Printed in Great Britain by WBC (Print) Ltd, Bristol
and bound by W.H. Ware & Sons Ltd, Clevedon, Avon

Earthscan Publications is a wholly owned and editorially
independent subsidiary of the International Institute for
Environment and Development (IIED).

Contents

Introduction

by Aamer Hussein

HAN SUYIN - her family name is Zhou, her given name Guanghu - was born in 1917 in Sinyang, Henan, in the brief period between the installation of Sun Yatsen's republic, which overthrew the corrupt Qing dynasty, and the student movement of 4 May 1919, the harbinger of a new intellectual epoch. Her father came from a landowning family, the Zhou clan from Sichuan. He had studied engineering in Belgium, where he met and married his Belgian wife, who accompanied him to China when he returned to work on the railways. Han Suyin grew up in a semi-feudal, semi-colonial Peking; Sun's revolution had been subverted by the new president, Yuan Shikai, and China was still in the hands of foreign and feudal powers.

Images of dead babies wrapped in newspaper, of stone-eyed beggars kicked as they clawed their way through crowds, of rickshaw-drivers whipped like beasts on the city streets, haunt Han Suyin's reminiscences of her childhood. This early recognition of poverty, of hardship and human suffering, led her to her initial sense of vocation: the elimination of disease. In conflict with a mother whose European values constantly undermined her identity, triply handicapped by gender, financial stringency and a convent education inadequate for her academic needs, Han Suyin earned her university fees by working as a typist for a fraction of the salary paid to a white employee in the China of the 1930s. Her knowledge of Chinese was also insufficient and had to be supplemented by private lessons. Nevertheless, in 1933 she succeeded in entering Peking's Yenjing University. When her savings ran out, she managed to obtain a scholarship to continue her medical studies in Belgium, where she studied from 1935 to 1938.

Her experience of Europe on the brink of war, its racist politics and imperial policies, strengthened her sense of Chinese identity; the news of Japan's invasion of Peking compelled her to return, leaving her studies incomplete. On her voyage home, she met the

1

Chinese military officer Tang Paohuang, whom she married the same year.

Trapped once again in a militaristic, feudal milieu, she used her medical training to work as a midwife in Sichuan province. Reconnected with roots, immersed in the life of China's rural poor, she became aware of the need for revolutionary change, though she had little or no contact with the burgeoning Communist movement and its theories and doctrines. Her sojourn in the Sichuan country-side, and her experience of the heroic peasant resistance to the Japanese invasion, inspired her first book, *Destination Chungking* (1942). She had never before thought of writing, and dismisses the book – a collaboration with an American missionary – as a fledgeling work. It is interesting to observe, however, that her literary career already closely paralleled her medical career; the two were to be intertwined for more than two decades. Obliged to conceal her identity for fear of her husband's conservative reprisal, she now took the pseudonym that was to bring her renown. Suyin, her chosen forename, means "little voice"; the surname Han evokes China's vast ethnic majority. (The surname is placed first in the accepted Chinese manner.) "The little voice of China" – the choice of a name signals her commitment. Already, she was compelled to give a voice to the dispossessed of her country: women, peasants, rickshaw-pullers, the victims of war and social injustice. *Destination Chungking* was also inspired by the need – advocated by Zhou Enlai, whom Han Suyin now encountered for the first time – for Chinese people of all political persuasions to form a united front or coalition, beyond ideologies, to resist the Japanese. Her choice of the English language, too, was a consciously political decision: she recognized the need to inform the increasingly indifferent West of China's need for support in its massive struggle to re-establish autonomy.

Han Suyin did not write again for a decade. Her husband was transferred to England as military attaché in 1942, and she followed him there with their adopted infant daughter, Yungmei. Exiled from the Chinese causes she had fervently espoused, alienated from her Kuomintang husband's increasingly Fascist ideology, she turned to the reading of historical and political texts that had been inaccessible to her in China. Edgar Snow's seminal work, *Red Star Over China*, with its documentation of Mao Zedong's Long March, filled in the gaps of her knowledge; she was now aware that revolution was inevitable, that it would be a peasant revolt, and that liberation, when it came, would come from the Communists. In 1944, she resumed her medical studies on a grant from the British Council.

Her husband left for China in 1945; she stayed behind with their daughter, supplementing a small scholarship by working, once again, as a typist.

Han Suyin qualified as a medical practitioner in 1949. Her husband had been killed in the war between the Kuomintang and the Communists in 1947. She was faced with an inevitable choice: to remain in the West, a permanent expatriate; or risk a return to Communist China, where her feudal origins would be further complicated by her status as a Kuomintang war widow. She decided instead to accept a post as a surgeon in Hong Kong, where she could wait on the borders of the mainland until China was ready to accept her.

The story of her years in Hong Kong, *A Many-Splendoured Thing* (1952), was the first major achievement of Dr Han's magnificent career as Asia's leading woman of letters. The rudiments of her political, philosophical and social thinking are clearly discernible in this early work, which describes in tense and teeming detail the difficult economics of being an expatriate, a woman and a professional in a colonial enclave. The novel, with its ingenious juxtaposition of poetry and polemic, had an immeasurable impact, articulating as it did the concerns of an Asian generation in the process of self-decolonization.

For another 15 years, writing was to serve as an escape-valve from her chosen vocation, medicine. In 1952 she moved to Malaya, where her anti-colonial stance was reiterated even more fiercely in her polyphonic recreation of the guerrilla war, *And the Rain My Drink* (1956). The British colonial establishment saw her as a revolution- ary writer, a threat to their values: her books were an incitement to revolt, feminist and highly critical of imperialist mores. For Han Suyin, writing is an attempt to shatter antiquated structures both mental and material. Her novels of this period are bulletins from the front-lines, erasing boundaries between literary and documentary texts, innovative in design and intent, prefiguring by a decade the still-emerging genre of the post-colonial Asian novel. Her writings included South and South-East Asia, engaging with the cultural politics of the entire region. *The Mountain Is Young* (1958) figures a woman in the act of writing, drawing parallels between feminist liberation and struggles for national independence. *The Four Faces* (1963) situates a debate on the uses of literature within the genre- bending framework of a suspense thriller. Her expatriate experience had made her a writer for all Asia; but a return to China was still necessary to her understanding of current events. In 1956 she was allowed to revisit Peking after twenty years. Her encounter with Chinese socialism had a profound effect on the evolution of her social thought; its tenets, embodied by her friend and mentor Zhou Enlai, bound together the varied strands of her intellectual experience in a nexus of ideas for a new, autonomous Asia, free of need, imperialist hegemony and the strangleholds of monopoly capitalism and of a neo-colonial economy. She had often discussed, in her fiction, the writer's responsibility, the need to polemicize, struggle and subvert. Fiction is, at times, an inadequate vehicle for the formulation of ideas; Han Suyin's observations of a rapidly changing Asia demanded a suppler, more transparent and succinct form. Then, as now, she insisted on the inextricability of art from economics.

The Hong Kong journal *Eastern Horizon*, then recently established, provided a perfect platform for Han Suyin to enter into a dialogue on an immediate polemic level with Asian writers and readers. Aware of the diversity of this polymorphous continent, she could nevertheless indicate areas of common concern. In her use of the flexible framework of the short essay, she was echoing the radical mode of the *zawen* or satirical prose piece, adopted by Lu Xun, the genius of the May 4 movement, to articulate his political preoccupations. Consciously or unconsciously, she was mirroring his move from fiction to polemic, her discursive prose, like his, pared down to its bones, its taut simplicity concealing obliquity and paradox. The essays of the early 1960s reflect her strong sense of Asian identity and, in the aftermath of her intellectual relocation in China, an interest in Chinese socialism, in its pragmatic aspects, as a possible model for other Asian countries.

In her longer works, too, she was exploring new horizons. The firm historicism of her world-view resulted in her masterwork, the serial autobiography which in its ensemble constitutes an unofficial or subaltern history of China, from the last years of the Qing Dynasty to the early years following the death of Mao Zedong and Zhou Enlai. In the mid 1960s she gave up medical practice to dedicate herself to the task of chronicling China's most tumultuous century in an ambitious interweaving of memoir, oral history, documentary evidence and lyrical reminiscence.* She left Malaysia

* *The Crippled Tree* (1965) was followed by *A Mortal Flower* (1967), *Birdless Summer* (1968) and *My House Has Two Doors* (1980), published in two volumes in paperback, the second volume entitled *Phoenix Harvest. A Share of Loving* (1987) is a memoir of Han Suyin's Indian in-laws. *Fleur de Soleil* (1988), which has appeared only in French, is a condensed account of Dr Han's life and an indispensable key/guide to her work as a whole.

that year to lead a peripatetic life, with Switzerland as a base. A new stage in her career, as an unofficial spokesperson for China's continuing revolution, partially imposed upon her by the exigence of the West's academies and their urgency to learn about China, left her with little leisure time.

She added another dimension to her career; having no formal education in political theory or history, she began to lecture regularly all over the world. The publication of Han Suyin's autobiographies coincided with the crucial events of the 1960s: waves of protest in the wake of escalating American violence in Vietnam, the Cultural Revolution in China, the student uprisings of that period. Dr Han's best writings of the decade 1965-75 reflect her involvement in current affairs all over the world. Her series of essays recounting her American lecture tour are the most perfect examples of her skill as a polemicist and satirist. Her acerbic critique of US policies, both domestic and foreign, gained her many enemies; she was also iconized for her forthright position on Vietnam and her firm stance against imperialism and Western patriarchy. She had been blacklisted during the McCarthy era for her radical sympathies, and until 1977 was barred from visiting the USA without a special permit. Her account of her visit transforms realistic social reportage into an allegory of political paranoia and delusion akin to her later imaginative work, *The Enchantress* (1985). In other accounts of her travels – her Australian and Algerian journeys – she pauses to speak for a significant minority, the Aborigines, or to deconstruct the myth, and question the politics, of a colonialist writer, Camus.

In the first half of the 1970s she laboured on her massively detailed history of Mao Zedong and the Cultural Revolution, entirely unable to write in a more personal vein during that turbulent period. The publication of further instalments of her autobiography was also suspended until the end of the decade.

Han Suyin's first full-length work about the Cultural Revolution, *Phoenix Harvest*, was published in 1980, but several of her shorter writings offer first-hand accounts of the period. A hitherto unpublished piece from the 1970s, "Water too pure", employs the techniques of fiction to offer oral testimonies of the victims and survivors of the upheaval. After the death of Mao and the fall of his wife and her acolytes, Han Suyin's articles reflect the euphoria of a newly discovered freedom and the optimism of a new age.

In the 1980s, Dr Han continues to lecture and write about Chinese economics and political events, combining a scientist's precise analysis of technological and ecological facts with a seasoned political commentator's analyses of social change. A continuing critique of the First World's economic and technological domination of the "developing" countries underwrites her research and documentation. Though she has often been criticized by Western sinologists in the post-Mao era for her supposedly partisan politics, a careful reading of her work displays her distance from all ideological closures and political orthodoxies. However, she is not prepared to disclaim her contentions and beliefs of the early years of the Cultural Revolution, preferring that her writings of the time be read in the context of her entire oeuvre, to trace the itinerary of her thinking and the parallel movement in contemporary historical thought. A forthcoming work is her biography of Zhou Enlai, which should give her an opportunity to conduct a trenchant enquiry into the events in China's history which she believes should be re-evaluated: Mao's career, the Cultural Revolution, and the positive lessons of both.

Constantly aware of the reversals to feudal modes and actions that bedevil China's route to progress, she still believes that China's liberation by the Communists was a significant advance, and she remains deeply involved, part-participant, part-observer, in China's long march into the twenty-first century. China, she says, like all Asia, must find its own road and its own models: no Western model will suffice.

Here, in *Tigers and Butterflies*, is Han Suyin's voice at its most engaged and personal: this selection of her hitherto uncollected writings bears witness to the amplitude of her vision and the singular integrity of an exceptional writer.

London, November 1989

Acknowledgements

Thanks, above all, to Han Suyin, who as always proved an invaluable source of support: she led me to many unpublished pieces, and provided information on others, some of them pseudonymous, others published in journals. However, aside from suggesting a certain cohesive outline, she left the final selection entirely to me. Given the density and diversity of the materials at my disposal, I could not have made the final selection without the expert editorial guidance and discretion of Margaret Busby, with whom I have always agreed on essentials, including the title. All the essays in our selection are taken from the Hong Kong journal *Eastern Horizon*, except for "The Aborigines", which first appeared in *The New Yorker*, "Land and water in China", which was published in the *Great Britain-China Journal*, "Two weeks in Beijing", which has appeared in *China Review* (Hong Kong), and "Water too pure", which will appear in a forthcoming anthology of fiction in support of the ANC, from Lawrence & Wishart. "Zhou Enlai: a personal memory" first appeared in *China Reconstructs*, and "Looking forward", hitherto unpublished, is based on a lecture delivered at the University of Edmonton, Alberta, Canada.

AH
November 1989

A note on spelling:
In keeping with the current trend in Chinese studies, Dr Han has recently adapted her spelling of Chinese proper nouns from the Wade-Giles to the Pinyin system. In most cases, we have preferred to retain her original spellings.

AH and MB

Social Changes in Asia

WHEN I was ten years old I went to school in Peking in a rickshaw, a vehicle pulled by a running man. In the winter I could see along the sidewalks big or small bundles of rags. They were the dead bodies of men, women and small babies, dead of cold and starvation. There were many babies.

When I was a doctor in Hong Kong it was my job to look after the emergencies and accidents, people suddenly taken ill but too poor to call a doctor. What I remember best were the suicides. They were brought in, mostly people who had jumped in the sea because jumping in the sea cost nothing. There were sometimes five or six a day. These people killed themselves not for love but because they were dying anyway – dying of hunger. Brought back to life they cried: "Now I shall have to die all over again."

A few weeks ago I was in Central India, travelling by train through a region made desolate by famine. Forty thousand people were dying of hunger, and relief was inadequate. At every station hordes tried to get on the train, which was already full, running away from death to the big city. But it was no use, for in the city they lay about the streets, too weak to beg, waiting for the mercy of death.

This is the fundamental, inescapable fact which rules and destroys the lives of millions today: hunger, death through hunger. In the United Nations Charter are listed Four Freedoms, the first one being Freedom from Want; and without this Freedom the others are nothing but words written on the wind. It is true that man* lives not by bread alone, but without bread he cannot live at all.

No wonder that in the face of this overwhelming need Asian countries and their peoples should clamour for change, sometimes at what seems to you a heavy price in personal liberty, but not so where the only liberty left is that of death.

What do Asians want? They want freedom from want. Today's

* The term "man" is used in a purely neutral and philosophical sense here. AH.

Asians no longer believe that this freedom will be a gift of the gods, they *know* it will be a freedom *made by man*. This rediscovery of man happened to Europe during the Renaissance; it produced science, and brought about the changed world of the industrial revolution; today it is leading man to the conquest of the universe. This same belief in man's right and his ability to master his environment is strong in Asia today. Disease, ignorance, want, can be conquered by the collective, united efforts of human beings working together for the good of all. This is the tremendous change in thought which has occurred, and it cannot be stopped. Asia is undergoing, four centuries later, its own renaissance, its own industrial and technical revolution; and the only difference today between the countries of Asia is in the *speed* with which this process occurs, the methods used to achieve this aim, and the results obtained.

The more I travel, the more I realize that the fundamental differences between Asian countries today are not political. To divide the world into communist and anti-communist faiths is to obscure realities, not to explain the monstrous necessity which drives men into action. The differences are in speed and method towards a common aim: food, shelter, social security, a living wage, social justice, education; what man wants everywhere, what millions in the West have got, what millions in the East have not. In Asia today whichever country or nation is going to achieve this basic social security within the next twenty years, for the greatest number of its people, is likely to set the pattern for others. Not a pattern to imitate exactly, but a frame of reference, powerful because successful.

Here the division between technical, economic and social progress is arbitrary. Better tools and equipment, improved methods of cultivation, are both the cause and effect of higher standards of living; advances in literacy and hygiene create further demands for commodities. All advances are cumulative, each tending to reinforce the other. Ideas and concrete factors go hand in hand and mutually interact upon each other. Progress is its own motive for progress.

In this enormous revolution of Asia the fundamental relationships of the person also change. There is sometimes concern in the West over what happens to the traditional Asian big family in such countries as China, where the Asian revolution has assumed its most extreme form in speed and collective effort. I think such fears as groundless as when expressed about Russia ten or fifteen years ago. As in Europe, the patriarchal, clan family, in which all members functioned as units in a collective, now consists of the parents and their direct products, the children, and these only up to a certain age. The kindergarten, boarding school and university take on educational and parental functions to release adults for other work in the social group to which they belong. Of course feudal, big family, joint families or clans, still exist in many Asian countries, but they are getting less viable and the smaller unit is taking over everywhere.

It is incorrect to state that in China children are being taken away from their parents. On the contrary, after an initial period (as in Russia) of over-emphasis on institution life, every effort is now made to induce parents with children at the kindergartens to take them back at weekends and every night, and a home life, with separate housing for each family, is guaranteed by law. In the West this process of family fragmentation has happened slowly, and has come to be regarded as "natural evolution". In China it is the speed and scientific blueprint approach that is so much in evidence, with changes telescoping into each other at an accelerated tempo.

The problem of the relations between the sexes, woman's place in relation to man, appears to me governed by economics more than we dare to acknowledge. Equality of the sexes and emancipation of woman are ideas which have become acceptable both in East and West for the last fifty years. But many Westerners still feel that "woman's place is in the home", if no longer entirely true in the West, should be the slogan of the East. The facts are different. For a certain minority, the middle and upper class, leisure, in the guise of non-participation in work outside the house and the family, was regarded as befitting women, though it is not certain that this was truly leisure. Certainly the modern unpaid housewife, always on the go, toils harder without servants in her modern home today than her grandmother did fifty years ago when servants were plentiful. Both in the East and West woman became an object, a property acquired, her adorned idleness a way of reinforcing her owner's ego and economic importance. But everywhere in the world the majority of women of what were once called the lower classes have *always* worked, in factories, in fields, side by side with men: housekeepers, family-makers, breeders of children *and* income earners all at once. The industrial revolution in Europe had quite as many women and children working in its factories as men, because women and young children have always been paid less for their labour. In my journeys through Asia the outstanding fact to me is woman-labour, although unlike the industrial revolution in Europe child-labour seems frowned upon and condemned in most countries of Asia. I recently visited an iron mine in India with many thousands of workers: more than half were women paid at 12 annas, which is 15 Canadian cents, a day, while the men were getting 25 cents a day.

Even in certain countries where there are religious taboos against women (including religion-sanctioned polygamy), it has been a matter of course to write into constitutions equal rights for man and woman, and to give some measure of legal protection to the mother and child. Women not only have the vote, they are often asked to vote by politicians. In Malaya, for instance, women in the small villages sometimes walked for two days to get to the polling booths to vote. In Nepal, that little kingdom at the foot of the Himalayas, whole families last year in the first election ever held spent a week walking to reach the polling stations, as if they were going on religious pilgrimage. But even if equality in law is achieved, there are often slips due to tradition, prejudices or religion.

In China the new marriage law passed in 1953 provided that in cases where coercion had been used to force a girl into marriage, the wives could appeal to the courts and obtain a divorce. This was followed by a spate of suicides among men: not young people, but the middle-aged group, the round-about-forties, whose wives left them, thus causing these unhappy husbands an irrecoverable loss of face. A grim retribution for the good old days when often the only protest a wife had against ill treatment was to hang herself at the door of the house to curse it for ever. But the suicides led the government to modify the marriage law, and now divorce is difficult to obtain in China. The marriage law also established monogamy; this also created problems when a husband, faced with five or six wives to all of whom he professed equal devotion, had to choose one and let the others go. The establishment of some sort of Marriage Counsel Bureau in the People's Courts, where each individual problem was discussed over and over, was brought in to smoothen the application of this law. In other countries of Asia polygamy still exists, and there is often the complex situation of a wife becoming a lawyer, doctor or even minister in government, but at home having to share her husband with a couple of other women.

In the direction of equality, monogamy, equal pay and opportunity and education for women, no country in Asia has gone as far as China has, or in a shorter time. This works at all levels of society. With the new release of woman for productive work, tasks once considered feminine because they were menial must be taken over by organizations, such as canteens, laundries, department stores for consumer goods. In many Asian countries these facilities now exist and function round new industrial and technical projects in large cities. In China, however, where the structure of the state gears everything to the majority working class, the peasant 80 per cent of the population, canteens, homes for the aged, welfare centres, kindergartens, schools, hospitals, *must* be made to function in the countryside, and the tendency to accumulate these facilities in big cities only must be resisted. This is one of the factors which, along with the need for large aggregates of manpower for the accomplishment of big-scale projects, has shaped and brought to function the commune in China today, which I will discuss now.

But first a few words about the Asian peasant, the 80 per cent backbone folk of Asia. The Marxist idea of the industrial worker being the "working class" *par excellence* is not applicable to Asia, because in Asia it is not a fact: the term "working class" still means the worker on the soil rather than the industrial worker. This concept was developed by Mao Tse-tung, the leader of China, and is of tremendous importance; it has changed the aspect of the industrial revolution in Asia. The peasant masses, not the factory workers, are the backbone of the Chinese revolution, and remain its mainstay. Social progress must begin with the farmer, must go on in the countryside, must never forget the countryside, and from the countryside proceed to the towns, rather than the other way round. This is the reasoning followed in China today, and the much criticized commune is its concrete embodiment.

The aim of the commune (of which there are 26,000 in China) seeks to abolish the gap between town and country, between the peasantry and the beginning industrial worker, to provide a smoother switchover from peasant to mechanic, from the skilled tiller of soil to the skilled factory man. In the industrialization of Asian countries emphasis on heavy industry and its workers is apt to be done, as it was in Russia, at the expense of the agricultural proletariat. The *object* of the Chinese commune is to create the many-sided social organism whereby the agricultural worker begins to feel, think and act as industrial workers do, whereby the product of labour in the field is brought at a par with the produce of labour in a factory, whereby there can be interchange, understanding and co-operation between the peasant in the field and the worker in the factories. Perhaps it is a Utopia, but only time can tell.

The *effect* of the commune is to carry out large-scale projects, such as dam building, afforestation, killing of insect pests, improved methods of planting, and cattle and pig breeding, on a scale which individual farms or co-operatives would not be able to carry out, mobilizing large groups of people for such enterprises which otherwise would be impossible without advanced mechanization. To achieve the concrete results of mechanization *without* machines is only possible when, instead of machinery, there is a large reservoir of man-labour available. A lot of moral indignation has been cast upon this way of doing things, and certainly it does imply discipline and regimentation, not of hundreds but of millions. But there is also a great sense of togetherness, of participation, achievement and triumph over difficulties. I, for one, would prefer to see social security achieved without the harshness, the iron control and the continuous effort which strains China's people today. The question for all Asia is: how else can it be done?

It is yet too early to say whether the communes will be entirely successful. In their short life a number of modifications have been brought in, because the first blueprint was impossibly Utopian and there was strong criticism in China. It is certain that there are and will be for years problems, teething troubles, difficulties, bottlenecks, for the whole country is still in total ferment and experiment. Suppleness in agricultural policies *must* remain the keynote.

One question asked is: what are the reasons for the comparative lack of resistance, the ease with which co-operatives, then communes, were received by the Chinese peasant, as compared to the stubborn resistance to collectivization still going on in other parts of the world?

One of the emotional reasons, it seems to me, is the enthusiasm of women in China for the new social system. Perhaps because, like the landless peasant, woman has been the oppressed class, she finds a new sense of liberation and an unfolding of potentialities now which were never within her reach before; and just as the Malay or Nepalese women will walk days to vote, Chinese women are strongly in favour of the new order.

Besides the enthusiasm of women, there are other reasons: the smallness of the rich landowning class compared to the poor peasantry; the fact that in China both the army and the communist party derive an overwhelming majority of their numbers from the peasantry (the communist army has always practised the policy of helping the peasant gather in the harvest); the fact that always and at all times efforts were made to win over by persuasion and indoctrination the small landowner and capitalist, rather than by extermination; and finally that, where education of the young is concerned, no distinction is made between children of the erstwhile exploiting classes (so-called) and the exploited. In some other

14

communist countries (I am told by well informed sources) there is still discrimination in education against the children of former capitalists, but this is not practised in China.

In the attempt to break down the barrier between city and countryside, between peasant and industrial worker, China is now operating another social experiment: the breakdown of the discrimination against manual work in favour of mental work.

All societies in the world have a tendency to consider manual labour undignified, repulsive, degrading, as opposed to intellectual pursuits. People who toil physically are regarded as lower in intellect and the social scale than those who use their brains. The man who sits behind a desk and wields a rubber stamp is at an advantage over the man who walks behind a plough. In China the lettered man, the mandarin, lorded it over all others. It became an indignity to do anything with one's hands except painting or calligraphy.

In Europe too this aspect of work prevailed, a snobbery which has not disappeared, in spite of the Industrial Revolution. As Sir Charles Snow said recently (he is both a scientist and a novelist), it is a fashion of Western intellectuals to scorn the gains of industrialization, and to look upon practitioners of applied sciences, as distinguished from pure scientists, as second-rate minds.

This looking down also falls upon craftsmanship (except when dignified as Art). It becomes foolish and dangerous in an Asia beginning to be industrialized, because it means that manual work connected with the assembly and use of machinery is left in the hands of people looked upon as only capable of menial work, who therefore have no pride in their work, and are not even adequately paid. This divorce between brain work and the technical side makes for incompetence, waste and unrealistic muddle. In Europe and America people grow up with machines round them; any American child plays with machine toys from the toddler stage. This must also happen in Asia, where engineers, technicians, agronomists, doctors, are needed on a vast scale. It can only happen when people think becoming farmers or mechanics a fine thing, instead of merely studying books which have nothing to do with the realities they grapple with, then drifting into unemployment in the big cities.

The aim in China, where everything is planned and blueprinted to a degree almost impossible to imagine, is to bring mental and manual labour on a more equal basis. Education must be also the learning of techniques, agricultural and industrial, so that the same person can be a bachelor of arts, able to look after pigs, drive a bus or repair a motorcar. Thus 50,000 students, intellectuals, professors in universities, constructed a dam for water near Peking the year before last (1958), completing the work in 148 days by giving two weeks of labour each to this project. No machinery was used. I saw afterwards several of them, all pleased as boy scouts at having thus proved themselves capable of "roughing it".

In other countries of Asia we find thousands of university graduates perfectly willing to sit behind a desk and look on while other men toil; but the idea of dirtying their own hands along with workers, shoulder to shoulder, is not only unpleasant but revolting. In China all university students are required to do manual work in factory or field for part of the year.

I wonder sometimes whether this Utopian scheme, this return to a primitive, golden-age type of communism, can succeed. The tendency to prefer a desk and a rubber stamp is very strong. It is shown sometimes by the very people who made the revolution, i.e., the communist cadres. Time and again the cadres have had to be shaken up and sent down to do a bit of manual work in the country because they were committing the fault of all bureaucrats, commandism (which is sitting behind a desk and giving orders), shirking work in the villages in order to congregate in city offices to sit behind desks. In the last two years an intensive drive has sent back to the countryside for agricultural work, varying from two weeks to six months up to three years, 60 per cent of the communist cadres, and even Cabinet Ministers have had spells of four weeks each at dam building. This policy, say the communists, restores the dignity of labour, destroys the delusion that book learning alone will solve problems, brings intellectuals into contact with the actual practical aspects of the problems they discuss. But it is also a shrewd policy to keep the government in close touch with the people in the countryside and to control the young by employing them on farms during the holidays instead of letting them roam about. Certainly it makes for very little leisure for the individual in China today.

I have tried to give here an idea of the industrial revolution of Asia, illustrating from China not because I admire everything that is done there, but because it is the country that is changing most rapidly. The most important single factor of the industrial revolution of Asia is its *acceleration*, when we compare it to the industrial revolution of the West. That one took its time; this one is in a hurry. That one happened half unconsciously, so that some of its man-made developments appeared natural or God-made. But in this one there is a total and ever-present awareness that the future is just round the corner and can be shaped by the present, that the means of determining future prosperity depend upon the work done today, the development of national resources by the people themselves, by their own efforts. The sooner this speed, this hurry, is recognized as legitimate, the quicker will adjustments be made to needs; the sooner can we all, East and West, go forward together towards a world of co-existent prosperity and peace.

(1960)

Tigers and Butterflies

L AST night I read what I think one of the funniest
books I ever came across: *The Memoirs of a Tattooist* by
Gerald Burchett. I sat, lay on my bed, and laughed till
I couldn't stand up. Maybe there is something wrong
with my sense of humour (humour: one of those things
which each country claims for itself, but not for export; humour
doesn't travel well – Thurber is solemn to Singapore); the book itself
is written earnestly enough. The last illustration convulsed me: it
was the photo of a lady with Victorian top-knot and affable and
virtuous expression, a timid locket round her neck, modestly holding
against her breasts a piece of material. From the wrists up, from the
neck down, all over the uncovered chest, shoulders, arms, and
disappearing under the wrappings further below, were interlaced
posies of flowers and baskets of fruits and hordes of butterflies.

The author is, I think, a genius. I mean, he is a man who was born
to tattoo as others are born to write, paint or compose music. When
small, he used to scratch his schoolmates with soot and his mother's
knitting needles (and was duly thrashed). He absconded from the
Royal Navy because they cramped his aspirations, and set up finally
as a tattooist and became very rich at it. He's done the skins of
thousands of people, from royalty down. The difference between a
tattooist and a tattooer, he tells us, is the difference between an artist
and a dabbler. Mr Burchett is an artist.

I learnt more about a side of human nature that I hadn't suspected
until now than if I had read a dozen Chessers and Kinseys. In the
last chapter Mr Burchett tells us how his wife (the lady described
above) was his best model. She is tattooed from neck to foot, carries
the Crucifixion upon one leg, a reproduction of some famous
Rembrandt painting on the other, and I forget the rest. With a touch
of chagrin the author tells us that she has taken to wearing gowns
with long sleeves and a high collar. He wonders why. Elsewhere in
the book he tells of the itch of lovers to get their epidermis pricked
with some enduring memento of their emotions; of the painful

erasures he undertook when the recipients of these emotions changed; and of the famous lady who carried a heart, enclosing some initials (these were changed again and again; he went through the whole alphabet with her) upon the unrevealed small of her back.

This is a book I recommend to all, the prude and those who take pride in tolerance. It made me muse upon that impulse which drives some to drink, verse or murder, and others to tattoo. I personally would hate to be tattooed; my emotions seem to get on well without the stimulus of an undying pigment set as a seal upon my skin. (Perhaps that was what *Song of Songs* meant when it said: "set me as a seal upon thy brow ... thy heart ...," but I hate to believe it, it's too awful. The seal must have been metaphorical.)

The morning after (this morning), I went into the subject of tattooing in Singapore. I already knew a fair amount, in a disorganized manner, about it. No doctor can escape it. After all, the skins of our patients are forever laid out for our inspection. Tattooing is performed in Chinatown chiefly; practitioners of the art are Chinese, and some Indians. Among Indians it is chiefly of religious significance: emblems for the pious inscribed upon their shins and ankles and wrists and sometimes foreheads. Among the Chinese it is supposed to have a sociological connotation: employed by the secret societies as a sign of brotherhood. In fact, for many years young people had been shoved into jail in Singapore because of tattoo marks upon their bodies.

Time and again newspapers carry such items:

Chong Ah Sik, aged twenty-two, waiter in The Laughing Heaven Restaurant and Dance Hall, was arrested as secret society man. He was found to have a tiger tattooed upon his shoulder. A police expert explained to the Magistrate that this was a secret society emblem....

Two years hard for Ah Sik.

Tuck Wing, aged nineteen, was arrested last night. Burn marks were found on his body. [Area not mentioned.] It is suspected that these burns were due to strong acid which he used to erase tattoo marks. Suspect denied being a secret society member. The Magistrate sentenced him to two years' hard labour.

Tattooing in Singapore is more hazardous than in London, where Mr Burchett practised.

I have often seen tattooed men in my clinic. Tigers were the most common design, and I disagree with police experts (who are *they*, anyway?) who think them only a mark of secret societydom. Tigers are associated with virility, with courage. Chinese drink tiger-bone wine, and in their dreams at night tigers burn bright to compensate for daytime miseries. I have a dear friend who every time he loses money in business dreams he is a tiger with wings, soaring high above the clouds. Hearts with arrows, according to Mr Burchett, are the most common form of expression of the love tattoo in Anglo-Saxon countries, "Love to Mum", second most common, joined hands, are non-existent among the Chinese and the Indians (the Malays don't seem to tattoo at all). Mr Burchett wonders why it is that so many men express "Momism" in tattoo, he got tired of doing Mum in London; he would get tired of tigers over here.

Coming to naked girls, etc., I've only seen a few, and they were done on Chinese who had been to Japan. They were most artistic, for as the patient moved and his muscles bulged the figure swayed and swivelled temptatiously (if there is such a word, but it sounds right for a tattoo pin-up). Our local tattooers can't do these things yet.

But I'd never seen a girl tattooed. Never in Singapore. Until today. At lunch time, I saw one.

I'd seen her dozens of times, but never noticed. However, today my mind was on tattoo. There she was, arms bared, ably shovelling back and forth the gooey shampoo suds over a head of curls. Lucy Teo is

20

a hairdresser, one of three in a shop open from 8 a.m. to 12 midnight. Before Chinese New Year they are so busy in her shop that she has benches put outside on the pavement and lines the women there, their hair in curlers, waiting for the perms to set.

As Lucy raised her arms in her tight white sleeveless dress I saw the tattoo, blue, in the armpit (which, she being Chinese, is hairless). It was a small butterfly.

I know well enough to stop and make talk, and I asked her: "What's that mark under your arm? A tattoo?"

She giggled. Yes, it was. A butterfly. Oh, couple of weeks ago. A beautician, a girl. Just returned from Japan. Studied beauty culture there. Two thousand dollars it cost her, all her savings. "It's the new fashion-lah, Doctor." A small butterfly, on leg or arm. Apparently she thought of it as in keeping with the new Dior line and the frosted lipsticks of this year. "Very fashionable now, Doctor."

I didn't tell her about Mr Burchett, and his wife covered with butterflies twenty years ago, in London. She might not have felt so fashionable. Did many girls do it now?

"Oh, some," said Lucy Teo, "but only butterflies," she specified. "It's quite smart."

"What about tigers?" I asked.

"Oh," said Lucy haughtily, "no, Doctor, too big. Tigers is vulgar, all the waiters have tigers."

Lucy has promised to take me to the tattooer (—ist) next week. The nurse in my small clinic is also going; she thinks she may have a butterfly ("Perhaps on my knee, Doctor, where no one can see it."). I say firmly that I won't be tattooed. I'll stay and watch, but I won't be tattooed. And yet, dimly, I feel, I just feel, that I might, might be tempted by just a little butterfly, for curiosity's sake. A little butterfly where nobody can see it. I hope I'm not.

(1960)

Aborigines

WHEN I landed at Dum-Dum Airdrome, in Calcutta, in the ochre dust of a spring evening, I was returning to Vincent and to home, though it was to a home I had never seen. This wasn't the first time that had happened, for we are a peripatetic couple. While I had been away, Vincent, who is an engineer, had got a temporary job in an iron mine near a village in the province of Orissa, about two hundred miles to the south. Vincent was at the airport to meet me, and the first thing he told me was that we would have to extricate from Calcutta's four million people not only ourselves but one other person - a cook. The week before, Vincent's old cook, Krishnan, who came from southern India and cooked very well, had run away with a woman from the aborigine village near the mine, and with Vincent's gold Omega watch and a bottle of whisky. The police had come and shaken their heads and taken notes. Later, they had found the woman, but she did not know where Krishnan had gone; beyond being taken to a film and being given toddy to drink, she had not received anything for letting Krishnan use her body one night through. And she had been beaten by her own man later.

Vincent knew how to accomplish things in Calcutta, and the day after I arrived we got our new cook - Abbas, thin and sad-looking, with a ravaged face arranged in wild pleats around brilliant black eyes. His left hand was crippled with rheumatism. He looked hungry and tired, but that was merely the habit of a lifetime. We thought he was nice.

That evening, after Abbas had collected his earthly goods - a small bundle, and a blanket, which he wrapped around his shoulders, and an army-issue khaki scarf, which he wound around his head - the three of us set out for Orissa. At the railway station, a clamour of porters surrounded us, wrestling for our luggage with quick but deliberately unforceful motions, in the solidarity of the poor. After a time, the chosen arranged themselves in Indian file (Indians seem to walk always separately, one after another, even when there is ample space, so that I forget that American Indians originated the word picture, and think of it as plain Indian), each with a suitcase balanced on a red scarf that he had arranged in a protective soft hoop around his skull. Vincent led, and Abbas and I followed, threading safari through the jungly tumult of moving bodies, through the iron gates and on to the platform, where the train waited, with its blind air-conditioned cars and its open third-class coaches asprawl with people.

A train official came in diffidently for a small bribe. "We have kept the compartment, sar. I myself personally saw to it. I have eight children."

A wisp of crumpled rupees passed from Vincent's hand to his.

At six in the morning, the train stopped, and bending out of the coach's sliding door, I saw Abbas, with his bundle, on the platform. This was Tatanagar, a steel town north of Pamposh, the village where we would stay, and the rest of the trip was to be made by jeep. Of course, the jeep was not ready; it was being repaired, so all that day, while Abbas and the luggage waited at the station, Vincent and I ambled about Tatanagar, with its bunched blast-furnace chimneys spouting nasturtium smoke. There was a place where ice cream could be had. It wore a proud sign across the door: "Foreign Liquor Is Sold Here Off and On." We got iced coffee with floating curds of milk that never dissolved. Later, we went to the market and bought bitter gourds and breadfruit, calabashes and jackfruit, bananas and new potatoes and cabbage, two kinds of spinach and some tomatoes and peas and papayas, tamarind and saffron, and brinjals and ladyfingers, tangerines and chilli peppers, and small fresh limes. And finally we picked up the jeep and drove to the station.

Abbas looked much better. He had had a bath and been shaved, for two annas, and he had prayed (being, like most cooks who work for foreigners, a Moslem), rolled his blanket, and acquired authority over our luggage, having spent all those hours in its company, so that it was he who now ordered the bearers to heave the suitcases on to the jeep, and he who peremptorily arranged them. Then he sat atop the most solid, holding on his knees the large basket of vegetables we had bought.

We fled through the dusk, the half-light tiring our eyes with deceptive amber shadows. Handfuls of people were returning to the villages strewn along the road, the women, with auburn clay jars upon their heads, scattered as sparrows and heedless of our jeep. Night came, and we stopped at a wayside Moslem inn with

Rembrandt lighting effects and a strong smell of the local sour beer. After a meal, we took a rough dirt road with unavoidable potholes and a smell of dust, and at length reached a cluster of huts at the foot of the iron mountains.

"We're home," said Vincent.

Home was a variation of the Nissen hut, 20 feet by 16, with a rounded aluminium roof that expanded in the heat of the day and contracted at night, with borborygmic noises. To allow for these thermal motions, the roof was separated from the walls by wire netting, through which seeped incessantly a fine red dust - iron-oxide dust - settling upon and gritting its particles into everything at all hours of the day and night, but especially around noon, when the wind rushed down into the valley from the iron mountains around us, bringing on its billows a rustle of leaves like sudden autumn. The huts had been designed by an Englishman who had seen their counterparts in a sheltered valley somewhere in a lush tropical land. Partitions of concrete, five feet eight inches high, divided our shack into cubicles - a bedroom, a bathroom, a kitchen, a living-room. Complete unprivacy was the main feature of the habitation, but it was home, full of dust and happiness, and from the start Abbas was in masterly command of the kitchen, producing Indian food and, now and then, cheese on toast or *crème au caramel* for me. There was no pork and, of course, in the land of the sacred cow, no beef, so we ate goat most of the time, salted fish occasionally, and chicken when there was no goat or fish.

"Abbas is a nice chap," Vincent said one day. "I hope he doesn't make a pass at any of the aborigine women."

He warned Abbas, who blushed and grinned and said the equivalent of: "I'm too old for that sort of thing."

"That's what Krishnan said, too," replied Vincent. "And if he hadn't run away I guess he'd have had an arrow through him by now."

Besides Abbas, we had a water boy and a sweeper, both aborigines. They cleaned the hut with docile lack of conviction. The water boy was sturdy; the sweeper was thin, and coughed, and wrapped a thin pink blanket around himself in the sharp, cold mornings. There was little to do, but their service required them to be on hand to do whatever was needed. I was irritated by this wholesale waste of manpower and work hours - three able-bodied men hanging around a small hut all day merely to pour water for baths, clean the floor and the furniture, cook three meals, and empty the commodes - but that is the way things were done, and as a transient I didn't feel I could challenge the old order. Then, there was a dhobi, to wash the clothes, and a dog boy, who came in every evening to take our dog for a walk.

We had neighbours - a couple called the Farringtons and a couple called the Teviots, both English. They lived in huts like ours. The Teviots were genuine English from England. Mrs Teviot, who read the *Observer* and the *Economist*, was obsessed by the red dust that fell, seeped and even slid into her closed suitcases, and she boiled all the water for washing the dishes and pots and pans. The Teviots had built a special stove outside the kitchen that boiled water all day, and it smoked, and the smoke drifted, with the red dust, into our hut. In spite of the stove, the Teviots both got dysentry off and on, and that, to the rest of us, was proof they were genuine English. I myself had a bout and was ashamed of this weakness, but, being "local", I recovered after a couple of days: the Teviots kept taking antibiotics, and finally came down with a vitamin deficiency. Mrs Teviot was very charming and sweet, and we got on quite well, talking about England.

The Farringtons were old India hands, and their conversation was mostly reminiscences of the old days. Mrs Farrington was worried about her weight (she was stout, on thin legs), and occasionally she mentioned going home, though she said she was happy only in India. She had acquired a few British-Indian (or Brindian, as people say in India) ways of speech; she said about sherry that it was "too heaty" for her. Mrs Teviot believed in carrying on with a smile, but Mrs Farrington believed in blowing up when necessary. Still, Mrs Farrington was very kind, and she bravely grew a garden in the midst of all the dust. She never had servant trouble, and her cook, Sethi, who wore gold rings in both his ears and had a beautiful moustache, was a marvellous cook, and always dressed in resplendent whites, with a gold-and-purple sash and headdress, as if he were the High Commissioner's butler.

On the slope above us were the mines, and round about us were the servants' houses and the homes of some Indian families, and half a mile below us was the aborigine village - thirty to forty huts of plastered mud and leafy branches thonged together with straw ropes. The aborigines are dark and quiet, with curly hair, and quiet eyes moving as do the eyes of deer. They belong to the Adivasi tribes, who live among the iron mountains of Orissa, but they go by many names, being also called Mahathos and Huths. The Adivasis are descendants of the people who lived in Orissa before the Aryan invasion from the north, over three thousand years ago, and their tribes have been gradually pushed into the least fertile places. Now they are nominally protected by the Indian government from the rapacity of the more sophisticated peoples around them. The valley fields are theirs, and they are not allowed to sell land without the permission of the government authorities, who side with the aborigines whenever it is possible. No outside unskilled labour may be introduced into these valleys; only the Adivasis are allowed to work here, so that they may not be displaced into worse poverty. But in spite of all this they are becoming steadily poorer, in the real sense of approaching total insecurity. For they are now employed to mine the iron ore in the open-cast mines - owned by a private mining company and staffed at the top levels by English and Indian managers and engineers - and have given up tilling fields. The pay is extremely low - the equivalent of 16 cents a day for a woman and 24 cents a day for a man - and as more and more land (not their own small fields but the unused mountains and valleys) is shorn of trees and turned into bare red earth by the mines, they are getting hemmed in and their fields are being smothered with red dust. They have to buy food, and although the price of food is going up all the time, their wages are the same as five years ago. And even with the government watching over them, there are many ways to cheat an aborigine, for there are still many things that he does not know. He is learning, not as slowly as some people imagine, but stumblingly, for, like all people, he is making his own mistakes.

The aborigine is darker than the Aryan Indian, of the north; he is more like the Tamil and Malayalee, of the south. His skin is reddish brown with a blue glint; as if the iron oxide of his land had been turned by alchemy into fine steel, his body glitters blue in the sun. Both the men and the women are stunted, possibly owing to malnutrition. The men, in loincloths and sometimes with blankets on their shoulders, go about carrying spears or bows and arrows in their hands. The women wear only a sari, with no choli to cover their breasts, and they twist the garment differently from the Indians elsewhere - tight around the waist, with the red border of the homespun right under the buttocks and a layer lower down, ending at the calf, and one fold brought forward over the breasts. The women's breasts are usually full and upstanding and singularly large for their small bones, perhaps because they are always carrying things on their heads - jars, bundles, kerosene tins full of water, large baskets. Their babies they carry riding on one hip. They are much freer than Indian women; they divorce and remarry easily, and they walk hand in hand with their lovers - something that is seen elsewhere in India only among the very sophisticated and the

Western-educated, and even then is considered "fast". The aborigines are animists, though their old backlog of plant-and-animal worship has an overlay of Siva Hinduism. The men drink hard – they brew their own rice beer, a muddy white liquid – and both the men and the women dance. They have communal dances – a whole village, or even two or three villages, assembling in an open space to the sound of drums, and dancing for hours or days, until everybody is tired out.

Every morning, Vincent got into the jeep and went to the deep gashes of the iron mines, eight miles from where we stayed. Sometimes I went with him. The valley was very dusty; the new roads pounded out by bulldozers and the trenches of the railway lines gouged out of the red earth were shedding and spilling and smoking red iron dust over everything at the least lift of air. Many trees had been felled, and the ones remaining along the roads were brown-red with mud and clotted dust raised by the passage of trucks and jeeps. The open-cast mines were immense red gashes lying low among the hills, some of which were 3,000 feet high, with bulldozer tracks coursing up their sides. It was a ravaged landscape, to be fled, and one could flee it by getting high enough above it among the remaining forests on top of the hills. But one day, fifty years from now, all the heights will have gone, leaving only immense areas of slag and dust, for the mountains are full of iron. Here and there were the patchwork fields and villages of the Adivasis, but since most of the able-bodied worked in the mines or on the railway, there were only old men and old women and young children about the huts.

At the mines, the men pickaxed the soil; the women filled baskets with the lumps of ore, walked over to large sieves standing here and there, sifted the rubble, filled the baskets again, and, in steady single file, with the full baskets upon their heads balanced by their swinging gait (the narrow or broad hips going up and down evenly), bore them to the cars of the small train that ran down the line. The women did most of the work – collecting, walking, and carrying. There were nearly twice as many women as men working in the mines; they put in the same hours as the men and expended more muscular energy, yet classically they got less pay. There was about them – men and women alike – gentleness and docility, patent in every movement, smile, and gesture. They caressed what they handled, brushed and swept with delicate tenderness, laid their feet dreamily on soil or grass.

Arjun Matho, the village headman, came to call at our shack one evening. He came softly – an ugly man with seamy features, eyes unevenly set and bloodshot from too much local beer, and the most hideous smile I've ever seen, black, crumbly, decayed teeth jutting toward us from a mouth whose thick lips could never meet. He wore a blanket on his shoulders, a pair of frayed khaki trousers, and laceless black Army boots, which he removed as he entered our house. He extended his right hand and arm in front of him as he came, as if cleaving the air for his body to follow. Thus he protected himself from the pollution of our shadows and our touch, made for himself a passageway of clean air through our room.

Vincent sprang up and tried to give him a seat, but Matho would not sit, though he accepted a full glass of Scotch whisky without soda and tossed it down in one gulp. He had come to ask us to a dance. His village was giving a dance in honour of the Lord Siva. The invitations, typed on slips of paper by an obliging Indian clerk in the mine office, read:

> Arjun Matho and his Adivasi village require the honour of the presence of — at their dance in honour of the Lord Siva at 7 p.m. on this tonight.

Later in the evening, we went down to the village with the Teviots.

"I do hope the Hawthorns have also been asked," Mr Teviot said.

Mr Hawthorn was the administrator of the local office of the mining company at Nalda, ten miles away. (The head office was in Calcutta.) I knew that there had been "some trouble" with the aborigines, and that Mr Hawthorn was not popular at the moment. What the trouble was I would have to find out for myself. Vincent would not tell me. "If I tell you, you'll feel there's no investigating for you to do and you'll get bored," he said.

The Hawthorns were there, standing on the edge of the flat, dusty threshing ground. Two arc lights were suspended from an electric cable that had been hooked up for the occasion to one of the mining company's shacks; ordinarily, the aborigine villages had no electricity. Silver-grey powder rose under the desultory feet of groups of girls with their arms clasped around one another's waist; they were trying out their dancing feet with tentative hopping and gliding steps. In the night, the dust smelled strongly acid and made us cough.

Arjun Matho came to salute us, and led us to an enclosure made of boughs hewn smooth and straight, and containing a table on which bottles of beer and glasses stood. It was for us, the British and the Indian administrative staff of the mines.

"For us, the untouchables," said Vincent gaily.

Matho gangled forward to Vincent to say that it was too early – the drummers were not yet ready to thump the drums. And it was so; the air was still inactive, the ferment of the dance absent.

"Come have a drink with us," said the Teviots, and we all – they, the Hawthorns, Vincent and I – went back to their hut. Mrs Teviot kept bunches of peacock feathers in pewter and silver vases, which gave the living-room an odd Victorian look.

We sat around and had drinks – gin and fresh lemon – made by Mrs Teviot and served in small pewter goblets by her bearer. Her cook was sick, not with dysentery but with tuberculosis. He hadn't felt well, and the doctor, suspecting appendicitis, had had him removed by jeep to the nearest hospital, 90 miles away; there it had turned out to be tuberculosis.

Soon the Teviots would have to go to Calcutta to find a cook, and Vincent told them how to go about it. I praised Abbas, thinking Mrs Teviot might want a cook of his sort, but she was dubious. Upon questioning me, she found that the cooking I extolled was Indian, and she and Mr Teviot liked curries done the English way. India is still full of Indian cooks brainwashed into cooking English curries; after that education, they don't know how to cook the Indian way any more and no Indian will employ them. Abbas was the unspoiled kind, and his curries raised the hair on my head. Mrs Teviot was therefore not convinced that Abbas was a good cook, or a clean one.

Mr Hawthorn talked about the Adivasis, his point being that since they were "children of nature", they "ought to stick to their own traditional ways" and not "meddle" in things they did not understand, like business administration and trade unions, or do anything except carry the iron ore in baskets and be grateful for their daily wage.

I stared at him with as much self-control as I could muster while he unwound about the aborigines. I had heard this talk, with no variations, about the Chinese, the Japanese, the Malays, the Indians, the Siamese, and other Asians who have lately taken to new ways and made neither more nor less of a mess of them that the Whites, who, according to Hawthorn, were naturally endowed with more steadiness, caution and foresight, were capable of the scientific approach, and were less impulsive. "Less children of nature," I interpolated, at which he nodded, very pleased with my co-operativeness.

"Why," said Mr Hawthorn, growing lyrical, "d'you know what happened only fifteen years ago? For a case of whisky – twelve bottles, to be exact – our company was able to buy twenty-five square miles of ore-bearing country. Twenty-five square miles!" He beamed all over his face, his voice choking on a baritone tremolo of greed and awe. "Millions and millions of tons of iron ore for one case of whisky. But now you have strikes and Communist ideas, and – would you believe it? – they assaulted my Indian manager, the women workers did, some years ago. Our lives were in danger. I'm not exaggerating." And then that chap Matho, the headman, had made such trouble about the shrine.

"The shrine?" I asked. "What shrine?"

Mrs Hawthorn turned to her husband a face screwed up in warning. "Darling, argling-bargling again about Matho?" she said. "The poor man has had such a lesson with his construction débâcle."

"Just what I was saying," Mr Hawthorn replied. "I told Matho to stick to what he knew – a bit of farming, growing vegetables for us, and keeping poultry. *We* could use his eggs and milk and cabbages. We'd pay him well. But no. He's got to go and lose a packet on construction. Buildings for the workers! The chump didn't know the first thing about building. He went and lost a packet. They *will* go and try to ape their betters."

"What about this shrine?" I pursued, tactless and tenacious.

Mrs Teviot and Mrs Hawthorn spoke of cooks and laundry, and, outside, Mrs Farrington's laughter boomed as the couple passed the Teviots' shack on their way to the village dancing ground.

"Well, m'dear," said Mr Teviot. "It's time we went, isn't it? Mustn't be late, you know. They might not like it."

We walked down the slope again. On the flat ground, the drums were beginning to boom.

Vincent grinned at me and said, "You find out, Sherlock Holmes. I won't say a word." And he didn't.

The Siva festival was not a success. The village was tired and surly; there was something tense and bad-tempered in the air, in spite of Matho's good manners. There was too much dust on the threshing ground. The drummers banged on their drums – large drums tied to their bodies, and small, long-stemmed drums – but in a rough, angry way. And although the dance leaders, one at each end of a long row of dancers, had devised some intricate new steps, they tried them only half-heartedly, then gave up. The atmosphere was oppressive, like the dust that swirled round and reached us in the reserved enclosure, and after an hour or so we left, a little sick with sour, milky beer.

The next morning, Mrs Farrington dropped in, and I thought she might tell me why the Siva festival had been so unhappy.

"What about the shrine?" I asked.

"Oh, we don't like to talk about it," she said. "Didn't Vincent tell you? No, I guess he's too new. Between you and me and the gatepost, it's Hawthorn's fault. Now, don't go repeating it. I guess all the higher-ups in the Calcutta head office know about it, but they like to keep it quiet, though I'm not telling you anything new. You'll hear it from other people, though no one likes to discuss it." Mrs Farrington paused and then added sagely, "It just comes from not knowing the customs of the country, however long you've been here. What my husband always says is, 'Give the native his due, don't mess about with his gods, and he'll be all right.'"

"What happened?"

"Why, Hawthorn tried to blow up the shrine," Mrs Farrington said. I must have looked blank, for she went on, as if she thought me rather obtuse, "The shrine is up by the waterfall, in the gorge. You see, they've got one of those things there – stalee ... stala...."

"Stalactite?" I suggested.

"That's it," said Mrs Farrington. "Anyway, one of those jutting rock things, and, of course, they say it's Siva. And then one day, up comes Hawthorn and decides that he wants to blast a new road right through the shrine, because he wants the road to go to the top of the range and on, and he wants the road to go right through where the shrine is now. Absolute foolishness, I call it. There are a dozen other places he could have blasted, and Pamposh Gorge is the only thing really worth looking at for miles around, with the waterfall coming over the rocks and down. It's really beautiful. You go right up among the rocks, up and up, and into the heart of the mountain, and there is the cave with the shrine, and there's a hole, a round hole right at the top of the cave, through which you can see the sky. And the water bubbles up out of the earth right under that hole. Oh, it's quite lovely. I like to go in the hot summer and sit in the water and keep cool. So, of course, Mr Hawthorn decides to blow it all up. His idea was that we could get water by lorry from the nearest river, four miles away. And Matho said if they blew up the cave and the shrine, his village would kill the whole lot of us, and then the government stepped in and there was no blowing up, though the dynamite charges had already been laid. But the harm was done, I'm afraid, and Matho has been sticky about lots of things since, like the water supply. The water here actually comes from the shrine, and Matho says it all belongs to his village and we can't have any. I guess that's why they asked us to the festival and then it went so dismal – just because they wanted to let us see that they weren't happy about things. I guess Hawthorn just wanted to show them who is master round here, but he's hurt their feelings. It's what my husband always says: 'Leave their gods alone....'"

After that, I had to see the waterfall, the shrine, the hole in the mountain through which sky could be seen. I went with Fatso, Vincent's silly curly bull terrier, who was indomitably addicted to charging bigger animals and biting the exhaust pipes of jeeps.

We proceeded up the mountainside, first following one of the bulldozed tracks contouring our camp and then, when it ended, walking along beside a narrow brook with slippery sides, where the iron earth became porous slime, dark green. The path wound upward, foot-stamped. It was very cool and the sound of the water was always there, a quiet murmur. There were many trees now, with small yellow buds; soon, when they blossomed, the bears that lived in thicker, untouched forest on the farther slopes would come over at night to pick and eat the flowers, which are sticky sweet with a dripping juice. Sometimes in the late afternoon, one heard a bear scream; it was the noise they made waking up for the night. They prowled not too far from the shacks, and everybody's dog howled, Fatso most of all.

We climbed the winding path, Fatso first, quivering with energy – the same eager force that threw him against cows, jeeps and bulldozers, foes worth attacking. He spared the aborigines. We met some of them – women with large jars of water poised on their heads and other jars or babies resting on one hip, older children following behind, and men holding spears or bows and arrows. All of them had damp hair, from having washed in the brook. The water served for bathing and laundry; they collected drinking water high up, and descended to wash at a lower level. Matho's village depended on this one thread of water trickling from the mountain for all its needs and for the fields, and what would the aborigines do if it disappeared? Looking at the aborigines walking their washed brown bodies in quiet files down along the brook, the wet children with tin cans full of water in their hands, I wondered that they did not get more angry with us and what we were doing to them and to their land.

Now the slope was covered with great boulders, and the stream was thicker, leaping from the rocks. The only way to climb was up rickety wooden ladders placed against the rocks, the rungs insecurely tied with grass ropes. I left Fatso at the foot of the first ladder. He sat and howled. I climbed one ladder, and another; the rock began shelving overhead, and in a moment I was entering the mountain itself. The tumbling water had scooped out a series of shallow basins, one below another. Ahead of me, the rocks rounded like a dome, and I stepped into a very large cave. In the cave was a tight nest of boulders, out of which the water spurted from the inside of the mountain. Through a hole in the top of the cave I saw the sky. Around the rim of the hole, trees bent down, as if to peer at the spring bubbling out of the earth.

On one side, under an arching rock wall, I came upon a small platform curtained off by a palisade of green boughs. A red brocade banner was strung across the palisade, as if it were a ceremonial gate. Inside this palisade was the god: not a stalactite, which hangs downward, but a stalagmite – a conical projection of stone about half a yard high, protruding from the rock floor, hoary with lime and iron, surrounded by candles and flower petals. Siva, of course, in his favourite shape, the linga. Two aborigines, wearing chaplets of flowers, sat tailor-fashion beside the stone. I knew they would not like me to come near, so I went down.

Another fortnight or so and we would leave, Vincent's job ended, so we drove about a lot, though the dust was terrible.

One Wednesday – market day – we went to Nalda in the jeep, to get a load of fresh vegetables. With us went Abbas, and the water boy and his fiancée, an aborigine girl of about fourteen with dimples, who wore a small gilded bangle in one nostril. The three of them sat in back and we sat in front.

In Nalda, the market was full of staff people from the mines buying green coconuts, vegetables and goat meat. Some of the aborigines were selling diminutive chickens and tiny eggs. Here and there, fat-buttocked and barrel-chested, plump fingers encased in rings, wearing turbans of fine silk gauze with the ends trailing and tight little embroidered jackets and enormous pantaloons, wandered the Pathan money-lenders carrying briefcases of black or brown leather under one arm. I had seen them, colourful and bulky, sinister on their motorcycles, in Tatanagar the day we spent there waiting for the jeep; now they were here, too, getting a hold on the aborigines, lending money to them at 25 per cent interest a month and squeezing it back from them for years, often for the rest of their lives.

Vincent and Abbas walked among the stalls, buying chillis and jackfruit and tomatoes and chickens. Here, as in some other parts of India, it was usually the men who bought the food, and usually women who sold it. A butcher came up to tell Vincent that Krishnan had collected some ten pounds of goat meat for himself and never paid. "I didn't eat that meat," said Vincent, and they both laughed and agreed to forget it.

When Vincent came back to the jeep, a smiling, dark-faced Indian with a small black moustache, wearing a white shirt and khaki trousers and white rubbers, walked over, put a hand on Vincent's shoulder in the assured way of a friend, and said, "No news yet of your cook Krishnan?" It was the district magistrate of Nalda. He and Vincent had struck up an acquaintance over Krishnan's case.

He asked us to have coffee with him at his house in half an hour, smiling with very white teeth under the black moustache, and we accepted. Our water boy had disappeared, perhaps to get drunk, perhaps to borrow money for his impending wedding. He was a widower of nineteen, his first wife having died three months previously in childbirth. We set off without him, and Vincent parked the jeep in the shadow of a mud wall. The fiancée of the water boy waited in the jeep, sitting straight and mothering some coconuts, and Abbas chivalrously sauntered away, for even though the girl's fiancé had left her alone, to remain with her would have been highly indecorous and possibly dangerous for him. Thus reassured that the proprieties would be observed, Vincent and I strolled across a couple of fields toward the house of the district magistrate, whose name was Deo.

The house had the usual thick concrete walls, with a tiled roof and a broad veranda; at the few, deep windows and at the door flapped the usual curtains of plum-coloured cloth. Seated around a table on the veranda were four men – Deo, the magistrate; the Nalda chief of police, with his tunic unbuttoned, and his cap on a chair nearby; and two Indians in white shirts and long pants, who, I learned, were the manager and the sub-manager of the mining company's Nalda branch, working under Hawthorn.

"You are welcome," said the magistrate, smiling again. He was very relaxed. He had a manuscript on the table in front of him, and he told us, "I have written down some of my ideas about harmony between man and man."

"We were talking about *justice*," said the Indian manager. He was corpulent, and kept his arms away from his body, sitting semi-regally, with his hands on the arms of his chair. His stomach bulged, and his feet, in new brown leather shoes, hung slightly above the floor; he would have looked much better in loose Indian clothes, with his feet tucked under him.

"We were," Deo said easily. "But I do not like the word 'justice'. It is a harsh word. I like the term 'natural retribution'. It is what I write about."

He handed me the manuscript. There was a lot of it, and it was written in Indian English, with vague and wayward spelling, and such phrases as "Now the nations roar in blind anger like bullocks left unfed and tied to their cartridges" and "Ah, how pitiable rendering the human attachments to Anger and to Gain!" It was long and discursive, and had an Indian quality that was all about us on the veranda: an almost sensuous consciousness of the motion of time, with no particular urge to do anything about it; a resignation and an acquiescence that freed one from worry, since worry did not help either the passage of time or the drinking of one's coffee, nor did it relieve the heat pressing down, or accomplish anything else, for that matter. It is a peculiarly Indian feeling, experienced only when one is with Indians in their full Indianness, which is when they are relaxed and talking philosophy; they love talking philosophy, which for them is a mixture of mysticism, transcendentalism, fatalism and elementary science, the wonders of electricity being easily comparable to the wonders of God.

The magistrate did not hurry me in my reading; he went on with his argument with the manager and the sub-manager. "You do not mean rights," Deo was saying. "You mean mutual respect of another human consciousness; you mean the harmonious knowledge of divine in human."

"We *do* mean rights," snapped the sub-manager, who was thinner than the manager and wore *chappals* - Indian slippers with crossed thongs. "Remember, sar, that both the manager and I were manhandled and mauled."

"You mean womanhandled," said the chief of police, bursting into laughter.

The manager made a polite, subservient smile with his mouth; it did not reach his eyes. His nose quivered a little with suppressed irritation. "The company," he said, "must maintain the correct relationship between the management and the workers."

"What is correct relations?" asked Deo gently, swinging his white rubbers on his toes.

"That, Mr Magistrate, is not for us to say. It is for representatives of justice like your good self to decide," said the manager, with the air of achieving a grand slam at bridge.

Deo moved his head from side to side, in the majestic and tolerant way of an elephant, and the chief of police rustled an enormous pile of files – sheaves and sheaves of foolscap encased in very English-looking tan file covers.

"What I am saying, what I say," Deo began, and the manager crossed his hands over his paunch in an exaggeratedly respectful manner to listen carefully, with just that overemphasis that shows a fundamental disagreement with what is about to be said, "what I say is that humans should not always want their rights but should preserve the ideals of a natural retribution."

"And what is natural retribution?" asked the sub-manager.

"Harmony in nature," said Deo.

"Sar, with respect," said the sub-manager, encouraged by a snort from the manager, "I do not think it was harmonious to tie us up, or make us carry the babies and the baskets, as they did."

"What's this?" I said. "What is this?"

"It is the trial," said the chief of police, shifting his files about. "The trial of the workers of the iron mine."

"It is a long trial," said the manager. "Four years this has been going on. I have been coming here twice or three times a month for four years."

"So have the workers," said the chief of police. "For you it is just a holiday, coming here in your car. They have to come, too; that is expense for them."

"Some of them have had babies four times since the trial began," said Deo.

"How many are there?" I asked.

"One hundred accused," said the chief of police, looking at his list, "of whom one hundred are women."

"*All* women," the manager said to me. "They are much worse than men. It was the women who went on strike four years ago. One hundred of them. It was terrible. They made us do *puja* to them – fold our hands and bow as to the gods – and carry the baskets on our heads and the babies on our arms."

"Because that's how *they* were carrying," said the chief of police. "You made them carry the iron ore like that. They had to carry their babies while working. Remember that."

"So that was what Hawthorn was talking about!" I cried.

Deo smiled at me.

"We didn't have nurseries at the time," said the sub-manager defensively, "but it wasn't our fault. It was Head Office. 'Don't pamper the workers,' they said."

"Natural retribution is strong in the heart of a woman," said Deo.

"Is that what happened – the women had to carry the ore *and* their babies?" I asked. "That's terrible."

"They have nurseries now," said the sub-manager.

"Nurseries!" the chief of police snorted. "There is a place under some trees, yes, where the children are put, yes, to wait while their mothers work. They sit in the dust, and an old woman sits with them. You call that a nursery?"

"Sar," said the manager to Deo, in an exasperated tone, "it is you who are judging the case, sar, according to law. There was attempt upon my person, sar; there was violence and personal violence and harm done, yes, and restraint by force upon me and my staff."

"We were shut up by the women for six hours in the office quarters," said the sub-manager to me.

"I wish I'd been there," I said.

The chief of police laughed. The manager and the sub-manager smiled dimly.

"Madam," said the sub-manager, "believe me, we, too, have sympathy for the workers, as you have – abundant sympathy. But that is not enough. The law must be observed."

"The strikers put themselves in the wrong," said the manager. "They laid violent hands upon us."

"You do not pay them enough," said Deo. "And you do not give them nurseries, or proper huts, or water. So all the villages are angry."

"I wonder if they are coming," said the chief of police. "It is long past the hour."

"If they do not come, we shall adjourn till next month," said Deo.

"Another adjournment," said the manager. "Sar, it is four years."

"There are many of them," said the chief of police, "and depositions have to be taken individually. It is the law."

At that moment, at the entrance to the garden, a group of women filed into sight. They were clad in cotton saris, their hair was carefully oiled, and they were carrying black umbrellas open against the sun, now very hot. Many had babies on one hip and were leading other children by the hand. The women walked across the garden, settled in the shade on the stone edge of the veranda – which came to about the right height for sitting – hitched up their saris, folded their umbrellas, eased their children, and turned their heads and stared at us, with neither resentment nor curiosity but in a tranquil, at-home fashion.

"Twenty-two, three, four, five, six, seven. Twenty-seven," said the chief of police. "I doubt the others will come."

The magistrate called out to the women, obviously asking a question. This made them look at each other, moving their heads in a vague, calm, reflective way. Two of the women extracted bottles of sugared water from their bags and gave them to the older children to drink. After a few minutes, one of the women answered – a tiny creature with smooth grey hair and sparkling, mischievous eyes. She was so short that the handle of her umbrella came up to her shoulder. Yet anyone could see she was a leader.

"What a sweet face that little old woman has!" I said to the manager in the long silence after she had replied.

"That, Madam," spluttered the manager, with the first uncontrolled anger he had shown, "That dear, sweet old lady possesses the *filthiest* language you have *never* heard, begging your pardon. I shiver when she opens her mouth," he added, subsiding into dignified sullenness once more.

"I think that there is something wrong that there should not be harmony between you and your workers," Deo said. "Perhaps you would like to give up the whole thing, yes? Forgive and forget?"

The manager raised despairing hands to the veranda ceiling. "How can?" he asked of it. "How can? Head Office will never agree. They want to see this thing through."

Deo and the chief of police looked at each other.

"Trial adjourned till next month, market day," said Deo. "Most of the accused have not turned up. Here are only twenty-seven out of a hundred."

As we left, I waved to the women, but they did not wave back.

And now Vincent and I were very near departure. Matho wanted to give us a feast, and we wanted to give him one, and our water boy was getting married.

One evening, Matho appeared with the father of the bride, both barefoot, treading the evening dark and grinning with atrocious teeth, both with right hands extended. We put 20 rupees in each one. Weddings are costly, and doubtless the bride's father had already pledged himself to long years of payments to a gross, gaudy money-lender.

On the nuptial night, we strolled down to the aborigine village. In front of the bride's family hut, three drummers banged away, refreshing themselves with frequent draughts of the local brew. The chief drummer was a wag; he somersaulted over his enormous drum, stood on his head and banged on the drum, and arched his back until his head touched his heels and banged on the drum.

We sat on a string bed, of the kind used by Indians. That was the only bed in the whole village, and was used as a seat of honour; the villagers slept on leaves on the ground.

The bride came out to thank us. For the last three days, she had been in retirement, away from the groom; before that, of course, they could be seen walking hand in hand everywhere. Aborigine marriages are love matches, and the girl chooses the boy. The Indian staff of the iron mine considered this immoral and said the aborigines were primitive.

The bride was enveloped in a purple sari secured by a large silver brooch in the shape of a fish. Why a fish? Matho explained that it was always thus for a bride, and he added that it was sure to be a good wedding, for the groom was a widower, the girl liked him, she was sixteen years old, she was healthy, and she had been married once before for a very short time and then divorced; there would be no sex trouble, both having had some experience.

There was some courteous arguing about the bride's age. I said I thought she was fourteen, but nobody really knew, because aborigines are not sure how old they are and it does not matter to them.

By three in the morning, the drummers were banging away louder than ever. The groom, surrounded by friends carrying torches, appeared and was immediately pushed into the hut. The couple stood in the doorway, giggling, holding hands, covered with garlands of marigolds. Someone knocked their heads together – a sign they were married. We went home, dead tired, our ears buzzing with the drums.

The next evening, we gave a party, and the whole village came, including the newly married couple; the aborigines came swinging to the beat of drums, arms linked, already dancing as they advanced toward us in a long chorus-girl row.

"It's going to be a good party," said Vincent.

Of course, the Hawthorns, the Farringtons and the Teviots came, too; a party always included everyone. Abbas and Sethi had made mounds of things to eat – little dumplings stuffed with spinach and fried coconut, curried meat balls, bits of pineapple and onion and cheese.

We sat outside the huts to watch the dancing. Two big wood fires gave light. Soon more people came, including Deo and the chief of police. All ate and drank, and watched the village dance.

The village was in great spirits, and the long row of men, women, and children, clasping each other's waist, followed the leading dancer's pattern of steps with happy exactitude. The leader was a young boy with an unsmiling face, which he kept slightly bowed to the right, as if listening. His right arm was free, and swung to the rhythm of his dancing; with his left, he encircled the waist of the next dancer, a diminutive woman with grey hair. She had one arm around him and the other around the next dancer, and so on and on – men, women, girls, boys holding each other and swinging, bent slightly to the right, following the steps of the first dancer. Down the line rippled the movement of the dance, straggling a bit toward the middle, where the children congregated, firming up toward the end, where a tall woman stamped round and round, rotating like the axle of a wheel as the line described a wide circle about her. The steps kept on changing – first up and forward with the right foot, then one-two and skip with the left, then back to the right foot nimbly. Suddenly there would be laughter as, down the line, helter-skelter, quickly, the dancers would stumble, their feet tangling, and then swiftly catch the new pattern that the leading dancer had just made up; by the time they had caught on, the leading dancer would have invented some new combination of steps, and the line would laugh and follow.

Bang, bang went the drums, the dancing line went round, the leading dancer revolving in his wide circle while the end dancer stayed put. In the fire-glow, as the leading dancer passed me, I caught sight of the face of the second dancer, the little grey-haired woman, and recognized her.

"Ah," said the voice of Deo at my side, "it is the lady chief of the strikers." He smiled at her as she passed, getting grins and laughter and cheerful jeers back when the women turned their faces and recognized him as the magistrate who was trying them.

A group of young girls broke from the row and came toward us. They clasped us both in their arms, Deo and me; their bodies smelled of coconut oil. We were dragged into the dance, our arms around the waists of others, their arms around our waists, and we all leaped and skipped, one step to the right, one to the side, two swift steps back, a swivel sidewise and forward to the left, and again one step to the right.

More women broke ranks. Hawthorn was seized by two sturdy matrons with swinging breasts. His wife was gaily being a good sport, and entered into the spirit of the thing with tremendous zest, shouting, "Isn't this fun!" Mrs Farrington proved an admirable dancer, and Mrs Teviot, a little reluctant at first, was soon laughing and stumbling with abandon. The little grey-haired woman would not leave anybody alone. She stood and pointed a finger and groups of girls rushed upon our guests and dragged them into the dancing lines; some extricated themselves but were dragged back. Abbas and Sethi, seemingly exempt, stood grinning at us. Suddenly the little woman pounced upon Abbas. He put up his hands in defence; she tore at his shirt; terror came upon his face; he beat against her arms; she pulled harder. He appeared to give in, then suddenly wrenched himself free and fled. She pursued. They circled a tree; then Abbas ran behind the huts, and she after him. They were gone from sight. The aborigines laughed so hard they stopped dancing; some groaned with hands on bellies, and one or two women sat down in the dust to laugh better.

"Wasn't it wonderful?" Mrs Teviot said to me hours later. "Wasn't it *too* beautiful?"

We'd been dancing and dancing; we were exhausted, all of us, panting, covered with dust and sweat and smelling of the coconut oil that had transferred itself to our skins from the skins of the aborigines. Now we waved goodbye to the village as it danced itself slowly away. The people would dance all the way back, and the drums would go on and on, on and on, the sound slowly dwindling until they reached the village, where they would go on dancing until they dropped. No work would be done the next day.

"It was *heavenly*, wasn't it?" said Mrs Teviot.

Mrs Farrington and Mrs Hawthorn and some of the men joined us. We stood laughing and wiping sweat and dust off our faces, all malice gone. For a little while, we could almost believe that only this exultant, sweaty contentment was real. The rest almost did not exist – the undercurrents, the backbiting, the threat to blow up a god, the sure destruction of the pattern of the aborigines' lives, the pushing of these villagers into becoming mineworkers on a wage, the razing of their trees, and the eating up of their mountains with bulldozers and trucks and shovels for the iron within. Those shaggy, bear-haunted mountains would one day be only vast sores under the sky. But at that moment, having danced together, we had nearly forgotten this. We said we hoped that they would go on dancing, that they wouldn't lose this kind of thing – but we knew they would. In the end, they would gain other things; they would become like us. But they would not dance any more – not like this – and we, who had made them change, would not be dragged into long, swinging rows to dance to the rhythms of a young boy.

The next morning, Abbas was gone. All day we waited for him; he did not turn up. We did the packing by ourselves, cursing him. Vincent jeeped to Valda to look for him, but no one knew anything.

"Maybe he's got an arrow through him. Maybe the damn fool had too much money on him and got murdered for it," Vincent said when he came back.

In the night, Deo and the chief of police arrived.

"Your cook is accused of kidnapping an aborigine woman," Deo said to Vincent. "Matho has just reported the case. Do you know where he is?"

"She probably kidnapped him."

"Possible. Probable," said Deo, and the chief of police slapped his thigh and roared. "I will tell you," Deo said. "The woman is the little grey-haired one who ran after him to catch him at the dance – the leader of the strikers." He nodded, moving his head reflectively from side to side. "It is quite convenient," he said cheerfully, "because now the trial cannot proceed. She was the chief of the union of women workers – their spokeswoman."

"She had a very big filthy vocabulary," said the chief of police with relish. "But the trial is now postponed indefinitely."

"Until she is found," corrected Deo.

"That is, if you wish to find her," said the chief of police, roaring again.

"Perhaps you want to find your cook?" Deo said to Vincent. "He did not take anything with him – not like the other one? He is not the thief to be pursued, no?"

"No," Vincent said.

And so the matter was dropped, and the trial, and everyone was happy. Perhaps one day the matter of the shrine would also be forgiven.

(1961)

Picnic in Malaya

———

WHEN Maimunah rang me I thought at first that it would be about the mass meeting, because we were trying to hold a mass meeting for marriage reform and Maimunah had written to the police for a permit to hold the meeting.

"Come quick," she said, "Hasnah is very ill."

Hasnah is Maimunah's sister.

"Is it her baby coming?"

"No," she said, "the baby is not coming yet. Come quick."

I went in my Volkswagen to Maimunah's place. At the door was Kalsom, the little Chinese girl whom Maimunah has adopted. Kalsom is terribly spoilt, and I always tell Maimunah: "You are nicer to your little Chinese girl than to your own Malay sons." Maimunah laughs and gives Kalsom another hug, every time.

Kalsom screamed (she always screams, clatters, hurls herself, an ebullient fat little girl full of energy): "Mama, Mama, your friend has come!"

Inside the house, behind the screen, were women, about a score, including old ones with veils half-drawn, surrounding a weeping Hasnah with hair undone and her five children all weeping.

"What has happened?" I asked, but already I knew.

"Divorced," said Maimunah, "three *talaaqs* all at once, Doctor, and she knew nothing at all about it, nothing at all."

"How did it happen, and what about the children?"

"Ah," said Maimunah, "we are women, Doctor, so it happens and we cannot do anything."

The story was simple, so simple and so common story of Malay woman in Malaya. Hasnah was happily married to Idris, and Idris had three other wives, two younger and healthier than Hasnah; but Hasnah had made up her mind about them, and there was no more than the usual small underground bickering between the women. It was Hasnah who had brought one of the wives and her little daughter, aged three, to me when they were ill with gonorrhea (caught from Idris, who had caught it from a prostitute) two years previously. Idris was now getting rich. Not only had he a good job in the government, but he dealt on the side in licences for transport, and he had bought a car and two houses in the name of his mother, so that the income tax man did not trouble him. Hasnah was very proud of her husband's business acumen, because many Malays were unable to make money, they did not know how to do business. "That's because his mother is Chinese," said Hasnah. In her mind, business acumen was an inherited trait from the Chinese side of Idris, and so a very good thing.

That morning, after a night of love, Idris had said to Hasnah: "Please go to your sister's house with the children. I have some business, and I will come round to pick you up.

At first Hasnah was puzzled. Idris was usually too busy to take her and the children out. Would he come to pick her up in the car, because of the children? She herself was six months pregnant, and with the usual anaemia became giddy at times, but she did not have the habit of asking questions. She dressed the children, and they sauntered off to the bus stop. They waited twenty minutes, and the bus came, and they all got on, paying 20 cents for herself and 10 cents for each child. Maimunah's house was about three miles away.

When Hasnah arrived Maimunah was busy with her sewing club. Maimunah is a born organizer, in fact she cannot stop organizing. Even jail for two years under the British had not stopped her. She had worked hard for *merdeka*, independence, as many Malay women had worked hard, believing independence would also bring them some measure of real rights, not paper rights, some true relief from the fearsome, man-made laws which had the sanction of religion and made it so easy for men to divorce and remarry, so easy for women to be thrown on the streets. "After *merdeka*, when they divorce us, they will have to pay for the children," they said. Maimunah had campaigned for women's rights. "After *merdeka*, there will be schools for the women, then we shall be educated, and if our men divorce us we shall be able to work for ourselves. We shall not have to become prostitutes to feed ourselves and our children."

But this had not happened for the poor women, though the women of the rich, the women of the upper class and the government officials' wives had gone to schools, and some of them even had jobs, and there were three women in parliament. For women like Hasnah and Maimunah there was no such protection.

So after *merdeka* and her release from jail, Maimunah organized sewing clubs to teach the girls to sew.

"You see, Doctor," she used to say to me when I visited her among the whir and tack of the sewing-machines, "if we women don't learn to work, we go on the streets. There are forty thousand prostitutes in my State. And what does the Religious Department do if they catch us? Put in jail, lah, and finished. And when come out, who is going to feed mother and children?"

It was through Maimunah that I began to understand the distress of the Malay woman. In the *kampongs*, the Malay villages, in times of flood, when the catch of fish was poor, when the paddy rice did not grow, to pay off debts (and all paddy planters were in debt), girls were married off at fourteen and fifteen, or sold to brothels.

"Divorce and marry, divorce and marry, Doctor," said Maimunah, laughing softly (she always laughed in sorrow, because she was polite and did not inflict a sad face upon the world, however bitter her heart became), "what else is there for us? In my *kampong* there is a girl of nineteen who has been married five times!"

That morning Hasnah came to Maimunah, sat for a while in the room below the stairs with the sewing-machines amid the girls sewing. But the children were restless, so she went to the inner room, behind the screen, to give them some sweets, and there the message came to her. It was a letter from Idris, her husband, in which it said briefly that he had spoken the three *talaaqs*, by which she was irrevocably divorced.

When Hasnah read the message, brought by a boy who was a distant cousin of Idris and who hastily went away after thrusting the envelope in her hand, she could not believe it at first.

"My eyes are not good," she said to Maimunah, "a devil sits in front of them. Please read this from Idris, my husband.

"Allamah," cried Maimunah, "he has given you the three *talaaqs*! You are divorced. And you were not even present. Hasnah, what did you do wrong?"

Hasnah was too stunned to reply. She searched in her mind for something wrong she had done. Only last night Idris was with her ... had she offended him in love-making? Had her breath, perhaps, been sour? Was it the child within her? She now felt, with terror, the child move, and beginning with a loud cry she wept, knocking her head against the wall, until her heavy hair fell from its bun on to her shoulders and back.

With the first sound of weeping automatically the women left the machines. The sewing girls, many of them married and divorced and remarried and redivorced again, and who knew without being told what had happened, crowded round Hasnah, asking: "*Apa*? What is it, why does she cry?"

"Three *talaaqs*," Maimunah answered.

And they whispered, looking at each other, round-eyed: "Three *talaaqs*? All at once? And not even in her presence?"

Some said. "What has she done of evil?"

Others said: "It happens ... it was the same with me."

And still others said: "Allah's will."

And others ran to chafe Hasnah's hands, and wept with her and also for themselves, remembering their own pain.

"It is not fair," said a sturdy, tall girl with a slight hare-lip and big round eyes. She was a Sumatran and Minangkabau, where matriarchal tradition is strong. She had been to school somewhat, for two years, had been accused at one time of being a communist which is why she had lost her job in the welfare office and was now learning to sew because she had two children.

"It is Allah's will," said another, and Kalsom, the little Chinese girl, repeated, bouncing up and down: "Allah's will, Allah's will."

"No," said the girl from Sumatra, and her thick eyebrows came together. "It is not the Will of God. In other Islamic countries it is forbidden to give three *talaaqs* together. A man can only say: '*Talaaqs*, I divorce you,' once, clapping his hands, and the wife must be there to hear it. Then he must wait a month and for his wife to be unclean and clean again before the second time he claps his hands and says *talaaqs*. And once more a month, and another cleansing, before the third *talaaq*. To give three *talaaqs* together is not according to the Koran."

"Three *talaaqs* can never be taken back," said another. "It is unfair."

"But what has Hasnah done?" said others.

"I have a child," shrieked Hasnah. "It is Idris's child." And she wept till they thought she would die.

Meanwhile Maimunah had asked Fatimah's advice. Fatimah was match-maker, physician and midwife, and did not know her age so that she at times said forty and at others sixty. She applied herbs to Hasnah's temples, meanwhile counselled Maimunah: "Send that cousin of yours to Idris's house, quick, but let him stay outside and watch, and come back to report." So this was done.

It was time for the morning rice, and no one had thought of eating, there was too much sorrow; but the children clamoured for food, and

Maimunah went to the kitchen to start the rice cooking. I sat with the women. The Sumatran girl said to me:

"In Indonesia now the husbands cannot be careless any more. They have to pay maintenance."

"My husband did not pay," said another, "and I had three children. He was in the police, and the government transferred him to Penang so he left me."

"How did you get your *talaaqs*?" asked the Sumatran girl.

"Post office," said the girl. "A letter, like Hasnah. I cannot read. The postman read it to me."

The children ate, the women talked, each one telling her own story, or rather the stories of her marriages. The divorce rate in Malaya is sixty per cent of the marriage rate, so there are many stories.

The cousin returned, a young man employed in the telecommunications who therefore owned a bicycle, which is why he had been selected. He spoke to Maimunah, standing on the other side of the screen. He had arrived to see Idris leave in the car with a tall young girl with curly hair, very *sombong* (proud), who used to work in a massage parlour. There are many massage parlours in Malaya, and their uses are obvious. He added that someone said Idris often went to this massage parlour. The back seat of the car had suitcases and parcels. Where they went, the cousin did not know, but "some people in the neighbourhood" said they knew Idris had had sick leave from a hospital doctor who was a relative, and that the certificate said Idris was suffering from typhoid and needed three weeks' sick leave. Idris had promised the hospital doctor to help him get a house from a Chinese merchant, hence the certificate. In effect, added the cousin, getting more loquacious, Idris had told some friends of his a few days ago that he was going to another job, in Kuala Lumpur, and that he would be leaving soon.

So now everyone understood why Hasnah had been divorced. Because Idris otherwise would have gone against the law, which says that a man can have no more than four wives at a time, and Idris had his quota. If he wanted a fifth, he had to divorce *one*. Now the older Number One wife was a rich woman with a fairly powerful family backing her; she lived for the greater part of the time at home with her own parents, her two sons were in England on government scholarships. Idris would never dare to repudiate her. Hasnah was not attractive now, five pregnancies had spoilt her teeth and her figure. The two younger wives would possibly join him later, in Kuala Lumpur, where he had gone to honeymoon with the new one.

Evening fell, and Hasnah stopped weeping from sheer tiredness, and by that time everyone in the *kampong* had added his piece to the story, and now Idris was rumoured to have gone from Kuala Lumpur by airplane to Hong Kong with his new bride to enjoy himself there.

"Just like the Sultan," said a neighbour, half admiring.

"When the Sultan of — took his twenty-fifth wife he went there for the honeymoon," corroborated another.

Others maintained he had gone to Singapore, where the sixth floor of a certain hotel was reserved for officials to enjoy themselves. Still others said no, it was Kuala Lumpur, because Idris, being a government official, had friends in Kuala Lumpur and the wedding would be celebrated there.

Hasnah went back to the house where the two younger wives, lids lowered, pretended not to see her, Maimunah and I went with her, since I had a car to convey them all, and Maimunah said sternly to one of the young wives: "Hasnah your sister was good to you. When you were ill with the dirty sickness she took you to the doctor to be cured. It was Idris who infected you, and also your little girl, and it was Hasnah who took her own money to pay for the doctor for you to be cured. Why did you not warn her?"

The young wife giggled and did not answer. She was an uneducated girl from a village, and whatever happened she only giggled, and never answered a word.

In the days that followed my Volkswagen was much used. I drove Hasnah, always with at least three children to cling to her, on necessary visits. The first one was to Idris's mother, a stout, powdered lady in flowered nylon, with gold pins in her false chignon and gold teeth gleaming in her mouth and gold bangles upon her arms. She believed in carrying all her cash upon herself, since one never knew when a man would clap his hands with: "*Talaaq talaaq talaaq*," and out was the woman, to fend for herself. And since the law said that the woman would take with her, when divorced, the clothes on her back and the jewels on her body, and her dowry and property, Idris's mother had always, and wisely, invested in gold and, now that she was a widow, in real estate.

Consolidation had made her portly, the desire for hoarding traducing itself in her appetite as well. She received Hasnah coldly, but gave sweets to the children. "I shall look after my grandchildren," she announced. "You can leave them with me, Hasnah, when you go back to your *kampong*."

Hasnah, who now wept as easily as she breathed, wept and said: "But I love my children. I do not wish to go back to the *kampong*."

"Hasnah," said Idris's mother severely, "it is too late now. Hasnah and Idris are divorced, and it is best that Hasnah should marry again."

"Hasnah has a baby from Idris in her belly," said Maimunah. "To divorce her at this time is against the law."

Idris's mother looked round-eyed with anger at Maimunah. Then she spoke again in the third person. "Here is the crab that tells its young to walk straight. What does Maimunah know of the law, who has been, so I am told, in jail? I hear Maimunah is sub-versive." She pronounced it with weight, in English, soob-versiff.

"I went to jail under the British colonialists, yes," said Maimunah, "and I fought for *merdeka*, independence, while others went gazing at the sweet water." This she said because it was whispered that Idris's mother had had an illicit affair with a man from a village called Ayer Manis, "sweet water".

"Ah," said Idris's mother, looking into the air reflectively, "the turtle lays thousands of eggs and not a word says she; the hen calls the whole country to see her hatch one chick."

"Come, Hasnah," said Maimunah, "you can boil a stone, but you cannot make it tender." And after this parting shot Maimunah in great rage took Hasnah away.

The next visit was to the Kathi of the Religious Affairs Department. Hasnah and Maimunah had to wait some time, and Hasnah, never strong in mind, in the dim corridor began to feel that truly she must have done something wrong. "It is no use, Maimunah," she wailed. "Let me die, that is all. Let Idris's mother take the children, I will die and the earth will be the lighter for it. It is Allah's will."

But Maimunah wanted to fight. "You must have maintenance at least until the child is born," she said.

The Kathi of the Religious Court (Divorces section) was a frail man with a fine Arab face under his white corded cap. He spoke sparingly, his cheeks were sunken and his eyes brilliant. When Maimunah had finished, he said:

"Idris has recorded divorce. He pleads unfaithfulness on the part of Hasnah his wife; hence gave her three *talaaqs*."

At this Hasnah threw her veil across her face and fainted. Maimunah and I carried her out. Then Maimunah returned to the Kathi. She came back pale with anger.

"It is no use," she said. "Idris has witnesses, he says. Now we must get a lawyer."

We went to the Indian lawyer, because he was cheaper than a

Chinese or a European lawyer. He listened, and then he said that this was Religious Law, and in the state it was not against Religious Law for a husband to give three *talaaqs* at once to his wife, and it would be difficult if Idris had witnesses, even if witnesses did not tell the truth, and he was willing to take the case but five hundred dollars must be paid in advance.

"Five hundred dollars," said Maimunah desperately, "where can I get five hundred dollars?"

So I said I would lend them to her, and Maimunah said she would think about it, and the next day she came for the five hundred dollars for the lawyer to fight the case for Hasnah.

Hasnah went home, and now the rent was due, so Maimunah borrowed again for the rent; the other two wives disappeared. Maimunah asked Hasnah to come to live with her, but there was not room enough for six more people. Then Maimunah had another idea: she would speak to a Member of Parliament about this. She selected Che Marriamah, one of the three women members of parliament, and went up to Kuala Lumpur to speak to her, borrowing the train fare.

Meanwhile Hasnah moaned, and became persuaded that she had sinned. The habit of subservience was too strong. If Idris had said she had been unfaithful, perhaps it had been so, unknown to herself; she had been the victim of the demons, of evil spirits; perhaps she had unwittingly stepped upon someone's blood; perhaps a spell had been cast upon her ... an incubus had come to her in the shape of Idris, hence she had been unfaithful without even knowing it.

So Hasnah hoped for death; did not die at once, managed first to deliver the child at six months, a puny two-pounder, at night, with old Fatimah helping, and died ten days later of an infection from a boil on Fatimah's finger; and I did not know, until told by Maimunah when she came back from Kuala Lumpur, that Hasnah was dead.

"Why did you not tell me?" I said to Maimunah. "Why did she not send word to me, I could have done something for her."

"Oh," said Maimunah, smiling with sorrow, "she had bothered you much already, she was so ashamed of being much trouble to you."

Then Maimunah told me about her visit to the woman member of parliament, or *parlimen* as it is called in Malaya. Che Marriamah had been very kind to her, asking her to sit and eat with her, but she could do so little to help. "Sister Maimunah," she said, "what can I do? Already the men in *parlimen* are so rude to me. When I get up and ask for schools for women, for education, and for protection for children, for reform for prostitutes and not jail, they clatter their desks and make a great noise and bang their briefcases and stamp their feet and go out and in, out and in ... so that I have to shout to be heard. And they do this because I am a woman and they are men."

Che Marriamah had been to jail at the same time as Maimunah, and now she too had to fight hard, and, she felt, fruitlessly, for the women.

"They promised us everything when they wanted our votes, but now they do little or nothing because they are men." One day, she told Maimunah, she had said at the end of a speech: "You seem to have forgotten the women who voted for you." And one of the Ministers, getting up, had replied in a smooth, silky, arrogant way: "Now, how can we men forget women? Of course we *never* forget them, neither day ... nor night." And all the honourable members of *parlimen* laughed at that sally, deeming it *so* witty.

"That is how it is," said Che Marriamah. "They will not move until we the women organize and force them to change."

"Then how about your mass meeting?" I asked Maimunah.

"Cannot, lah," said Maimunah. "The police asked me *why* I want to call mass meeting. Then they say cannot, it is subversive, because I have not registered our association, and it is subversive for more than five people to meet for a common purpose without notifying the police and without proper registration."

It was the day for the funeral. Maimunah borrowed two hundred dollars. It was a beautiful after-rain cool day, with a gusty breeze blowing from the sea at high tide, and burying was quickly over, and after it Maimunah and all the children and I went walking by the sea edge. Many people, European families with their children, had come to lie on the beach, to sun themselves and to eat food out of hampers. Maimunah was too modest to look at them because they lay with so few clothes, but she was always puzzled, she said, why they ate on the beach instead of in their houses.

"It is called a picnic," I said, "it is a habit to go out in the sun to a nice place and eat there. The children like it."

Maimunah decided, there and then, that the Friday after the next we should have a picnic for the children.

And so we did, all the girls and women of the sewing club, Maimunah and her children, and also Hasnah's children, and some neighbours and their wives and children. We went to a place by the sea. The girls sang, and the children played. Maimunah and the women cooked curry chicken, plantains and vegetables, and rice wrapped in leaves. Maimunah borrowed plates from me, and we ate with our fingers. The sun was hot and good, the wind blew, the tall girl from Sumatra began to sing. It rained a little, so that someone cried: "See, the frog croaks and the rain comes." And this made all of us laugh and laugh.

(1961)

Relations Between East and West

THIS subject is one much in the news today, and inspires a tedious flow of platitudes and clichés. It is a little staggering still to be greeted, as I am when visiting Europe, with the hoary misquotation of Kipling's unhappy phrase: "East is east and west is west and never the twain shall meet." I say misquotation, for this is not what Kipling meant at all, since he went on to say: "But there is neither east nor west, border nor breed nor birth, when two brave men stand face to face though they come from the ends of the earth." Unfortunately Western commentators forget this ending, and use with reverence a sentence today only a pointer to an attitude of mind, racialist and primitive. There are still people of little thought and much prejudice intent on this wholly artificial division, who speak of "east" and "west" as two opposites, and regard these points of the compass, applied to nations, as evidence of a state of the world inevitably pregnant with future conflict.

This is deplorable, besides being as invalid as Hitler's racial theories, and about as helpful to world progress. It is more accurate to speak of the haves and the have-nots *within each nation* of the world. For in every so-called "rich nation" there are also undeveloped regions and depressed areas, even in the United States, where a recent census showed that at least thirty million Americans live below the average standard. But since one expects me to write about relations between Asia and Europe, I shall begin by saying that the word Asia itself is vague, because Asia is a term to denote a vast continent which contains nearly two-thirds of the world's peoples, many huge countries and many cultures. These countries in their physical and cultural make-up are far more different from each other than European countries, and yet there is very definitely an "Asian identity and outlook", in spite of these differences.

This "Asian identity" is based on three things: the first is undoubtedly the common struggle against colonialism. Many countries of Asia have only emerged into independence after the Second

World War, and the bitter struggle against colonialism is, for others, not yet ended. The second common and binding link is common needs, for all of us have suffered, through past servitude, exploitation and despoliation, and we need to catch up with the twentieth century in technology and living standards. The third is a common aspiration and desire for total independence in the full sense of the word, for freedom from hunger, want and disease. In these three main ways, all countries of Asia stand together, and the term "Asian" acquires validity.

When speaking about "relations" between Asia and Europe, then, we must first define the word "relations". Actually there have always been "relations" between East and West. Going about Stockholm looking at the pottery, the ceramics, the glassware, I am struck with delight and recognition, because so many of the shapes and patterns are Chinese. This is not to accuse Swedish artists of copy or imitation, but on the contrary to appreciate how their good taste has rediscovered the classic shapes which have always been the aspiration of Chinese art through the centuries. In art there is a continuous process of borrowing and lending, of assimilation and stimulation. Symbolic objects of jade and stone found in the graves of China have their counterparts in pre-Sumerian epochs. The great silk road of Asia created in its passage a fertile cross-exchange of crafts and techniques, from China to Rome. In Pakistan are found stone figures of the Buddha with a Grecian face and Greek clothes. Medicine and astronomy were carried into Europe by the conquering Islamic armies of the eighth to the tenth century, and the first hospital for maternity was established in southern France by an Arab physician from Spain.

One can go on for ever citing examples of this continuous "relation" between Asia and Europe. After all, the cradle of the Aryan race, we are told, is in Central Asia, from whence great migrations led to the invasion of Europe by the Aryans, from whom Scandinavians descend. Christianity, properly speaking an eastern religion, migrated west, where it achieved success. And we could even go on to say that communism, which many westerners look upon as an "eastern" manifestation, is after all an economic science whose laws were formulated by a German, Marx, while studying in the British Museum.

But the main "relations", those which do interfere with normal and equal and desirable links of equality, mutual goodwill and trust, are economic and political. Europe accomplished, in a great tidal wave, an industrial revolution which was a revolution of science and technology, starting about three hundred years ago. This scientific revolution changed the whole of the politics, economics, social insitutions, ways of life and thought, of the peoples of Europe, and also altered their relationship with the rest of the world. Unfortunately the superiority conferred by this advance was employed by their ruling classes to further expansion into and exploitation of other countries in the world, hence colonialism, which has not yet ended even today. This whole process was, in Europe, carried out over a certain length of time. Nationalism led to the emergence of modern states; democracy, the liberties and rights won by the peoples, did not come without long struggle and often bloodshed, and the systems of law, popular representation, and other institutions now regarded as self-evident have to be constantly preserved by watchful vigilance. Even today, in certain countries of Europe, it is only too clear that a resurgence of despotism and tyranny in one form and another is only too possible.

As it was in Europe yesterday, so in Asia today the nations are going through a process which involves the total remodelling of the old societies. Nationalism is today in Asia the strongest force, a desire only too obvious and very often misinterpreted, or labelled "trouble making" or "communist influence", by a Western press which has forgotten its own past fights for democracy and freedom. Although the Atlantic Charter, evolved in the last war, promised all nations the right to independence and an end to colonialism, yet now, eighteen years later, this is still not quite realized. In some instances the colonial powers, after the war, instead of keeping their promises, tried to re-occupy their old colonial territories and were only thrown out after a second or third and even more bitter struggle. These kinds of "relations", which are relations between master and servant, exploiter and exploited, we in Asia no longer want. It has left many bad memories; it has also left behind much poverty and many deficiencies, which form the core of the problems of Asia today.

Although today, in Asia, political independence is acquired, yet often another kind of independence, which is economic independence, is not yet achieved. Too many of the resources, of the sources of production, are still in hands other than those of the people themselves. A foreign power still has a stranglehold on the economy, and the benefits of whatever industrialization there is either flow out of the country in profits to foreign companies, or even if part return to the country whence they are derived, they are ill-used or wasted by incompetent or corrupt politicians. Many countries of Asia lack technical competence, and the business of government is sometimes in the hands not of the best elements, but of those who have shown themselves *persona grata* with the departing Western power, and who, when the latter left, took over and then proceeded to exploit their own people. This is not new. All over the world, in history, are tales of rulers whose concern was to enrich themselves rather than to benefit their land. Therefore in Asia there is a continuous process going on, and which will go on for some time, the process we call "the long revolution", which is both political, economic and social, whereby one after another these corrupt politicians will be eliminated, and one after another the liberties and rights of the people will be achieved.

But it is a huge, an enormous task, and whereas Europe had so many centuries to carry out its industrial revolution and to achieve nationalism and independence, we in Asia have little time. We have but ten, twenty, or at the most thirty years to carry out this revolution, for our peoples, informed through mass communication of what is possible as a decent standard of life, will not wait, and they clamour for change. It is this constant turmoil, upheaval, this steady pushing forward of the masses of Asia for a better life, which Europeans, ill-informed of historical processes, are taught to consider with fear as a peril, as a threat. And yet it is not so. On the contrary, these convulsions and changes are to be expected, and the less interference there is with them, the better in the long run will they be solved. For it can be said, once and for all, that nothing will stop their advance.

In spite of all that has been said and written about the good done by colonialism, we in Asia do not feel grateful for the indirect benefits derived from roads, schools and hospitals which were created not for our benefit, but for the better efficiency of the ruling power, and which, compared to what was taken away from us in the form of wealth, are pitifully small benefits. It is something we can do much better ourselves, once given the equipment. The last fifteen years have proved that an independent nation in full control of its own resources, can do more than decades of colonialism. To quote only a few small instances: in 1956 when the Suez Canal affair occurred, many Europeans said that the Egyptians were incompetent, corrupt, and would never be able to run the Canal. Now, in 1963, seven years later, it is proved that the Egyptians have run the Canal through these years just as well if not better, since the volume of transport has greatly increased, and many improvements have been made. In Cambodia, after seventy years of French rule, in 1955 there were only seven doctors for five million people. Today there are 27 doctors. In Indonesia, when the Dutch left finally in 1952 there were 800 doctors, and there are now 2,500 for about a hundred million people. It is not true that the peoples of Asia cannot do, by themselves, what is necessary for their development, but it is that they are left deprived of technical competence, of help, of know-how. All this they need to get a good start, and in order to achieve their desire for a better life.

And now we come to another fallacy to be exploded, and one which also embitters "relations" between so-called West and so-called East. That is the fallacy of "aid" or "help to underdeveloped countries". There is in the world today a notion developing that the European nations are aiding or helping undeveloped countries a great deal.

Now it would be ungrateful and peevish to deny that the wish from the part of many people of goodwill to help the poorer countries is good and noble, and that the awareness which develops from it is most helpful. To realize that the world is one, that humankind must work together, and that no nation which has plenty should shirk the responsibility of helping those which are poor is indeed an advance from the barbarism which took it for granted that some peoples were "inferior" and therefore condemned to subjection and to misery. We still hear, but in diminishing numbers, people otherwise well-educated and intelligent tell us how "happy" the "primitive" peoples are, in the midst of their misery and their ignorance, as if poverty, hunger and disease were a kind of golden age of happiness, and that the peoples of Europe are "psychologically miserable" in the midst of their comfort. These silly and childish statements are sometimes made to me, and I always retort: "We would rather be unhappy in comfort, than go on dying of starvation and disease." Indeed, this extraordinary fallacy is another myth solely designed to ease uneasy consciences. It has no existence in reality. The peoples of Asia do not want to be told that they should be "happy" to remain deprived. They say: "We are grateful that you should think of helping us. *But we want to know what exactly you mean by help.*" One statesman of Asia said to me recently: "Help is sometimes more costly and more ruinous than no help at all."

What is the real story? The real story is both comic and tragic. It has been told, again and again, in reports and articles in economic magazines and publications of the United Nations. It is that there is a growing gap between the "rich" and the poor, and that the whole of whatever aid has been given has been *wiped out* by other economic measures which are still being applied against the underdeveloped countries.

To begin with, let me quote from well-known sources, on the *extent* of aid given to the "developing" countries, a euphemistic term to cover those countries of Asia, Africa and Latin America that are in the throes of this "long revolution". The amount of aid given varies from 0.2 per cent to 1.3 per cent of the total annual income of the "giving" countries. That is to say that the total extent of aid, which is supposed to perform such miracles as to put the nations of Asia on a good footing, and to prevent "communism" (for again and again it is said that all this aid has, as its avowed intent, the warding off of "communism" in the poorer countries), amounts to exactly 20 cents in 100 dollars up to 1 dollar 30 cents per 100 dollars of revenue.

Under what form is aid given? Here again, I will not cast aspersions on "intentions". But hell is paved with good intentions. Should all this aid be truly helpful, there would be no quibble. Some of it is in the form of technical aid, experts, machinery, educative and health schemes. But at the same time another phenomenon occurs. Owing to the very structure of the Big Business companies which, *at the same time*, seek good investment fields *with returns* from these same countries, there is a definite drain away of revenue from these countries, and the aid becomes nullified in the long run. This is giving with one hand and taking away with the other, and *taking away much more than is given*. I had a recent experience in this field myself, when a friend of mine advised me to invest some money (about US$25,000) in Latin America. "You will get back 30,000 dollars within a year," he told me. "These South American countries are desperate for money, and all you have to do is to write a note, backed by your bank, lending the money, and you will get 5,000 US dollars interest safely within a year." I fail to understand how such a system of usury, where without any work at all I can make twenty per cent interest in a year (possibly more than by writing a dozen articles or even a good book) can benefit the peoples of Latin America! No wonder even American newspapers, writing of "Alliance for progress", sound uneasy. Is this real *aid* or is it merely a new form of exploitation?

We in Asia are vitally interested in all this, because we are directly affected. We know how often this "aid" depends on whether a country is considered a "sound investment" against communism, and the word "communism" covers any manifestation of desire for independence, for national liberation in every sense of the word. We all know, from the American newspapers themselves, that large sums, amounting to something like US$200 per head of population, have been expended in Laos to keep it "safe", with the result that Laos is just as tragically unrestful and full of tension, if not more so, than before. Into South Vietnam goes an enormous amount of money. If this money were equally shared out, every head of population would receive something like US$35 per year. Is South Vietnam prosperous and peaceful? Nothing of the kind. Something like 18,000 Americans are there, to "help" President Ngo Dinh Diem keep in power. At the same time, the help extended to other countries amounts to something like 25 cents to 60 cents per head per year – a ridiculous amount, just enough to buy one "hot dog" a year per person.

All of us in Asia remember that before 1949, in order to "avert communism" in China, the United States gave six billion US dollars to Chiang Kai-shek to form a New Army. An amount of six billion US dollars mean that every American paid out about 50 to 60 US dollars out of his taxes to help fight communism – with the result that in 1949 the Chinese communists came to power in a tremendous wave of popular enthusiasm. For the people of China did not want war, after so many decades of war. They wanted peace, reconstruction and progress.

The lesson is clear: when "aid" equals interference, political manipulation, and outright business investment which means not wealth for the borrowing nation but profit for the "lending" nation, then it is only another form of exploitation, a new kind of colonialism, and it breeds communism more quickly, more efficiently and more surely than any kind of propaganda from Moscow or Peking could ever do.

It is a paradox, that actions which are anti-communist in intention are pro-communist in effect.

It is also a paradox that those of us who raise their voices to warn the nations on the so-called "giving" side of the dangerous courses they are taking, and of the failure which is inevitable if they pursue them, should be called names and labelled "war-mongers" or "leftists". In this context I always think of Winston Churchill, who for so many years warned his country against the danger of Hitlerism, but was hooted at and derided. Yet he was right in the end. No amount of name-calling can suppress the truth.

For at the same time that this hyprocritical sham of "aid" is being perpetrated, the nations of Asia and Africa are growing poorer, and more restive. Any relief, any halt, is but temporary. The "long revolution" has only begun; it can only stop when the peoples of these countries *themselves* have realized their apirations and needs. This is not being done; on the contrary, as described in the United Nations report, the problems are becoming more pressing and bigger.

For all this while, another phenomenon has occurred, again on the economic plane. And it is this: that the price of our products is going down, while the price of the manufactured goods of the industrialized nations is going up.

Many former colonial countries, both in Asia and in Africa, have to depend for their national income on the sale of primary products or raw materials, such as rubber, or cocoa, cotton, or coffee. In quite a few of them the economy is still geared to one or at most two of these "primary products", such as sugar in Cuba or cocoa in Ghana. This is a relic of the past, of a "colonial economy", when the colony supplied the mother-country's industries with raw material. All the newly independent countries want to diversify and to change this colonial economy, but the process is strenuous, difficult, and involves hardship. Meanwhile, on the world markets, they have to continue selling their "primary product" in order to live, and in the last few years *the prices of primary products have been falling steadily*. A fall from 7 per cent (for oil) to something like 20 or 30 per cent (for rubber) has been registered. Meantime the prices of machinery, obtained by these countries from Europe, are going up and up.

Then how can the nations of Asia catch up in this economic race, and build their economies? No wonder that so many countries of Asia are afraid and suspicious of the European Common Market, for it is a threat, a very real threat, to their already difficult economies. For with the grouping together of Big Monopoly business, it is more and more difficult for the weaker economic nations to "shop around", to try to buy cheaper, since it is inevitable that there will be all-round "price-fixing", and that the Big Trusts and monopolies will be able to dictate the prices they choose, both for the things they buy, and for the things they sell. And that means that the income of Asian and African nations will fall even more, and that all the schemes for progress, for education, for health, for building schools and hospitals, for equipping industrial plants, for diversifying the economy, will suffer in the process.

Let me quote one case only, the case of rubber in Malaya. Natural rubber grown in Malaya forms about 40 per cent of its total income. Now, with synthetic rubber, natural rubber is threatened, and the Malayan economy, until now considered stable, is becoming uneasy. Many people in Malaya are hoping to be able to sell natural rubber to other countries, such as China, but they are prevented from doing so by unnatural restrictions and threats. Malaya also mines and sells tin; but she is threatened by a stockpile of tin of 50,000 tons, which is held in American hands. The slightest move to sell out of this stockpile makes the price of tin stagger and fall and causes loss to Malaya.

How can countries, considered independent, live under a permanent threat of insecurity, not become restive, and seek other means and ways of achieving a stable economy than the ones proposed through "aid", which in the long run only amounts to political and economic manipulations, which make the situation even more precarious?

What is the answer? The answer is that in order to have real, permanent, stable relations of equality, dignity and respect, we must start again from first principles, and recognize that any interference, armed or non-armed, political, military or economic, from any side whatsoever, in the affairs of other countries, is dangerous from the start, leading to results diametrically opposite to its intent, and re-establishing, but only for a while, a kind of artificial "peace and stability" which is really only another form of domination whatever the label may be. The "long revolution" of Asia must be understood and recognized for what it is.

(1963)

Why Cambodia Rejected Aid

I HAD not been in Cambodia for two years, and very recently visited the country again: December in Cambodia is cool and sunny, and I was tired of Singapore, its monsoon dampness, the nervy, tense atmosphere fostered by confrontation, mass arrests and the speeches of bickering politicians.

On the morning of my arrival in Phnom Penh, 12 December, friends told me that in a speech at Takeo, some 80 km from the capital, Prince Norodom Sihanouk had not only reiterated his repudiation of all aid from the USA (first announced on 12 November 1963) but had now recalled his ambassador in Washington. He was also to recall the ambassador in London, and in several other capitals: these later moves dictated by the need for economy in foreign exchange spending.

All the Americans involved with aid, Usom, Maag, etc., were to leave Cambodia before 15 January 1964. "The Prince is right," said my friend, a UN expert working in Cambodia. "The Americans say that the rejection of aid is a threat, that Prince Sihanouk is mad, eccentric, irresponsible, that he is slipping into China's orbit. But it is precisely in order to maintain peace, to maintain the neutrality and the integrity of his country that he has taken this step."

This was not the version of events broadcast in Europe and in the United States and it took some time to disentangle fact from fiction. Fiction abounded: irresponsible reporting had helped to envenom the situation. For four weeks, between the decision to reject aid and the one to close the Cambodian embassy in the USA, the climate of communication had worsened to the point when it seemed difficult to re-establish a normal dialogue.

Sihanouk acted to maintain the dignity of his country and of his person; he would not yield to threats. This firmness has given an example of courage to some other countries, also irritated by "aid", but afraid to make a decisive break, afraid to say "no" to money, as Cambodia has now done.

Aid a "danger"

Ever since 1952 when aid first started the Prince made it clear that he did not like "aid". This is no "new" or "sudden" decision of his, not dictated by madness, threats from China, hysterics, or any of the other "reasons" given by certain newspapers. Sihanouk repeated to me once again that he had always taken aid *à contre-coeur* ("against his heart") even while receiving it, for the sake of speeding up Cambodia's development. Always, in his public speeches, he indicated that he did not intend to become a slave to this help, and that although Cambodia was grateful, aid could not buy allegiance, nor turn the country and the proud Khmer people into a Western base or a communist base: Cambodia would stay absolutely, positively neutral. This has been the Prince's steady and unswerving policy all along. In speeches made in 1961 and in 1962 (which I read) I found he had repeatedly warned the Powers that he would reject aid, if pressure continued to be applied to him, and if this aid was *harming* instead of *helping* the country. When did Sihanouk finally reject aid? This was announced in a speech to the public on 12 November reprinted in the local press; many thousands of Cambodians heard him. One likeable thing about the Cambodian form of democracy is that Sihanouk keeps his people totally acquainted with what is happening; in fact, they are always told before the Press is. Government officials sometimes complain that Sihanouk is too frank, too outspoken, but the people of Cambodia listen, they feel they are being kept informed, they follow what happens, and they trust Sihanouk. Among the small countries of Southeast Asia no other leader "goes to the microphone and thinks aloud", as Sihanouk does. They usually talk to the Press first, and the public learns what happened by reading the newspapers. In many places, the people are only told what higher-ups think they should know; Sihanouk gets in front of a crowd of peasants and talks exactly as he would at the UN, and tells all he knows.

American aid, said Sihanouk, in the form of money, was applied to education, agriculture, public works, private industrial concerns, defence and police. *In toto*, from the time of its inception in 1951, it came to 300 million dollars. Sihanouk expressed publicly, and more than once, gratitude for this aid. "I know, we have a difficult time ahead. I have no illusions on this score. We have utilized the money given to good use, and not wasted it. By rejecting money things will be harder for us." Cambodia would have to rely almost entirely on her own efforts. "But this is the only way. No country can grow strong on aid; aid is *helpful*; but it has also its bad sides. It may make certain things easier; but it also weakens a country. And so we had to cut it off, to go unaided, in order to remain ourselves."

What were the "dangers" of aid? To begin with, the Prince said, there were the multiple, incessant pressures of all kinds brought upon his government and himself in order to turn him from neutrality and "align" him with the West. This went on and on, aid became a kind of blackmail, an excuse for uttering "democratic warnings" humiliating Cambodia at all times. "People seem to think that if they help you with money, you are sold to them and must do their bidding." In spite of the fact that Cambodia used the aid as best as it could, nevertheless they were told they should "follow the example of Thailand and South Vietnam". This was said not only by American senators, but even by certain British officials on tour, and this the Prince resented. One of them, it is alleged, plaintively said to him: "Why do you insist on being different (*sic*) from the others (meaning Diem and Sarit Thanarat)?"

Apart from constant pressure to turn Cambodia into an anti-communist base (and, probably, into a battleground similar to South Vietnam), there were material reasons for discontinuance of aid. In spite of some practical benefits, there was also a steadily growing dislocation of the economy of the country, directly due to the effects of aid. One may term them side effects, since they are not what aid is supposed to promote, but it appears that in this case (as indeed in many other cases, such as in Latin America) the side-effects of aid are more pernicious and destructive than any benefits the avowed intentions of aid may bring.

"Aid proclaims itself unselfish, but is actually a thoroughly hard-headed business and profit motivated activity for the benefit of businessmen." Commercialized aid, the Prince called it.

The "compradore class" and aid

The "distribution of dollars" conditions a country receiving it by separating an upper, receiving class from the rest of the people. This small class in contact with aid is eager to import goods; and to re-sell them at a profit in their own country. There are consumption goods and equipment goods; a heavy and constant pressure is abetted by this class to import non-essential luxury objects, refrigerators, radios and motor cars which can be re-sold at vast profit. This awakens an insatiable appetite for dollars, coupled with a total disregard for the needs of their own people. Placed between making a lot of money from aid or rigidly refusing to accept anything which is not needed for economic construction, the "élite", already westernized, already sighing after all "the good things of the West" (which their own people cannot afford yet), are too easily tempted to corruption. Bribery becomes prevalent. Shoddy equipment for capital construction is passed as fit for use; machines disappear, sold on the black market. It is alleged that in building the American Friendship Road from Phnom Penh to Sihanoukville, the amount of money spent per kilometre was exactly TWICE what it should have been; half "disappeared" in private pockets and yet the road was unsatisfactory, it has had to be re-done in parts. Speculation, stocking of necessities (such as sugar in order to create a scarcity), blackmarketing, smuggling, delivery of old and useless machinery when new ones were contracted and paid for; refusal to aid state industries, exclusive direction of aid towards private industries; all this, said the Prince, gradually convinced him that he must do without aid, or else see his plans for a viable, healthy independent Cambodia be "gnawed from within", his élite corrupted thoroughly to the core and the country sink into subjection. "Another South Vietnam."

"The principal and fundamental error of aid," said the Prince, "is that it is the deliberate and relentless means of a policy which aims at the creation not of an independent and prosperous country, but of a small and corrupt capitalist class, in the pay of a foreign power, holding the economy of a country in its stranglehold, and maintaining the country as a dependant."

The creation of this small élite capitalist class, corrupt, money-grabbing, disloyal to its own country, devoted only to its own wealth, alarmed some of the honest officials and made the young restless and critical. Out of the money made by these means from aid, villas and houses were being built in the capital of Phnom Penh by corrupt ministers and bureaucrats to be rented at fantastic prices (60,000 riels a month) to American personnel, experts and technicians, of whom there were round about 130 in Cambodia. The rents were deductible from aid; so it did not matter how high they went. In this way a few villa-owning bureaucrats got richer and richer, but the people of the country saw little benefit out of all this. Thus slowly the profile of Cambodia was beginning to resemble that of other small countries (and even large ones in Asia) where unrest and inflation prevail, where the city gives an appearance of wealth, large motorcars rush by, and luxury houses are found; but the country gets more and more hungry and denuded of prosperity. "Cambodia until recently had no such opulent upper class, but now there was the beginning of one." It was high time, ended the Prince, "to stop this plague".

Development without US aid

From now on, instead of building villas, the rich would have to put their money in productive enterprise and in the creation of industries. "We shall have to re-educate the capitalists, the merchants, the profiteers, and the middlemen," said the Prince, "to forgo their transactions and to start putting their money into such things as flour mills, factories, plantations." In order to carry this out all import and export concerns were taken over by the State.

At Kep, a pleasant holiday resort by the sea, on 6 December, the Prince spoke to assembled businessmen, outlining the constructive efforts they could make towards achieving economic independence for Cambodia. As usual he was candidly frank; told them they would make less profit but would be emotionally sustained by doing the right thing for their own people; serving the country instead of helping themselves only. He advised them to invest their money in state enterprises, such as factories and plantations, to bring their talents as managers and technical experts from private concerns into public ones.

There would be no taxation on such productive private enterprises; on the contrary, they would be encouraged and helped with benefit and concessions of free land in sites selected for their industrial advantages or their fertility. Plantations of sugar cane, jute, copra, cotton and mulberry would not be nationalized. Efforts to utilize Cambodia's cattle to set up a milk industry would be made, instead of importing tinned milk. Fish, fertilizers, textiles, preserved foods, a tyre factory, an assembly plant for cars, a petrol-refining plant (to refine oil purchased abroad) would have immediate attention. A sugar-refining plant would be set up. These pioneer industries and their products would be thoroughly protected. Toys, shoes, belts, bags, which could be made locally (leather is abundant, from Cambodia's cattle) would no longer be imported. Import-export lists would be carefully studied and revised.

Education for development

Outlining plans for industrial expansion, the Prince emphasized that only by its own efforts could a country, ultimately, achieve economic independence. But in order to attain economic independence, Cambodia must also reform her education system. Educational reform is not only Cambodia's problem, it is the problem of every emergent country and even of many Western countries. France, England, the USA, are all trying to re-style the schools and the school curriculum to provide necessary technical, managerial, scientific talent. Most developing countries are grossly handicapped in this effort by the fact that their education is still colonial and therefore even less advanced in content, if slightly altered in form, totally unsuited to the realities of the country and its needs. Even today, in 1963, there are five times more students studying law at the university in Phnom Penh than there are engineers, yet it is the latter, not the former, that are needed. In every post-colonial country the pattern is the same, and in some it has remained unaltered even a decade after independence; lawyers predominate because in a colonial country they were extremely necessary as middlemen between the people and the colonial power; then come bureaucrats (studying Arts) doctors (often the "get rich quick" type who stay in large cities). Technical students, engineers, agronomists are remarkably few.

In Cambodia education is still a copy of the French curriculum, with a heavy tilt towards the "humanities". "We cannot go on doing patchwork reform in education, we must rethink totally, up from the very foundations, our educational programmes," said the Prince. For instance, out of 26 hours spent in school per week, 20 hours are devoted to the study of language (Khmer, French), morality (civic education), history and geography, leaving very little time for science, agriculture, mathematics, physics, chemistry, the educational infrastructure necessary for an industrializing country, including practical work in laboratories. "Education is a determining factor of technical progress, and hence must be an inseparable component of the productive forces in the economy." These words by a UNESCO expert were endorsed by the Prince.

In nearly every developing country the new literates are showing the same tendency; they prefer white-collar work to soiling their hands in manual work. This phenomenon is not particular to postcolonial regions: it is universal (exception perhaps made for China and only because of the heavy emphasis on the dignity of labour). In the West, as a recent UNESCO congress in Paris has shown, the "non-integration of youth in the world of tomorrow" has been dubbed the evil of this century. To quote the congress: "Our youth is not integrated. It is completely uninterested in the problems of the world. It drinks and dances, and could not care less. It lives as if there were no tomorrow; it has no faith and no beliefs. All it appears to want is a good time, today, now. It refuses anything that demands effort. Youth feels itself an orphan, separated, alienated, cut off from all the past...." Juvenile delinquency, a high proportion of mental ills, drug addiction are linked to this desperate state of mind.

For 30 vacancies as clerks in Phnom Penh, 2,000 candidates mill round the gate of the employment offices; 1,000 students take the first-year examination for law studies, although only 100 have any chance of being selected. The attitude that it is nobler to wield a pen in an office than to work a spade is unconsciously encouraged by present-day education and must be changed, otherwise the country will not be able to progress. The Prince spoke of a "morality of work"; in fact, for years Prince Sihanouk has personally tried to break down disdain for manual work by instituting regular sessions at manual labour and actively taking part himself. And now this emphasis will become more sustained. Certainly no one in Cambodia has illusions that all this will be easy; hard times will have to be conquered by grim determination, by slogging, patient effort. "There is no other way, except the Royal way, the way of work," said Sihanouk.

The Press reports ...

There remains one other event to comment, the imbroglio about President Kennedy's death. This demonstrates, I feel, almost malicious misrepresentations by certain sections of the Press. It is well known, and it was indeed reported everywhere, that when the American President was murdered in Dallas, USA, the Kingdom of Cambodia went into mourning for three days. Prince Norodom Kantol was sent to attend the funeral in Washington. Three weeks later (approximately), Sarit Thanarat, the Prime Minister of Thailand, expired; Cambodia rejoiced, for Sarit Thanarat was considered a vicious enemy of Cambodia. In the same way Cambodia had also expressed itself relieved when the Diem brothers were "suicided". However, the State Department and the American Ambassador in Phnom Penh took it upon themselves to "scold" Cambodia for expressing its feelings; and at the same time, some irresponsible television team and certain newspapermen asserted that the Prince had rejoiced publicly that President Kennedy, as well as Thanarat and Diem, had left this world. The television team, it is alleged, took pictures of two smiling Cambodians in front of the USIS building. Behind them (unperceived by the Cambodians, who had been told to "stand there for a picture") was a portrait of President Kennedy, framed in black. One smiles when posing for the photograph, and smiling comes easy to the Cambodians. This picture was later presented as "rejoicing at Kennedy's death". It is as absurd as accusing Mrs Kennedy of "rejoicing", because there are some pictures of her smiling at photographers a few days after the death of her husband.

Great ire was expressed, and not only by the Prince, at this distortion; but even more at the arrogance of certain powers whose representatives took it upon themselves to make official reproofs to Cambodia without first checking *carefully* the facts.

Although the rejection of aid had nothing to do with this uproar over smiles in the wrong places, the fracas serves, as did other pressures (such as the Free-Khmer radio inciting the people against Sihanouk), to convince many people in Cambodia that there was no other way out than the one chosen, of "cutting off" totally from such *dishonesty*.

Prince Sihanouk, by his firm refusal to be bullied, threatened or frightened in any way, has given a warning to the Great Powers. He has no intention of becoming a stooge, the plaything of one bloc or another, nor of letting Cambodia be turned into another Vietnam or another Korea, either through aid, or any other wiles, that may be thought up in the future.

A brief summary of aid received by Cambodia

American aid, 1951–1963 (twelve years): 300 million dollars, an average of 25 million dollars per year. This is the equivalent of three weeks of American expenditure to "combat communism" in South Vietnam in 1962. Breakdown of aid, in percentages (1961–1962):

Police and Army	52.2 per cent
Education	26.5 per cent
Public Works	0.5 per cent
Health	3.1 per cent
Agriculture	6.0 per cent
Other	11.7 per cent

Under this programme was built the road to Sihanoukville. Actually about half the road (100 km), had been laid down by the French as a dirt road previously, and was surfaced by the Americans. The remainder was

American built. The total length of road from Phnom Penh to Sihanoukville is 220 km.

One education centre was maintained and staffed; also one police academy, and one agricultural college. Aid provided for transport from the USA, salaries, rent of house and cars of six experts to teach agriculture, who lectured for a year through interpreters.

French contribution to Cambodia (last 5 years):

> The port of Sihanoukville
> The airport at Phnom Penh
> Besides these there are technical and educational personnel from France employed in Cambodia.

Chinese contribution to Cambodia, to date:

> 1 textile factory
> 1 plywood factory
> 1 paper factory
> 1 cement works
> 1 radio diffusion centre
> 1 hospital (joint contribution with Czechoslovakia)
> Some credits for industrial production in Cambodia

NB. Figures are from Cambodian Ministry of Information publications.

(1964)

The Rich *vs* the Poor

In Geneva a trade conference is considering ways to help the under-developed Afro-Asian countries. Instead of gratefully accepting aid when it is offered, these nations are now issuing impudent demands.

Without any further ado the saucy fellows should be told that beggars cannot give orders.

Daily Express editorial on United Nations Trade
and Development Conference

NEWSPAPERS sometimes coin unredeemable tripe. I do not know who, on the staff of the *Daily Express*, committed the paragraph quoted above when fulminating against the "underdeveloped" countries, but it can only evoke laughter from the beggars. And laughter is a sign of strength.

The United Nations Conference on Trade, Aid and Development (UNCTAD for short) gathered together 120 nations; of which 77 (78 when South Vietnam joined) were the "poor of the world" and the rest the "developed", "wealthy" or "industrialized".

Dr Raul Prebisch, as Secretary-General of UNCTAD, presented a report well worth reading. Although careful not to arouse the sensitive "developed" to irritation early on the proceedings, Dr Prebisch made it clear that there was a lot wrong with the present systems of trade, aid, tariffs, preferences, in fact the whole paraphernalia of world economic relations.

One is always glad to have been a minor prophet. I was pleased to read Dr Prebisch call movingly for a "new attitude" towards these issues, because I had suggested the same thing in a previous article ("Relations between East and West"). "Realism," says Dr Prebisch, "is the ability to discern what could happen when we do not know how, or do not wish, to take deliberate and timely action to shape the course of events." He warned that continued lack of realism, persistence in old, tried, and proved unsound policies, would lead to catastrophe.

The solid 77

The conference dragged its slow weary weeks of talk from 23 March to 15 June. Altogether 2,000 delegates toiled for three months. And what was the result?

To quote the *Economist*: "77 nations made an impact *out of all proportion to the material results achieved.*"

According to the *Far Eastern Economic Review*: "*The 75 stuck together.*" Both economic journals emphasized one phenomenon, the "unexpected" unity of the "impudent beggars", a sticking together which worried the wealthy 43.

A feature of this unforeseen unity was its non-racial, but economic, composition. For if Yugoslavia and the Latin American states were with the poor, Japan was reckoned with the rich. Furthermore this was no longer an east–west axis, but a north–south division. Two years ago Professor Keith Buchanan pointed out to me that the divide of the developed–undeveloped, rich–poor, became, on a map, a north–south delimitation of the hemispheres.

At Geneva the Unity of the Poor became a fact; as the *New Statesman* (almost mournfully) wrote: "If they (the poor) know what they want as a group, the great powers will find it hard to play them off against each other as has been done so often in the past."

The reactions of great powers to the new-emergent unity are amusing to record. Great Britain and France, it was felt, had behaved "almost decently"; at least with less rudeness than some other powers. France made a few suggestions regarding preferences. Britain's Mr Heath was suave, and in a pyrotechnical last-minute ploy was credited with salvaging the conference by his suggestion for a financial compensation plan to offset the price decline of primary products. This was described by the *Economist* of 6 June 1964 as the "one" constructive proposal from the side of the rich. But whomever they came from, these suggestions (for they were no more than that) to avert the crumbling of UNCTAD were regarded as mere sops, unsatisfactory palliatives for a situation requiring drastic and thorough overhaul.

The *Far Eastern Economic Review*, however, opined that it was a last-minute move from the President, Dr Kaissouni, and the Secretary-General, Dr Raul Prebisch, which had prevented a "total rupture", and not Mr Heath.

The rich

Most industrial countries had "approached the conference in the mood of giving as little, not as much, as they can". This mood was obvious in the attitude of the United States delegation, which seemed to draw most of the ire of the 77. "The anger of the developing countries ... was polarized against the Americans, who were not only negative, but hostile at many points."

The Russians remained "singularly silent", disappointing some African and Asian undevelopees; the Chinese were and were not there. Although officially absent, they attended the caucus sessions of the Afro-Asian groups, and the further meetings held after UNCTAD had wound up.

The "relative friendliness of the Russians" towards the European powers, and their "non-participation at the Afro-Asian caucus meetings", says the *New Statesman* of 19 June 1964, was "a significant feature of the Geneva conference". This left-wing weekly went on to say that the Russians seemed "unable or unwilling" to capitalize on their prestige, or their trade advantages, with the non-developed countries "against the manufacturing countries of the North Atlantic". This does not sound like the usual vigorous self-promotion propaganda campaigns which the Russians have carried out among the undevelopees.

This Russian "demonstration of solidarity" with the wealthy 43 rather than with the "poor" seems to have inspired Sir Alec Douglas-Home on the theme of "white versus the *rest*". Sir Alec assured the world that in case of conflict Russia would be "on our side", which sounds hardly reassuring for the already harassed "poor".

Apart from this manifestation of unity among the have-nots, very little was achieved in terms of new attitudes, breadth of vision, or concrete steps. The *Straits Times* of Singapore, in rapturous headlines (25 June 1964), described the 200-page Final Act, containing the recommendations of the Conference, as a "Magna Carta for the have-nots, to create jointly new trade and new wealth". But it is nothing of the sort, since the recommendations are not a charter, nor an action programme, but in fact a mere description of some of the events at the Conference, and not legally binding in any way.

The trade gap

At the Conference one of the requirements put forth by the 77 was to do something about their growth rate, which must attain, by 1970, an annual 5 per cent. Otherwise the trade gap between their export earnings and import needs would reach 20 billion US dollars a year, and their living standard, already low, decline further.

Even if the 5 per cent goal is reached, it will take 80 years for the developing countries as a group to attain the present average per capita income of Western Europe, and an additional 40 years to reach the present level of the USA.

For the have-nots, average export value, due to the decline in prices of primary commodities, was only 1 per cent higher in 1960 than in 1950, even when volume of exports had increased by 20–30 per cent, while the value of manufactured goods these countries had to buy from the wealthy nations rose by an average of 10–20 per cent. The resulting "price squeeze" reduced ability to import goods needed for economic-industrial developments.

Manufactured goods for export from the poor countries were handicapped; markets restricted, higher duties set at every degree of processing; quotas; tariffs, all imposed by the wealthy – hampered exports by the poor. Lack of technique, lack of capital to promote new markets; competition against large monopolies which can "wipe out" the less well-equipped producers – combine to discourage manufacturers, to raise the cost of industrialization in developing countries, and to promote once again a precarious fallback on primary commodities, which means a crippling return to economic dependence.

On both sectors of their economy, primary products and manufactured goods, the have-nots are having a tough time. The primary commodities sector is still for them the most important, the chief provider of income, forming 86 per cent of their total exports, while manufactured goods make up 14 per cent. Export volume may increase, but prices decrease, or fluctuate unpredictably, and they have deteriorated steadily in the decade. A very few commodities have recently achieved temporarily stabilized prices, chiefly by arrangement with one country (France and her former African dependencies). But this arrangement is not for ever. Price stabilization in the primary sector, though giving a respite to the poor countries in their ruinous downward course, tends to make them revert to an economy dependent on one or two primary commodities. Meanwhile the prices of manufactured goods sold to the have-nots by the rich keep on increasing.

A combination of two factors, i.e. the falling prices of primary products, and the difficulty of finding outlets for manufactured goods, spells severe balance of payment difficulties for the have-nots, and restricts their ability to earn enough for carrying through their development plans. As a result, the poor are getting poorer, and the rich are getting richer, and there is no end in sight to this process.

A yawning abyss

All through the conference, these points were hammered home by the delegates in one way or another. The gulf between the rich and the poor was becoming a yawning abyss; the terms of trade of the have-nots deteriorated by 9 per cent in the decade 1950–60, while the rich had improved theirs by 5 per cent; the development of synthetics had rendered the poor even more vulnerable to price squeeze in certain areas; the subsidized agricultures of the rich were now competing with the still primitive agricultures of the not-rich. World exports of main seeds and oils were 40 per cent higher in 1959–61 than in 1950–52, but the not-rich only earned 5 per cent more from such exports. In manufactured and semi-manufactured goods, the poor in 1960 accounted for only 5.6 per cent of world export, 94.4 per cent coming from the rich.

The development of export of manufactured goods in poor countries was rising only at half the rate of expansion of the rich countries. The tariffs imposed by the rich *against* manufactures from poor countries rose in progression with the degree of processing of products. One example was iron ore and iron goods.

iron ore	0%	tariff
pig iron	9%	„
ingot	11%	„
finished articles	14%	„
pipes and fittings	17.5%	„

Most speakers from the poor countries again and again laid stress on industrialization as being the key to economic advance, and asked for a policy which would place fewer obstacles in the path of industrialization; notably, a bigger export market for their manufactures, etc.

But the rich nations demurred, invoking the "dislocation of internal markets", "unemployment", and "industrial chaos" that any readjustment of existing conditions might provoke in their countries. The arguments were long and learned, but, surprisingly, the not-rich refuted them almost as learnedly.

It was pointed out that an arrangement to increase import of manufactured goods from the have-nots by a total of 10 billion dollars by 1980 would amount to only *1 per cent* of the additional demand for manufactures anticipated by that time in the industrialized countries. Such an "expansion" would hardly dislocate or displace, even under the most adverse conditions, *one-tenth of 1 per cent* of the total labour force of the developed countries.

"Invisible" account

Another drain on resources of the not-rich was "invisible transactions". These invisibles represent a loss of foreign exchange: shipping freights, insurance charges, interests on loans, dividends paid on foreign private capital invested from abroad, salaries and requisites for technical experts fròm rich countries (absorbing sometimes up to 20 per cent of any grant). In this pattern of "invisible" accounts, payments from the poor as a group exceeded their receipts, whereas in the industrialized countries receipts exceeded payments. "Because of borrowing, the rise in debt service payments has been more rapid than expansion of exports."

In certain areas, the loss in export earnings had cancelled out twice the amount of donations, and aid of all kinds, received during the period 1959 to 1961.

The terms of trade of primary exports had fallen by 26 per cent between 1950 and 1961, due in part to increase in price of manufactured goods.

The net inflow of finance (loans, investments, grants in aid) from 1950 to 1961 was 47.4 billions, but if remittance of interests and profits were deducted, the figure dropped to 26.5 billions. The 47.4 billions included figure for private reinvestment *after* interest and dividends have been paid. In the same period the *fall* in purchasing power of total exports from the poor was 13.1 billion, so that half the benefits of net inflow was nullified. Of what remained, outflow continued from the poor in the form of interest to pay, profits to be remitted abroad, etc. What percentage of these remaining 13 billions must be ascribed to military aid, which forms a large proportion of certain forms of aid to certain countries?

This phenomenon of increasing poverty was particularly severe for Latin America, where the deteriorative effect for the decade was 10.1 billion. Net inflow of foreign capital of all types to this region during the period reached 9.6 billion, but remittances in the form of interest, dividends, etc. reached the figure of 13.4 billion, so that the phenomenon of "more going out than is put in" was outstanding in that region, to the tune of 3.8 billion dollars.

At the end of the Conference an open rupture between the haves and the have-nots seemed imminent. "Faced with a situation in which communication between rich and poor had virtually ceased, the President (Dr El Kaissouni) and Dr R. Prebisch tried to bring the two sides together ... by persuading the Conference to adopt recommendations *which none of the western countries was prepared to implement.*"

Compromise was accepted by both sides "with visible reluctance" and only because time had run out.

To summarize:

a. The combined income of the 77 poor, who have two-thirds of the world's population, is one-tenth of the income of the rich.

b. The value of exports has doubled in the decade 1950–1960, but of this the larger share went to the rich (70 per cent).

c. The share of the poor in total world trade declined steadily from one-third in 1950 to slightly over one-fifth in 1962.

d. This decline in expansion is partly due to the *conditions* governing international trade, which are controlled by the rich.

A debating club

By 80 to 20 votes, the Conference passed a resolution for its Assembly to become a permanent organ of the UN; this permanent organ, however, is still to be set up; already the rich have given notice that they will not allow such an organ to be used as an instrument for challenging their "vital economic and financial interests". Such an organization, therefore, has a good chance of becoming merely another debating club.

Both the *New York Times* and the *New Statesman* cast doubt upon the effectiveness of a new organization "without the full consent and co-operation of the industrialized nations. The latter have the power to rewrite the rules of the game of international trade; they alone can make them work."

"The drama which marked the conference's closing days may be repeated at the UN General Assembly in the autumn," remarks the *Far Eastern Economic Review*, "but much will depend on whether the 77 maintain their unity."

Afro-Asian conference

Meanwhile another conference, the Afro-Asian Economic Preparatory Conference, was being held from 6 to 17 June 1964, also in Geneva. This meeting was attended by delegates from 41 Asian and African countries, including a delegation from China.

This conference, correlated at first with UNCTAD, later assumed its own existence, stressed the strengthening of mutual aid and co-operation, and emphasized the manifestation of "common action and unity of the group of 75" at UNCTAD as of "historic significance". But the fact that the UNCTAD conference, measured in concrete results, was neither adequate nor commensurate with the essential requirements of developing countries was also expressed. "Results achieved must be used as instruments of action in future efforts to set up a *new economic world order*," read the statement of this Conference.

The 41 recommended to all countries participating in the second Afro-Asian conference (to be held in March 1965) to "study and evaluate the results of UNCTAD" and forward their studies to the standing committee of that conference before it meets.

Asian economic seminar

Hard on the heels of UNCTAD and the Afro-Asian Preparatory Economic meeting came an Asian Economic Seminar, held at Pyongyang in North Korea, from 16–23 June 1964, and attended by delegates from 34 countries and territories.

The communiqué issued by the Seminar stressed the importance of self-reliance and mutual aid in the building up of an independent national economy.

It declared that, for the poor, the continuation of a pattern of colonial-imposed economy, *even after independence*, only prolonged the helplessness and undeveloped state with all its problems; it was therefore only logical that this pattern should be changed. So long as the machinery is only patched up, no amount of palliatives and placebos will work, because the basic factor, which is exploitation, remains. It would seem therefore that, for their own sake, the rich nations of the world should by now be convinced that the have-nots must be aided to become truly independent, and that means, financially and economically. But this cannot be done unless there are some basic, fundamental changes in attitude, as Dr Prebisch called for.

Land reform, a correct solution of the land problem, to solve the urgent problem of food and to develop the rural economy, is the crying need in many countries of Latin America, and also in India. Yet the problem meets with opposition precisely from the rich. As soon as land reform is seriously tackled, the cry of communism is raised, aid and help withdrawn, if not worse.

Nationalization of enterprises is violently opposed by foreign investment capital, such as in Ceylon. The tragedy of Indian democracy lies in the fact that aid was *never* forthcoming for the public sector, only for private projects. Genuine aid used effectively, for national interests and not as a source of profit and for the corruption of a small ruling class, should be based upon a Charter of Aid, something like the eight points brought up by Mr Chou En-lai during his African tour, which embody the Aid programme of the Chinese. And finally, industrialization is the key to a sound independent national economy in every country.

A new mood

To conclude: economic thinking has at last hit Asia and Africa in a big way. Large numbers of people are beginning to grapple with economic realities, to realize that independence does not only have a political significance but also an economic one. Who neglects the latter slides back into subjection. Many of the leaders of the new-emergent countries are brilliant politicians and gifted statesmen; but when it comes to economic thinking, to long-term planning, they are not so adept. There is a dearth of technical experts, lack of familiarity with statistics, a reluctance to do arithmetical homework, prestige considerations, the "soft sell" of easy money and short-cuts to success – these things are now being shed as the poor become more aware of their basic needs. Only hard work, self-reliance, and a complete dedication of people and leaders to the reconstruction of their own country can lead eventually to success.

A new mood has been introduced in Afro-Asia: a most far-reaching change in consciousness, a deepening of understanding of the problems which the poor must tackle with their own strength, through their own efforts.

The realization that nothing can take the place of self-reliance is one that surprisingly enough is meeting with joyful acceptance. At a student seminar some time ago in Kuala Lumpur, I was struck by the tenacity with which the delegates from Africa spoke of self-reliance, and voiced great doubts about international organizations with high sounding names which they termed "gimmicks to turn us into beggars".

To ensure "a new economic order", a "new attitude" on the part of the wealthy and the rich was called for by Dr Prebisch. But will this be forthcoming? Meanwhile the poor, *who do not want to be beggars*, have realized that, unless they stick together, they will go on being defrauded of even the little that still remains to them.

(1964)

The Troubles Miscalled Racial

WHEN my friend Victor Purcell died a few months ago, we were in the process of corresponding regarding the Nien uprisings in North China, a little known but enormous nineteenth-century peasant revolt, which took place about the same time as the Taiping and lasted five years after the defeat of the latter. I am an admirer of Purcell's last book, *The Boxer Uprising* (1963), knew he was writing a study of the revolution of 1911 in China and was looking forward to it. His bitter yet true indictment – *Malaya, Communist or Free* – had made a deep impression upon me, as I was at the time in Malaya, observing the Emergency there.

It is with pleasure that I re-read the second edition of his imposing work, *The Chinese in Southeast Asia*, and if I have certain comments to make, they are in no way derogatory to the vast erudition, the painstaking meticulous care in documentation which Dr Purcell exhibited at all times. Indeed he taught me much; and it is precisely because of this, and because I know he would enjoy our argument, had he been able to read it, that I feel bound to point out both the admirable portions, and also the defects of this new edition.

Five years ago, even two years ago, I might have had nothing but praise for the volume; for I myself then still lacked a thorough comprehension of the subject. But I have now spent ten years in Southeast Asia, intimately connected with educational work and the overseas Chinese, and also observing other groups, notably the overseas Indians, who present very much the same features as are ascribed to and regarded as particular to the overseas Chinese. The overseas Indians in the West Indies, Mauritius and Africa fulfilled and fulfil the same features as the overseas Chinese in Southeast Asia, and it is a pity, I feel, that in the second edition there has been no added material on the process whereby the overseas communities got there. In fact, some material has even been omitted in this edition. The socio-economic and political circumstances which fashioned these groups, and brought them to assume the role and importance they occupy today in countries away from their own, are mentioned in only one sentence, in the introduction: "it was in the great period of European colonial expansion, in the last quarter of the nineteenth century and onwards, that the 'immigration' of the Chinese increased to a flood to meet the demand for manpower." Which demand? By whom? This should be underscored, for actually this is the crux of the problem, the heart of the matter, and it demands more than a passing reference, here and there. If there are millions of overseas Chinese, if there are also millions of overseas Indians, out of China, out of India, surely something should be said about the *manner* in which these problems were created – "pigs" system, the indentured labour system in India, the press-ganging of hundreds of thousands of coolies, Indian and Chinese, for transportation to labour on American railways, the Panama Canal Zone, in Africa, in the plantations of Southeast Asia. How many of them died of disease, how many, having contracted for three years, remained for 30 to pay off debts contracted on the opium and gambling farms licensed by the colonial governments? The price per head, the profits made from such invisible slave traffic, the middlemen who profited, the plantation owners and the colonial governments which encouraged such practices because it brought in so much revenue, and which in fact made it their policy to procure such labour till 1915, all this surely amply deserves a chapter on its own.

This form of exploitation went on. The Manchu policy had been to forbid the Chinese from migrating on pain of death; but in 1860, when the Western armies occupied Peking, in the "peace treaty" which followed one special clause stipulated that this law should be repealed, and this was done, not in the spirit of charity, to allow Chinese to leave their homeland, but to facilitate the commerce in "pigs", as the trade in coolie labour was called at the time. The Taiping wars, the destitution of the peasantry in South China, provided an abundance of such labour. Even today, in the Nanyang (Southeast Asia), descendants of the Taipings will tell tales of how their ancestors came, fleeing in junks, and on their arrival were put in chains by the French or the Dutch, and sent to forced labour on roads or felling the jungle for years. And in India, the tale is the same, except that here, transportation as convict labour for minor offences was practised, as it had been in England a century before. The presence, therefore, of millions of overseas Chinese, and overseas Indians, and the problems which ensued, were due to the colonial policies; today's dilemmas, stemming from nonassimiliation of these overseas communities, can be ascribed to the same policies.

For neither in Africa, with the overseas Indians, nor in the Southeast Asian countries, with the overseas Chinese, was there a social-economic structure in which assimilation *could* take place during the colonial period. In contrast with former emigrants in previous centuries who had come on their own, settled and assimilated, intermarried, the colonial structure of the nineteenth century precluded assimilation taking place, for in the colonies the "opening up process" of the territories involved keeping the labour force concentrated, and under control; later it could seldom establish itself into agriculture, for the land was in the hands of the native peasant populations, still at the level of a feudal economy, self-sufficient, but self-enclosed, governed by landowning sultans, or rajahs or tribal chiefs, whose authority was carefully preserved by the colonial power. The native peoples did not share in the "opening up" process, refused to labour in the cash plantations or to toil in the mainly extractive mining processes, both these processes for acquiring raw material cheaply for the metropolitan power being superimposed upon an agricultural base, but unrelated to it. It follows that those of the overseas emigrants who did get away from plantation labour, and accumulated money (the reputed vast fortunes of the overseas Chinese are actually rare) found outlet as middlemen, small shopkeepers, import-export merchants, whose transactions of commerce are dependent upon the colonial power and are in fact endangered by a change in the status quo. Hence, in a way, among these overseas communities are found the most conservative and staunchest defenders of the prevailing order; there are no more reactionary bodies than those of the overseas Indian merchants in East Africa, or the merchant Chinese in Indonesia, or in Malaya and Singapore. Both tend to side with the colonial masters when the rising tide of nationalism hits these once colonial territories. This conservatism, however, is ambivalent; together with the economic dependence which particularly the wealthy feel towards the metropolitan power, there is also an emotional and cultural dependence upon the *old* culture and the *old* mother country; for since there has been no assimilation, there is only the old cultural pattern (with archaism preserved long after they had disappeared in the mother country) to express the community's personality.

No attempt, before the end of the Second World War, to fuse the various races into one, or to introduce a common citizenship was ever made; on the contrary, divisive practices were emphasized. Given all these conditions militating against national unity, it is indeed remarkable that assimilation did take place, in spite of all, though only fractionally. This assimilation is always more marked in small communities, in agricultural regions, where services are on a communal pattern, and the emigrant family becomes more easily integrated and identified with the general community pattern; or where the colonial mercantile power was least evident. In larger cities, the native tended to be in the minority and to occupy the lower, menial scales of society; and this is as true in Nairobi today as it is in Kuala Lumpur. It is small wonder, therefore, that troubles, miscalled racial, occur.

This is the heart of the matter, fountainhead of today's problems which are actually socio-economic, in Africa, in British Guiana, in Malaya and Singapore; often the new order, advent of political independence, has done little to modify the old economic order; and the subterfuge by which ostensible colonial superiors are replaced by "national" politicians, themselves products of colonial education and more anxious to maintain their self-interest than to promote social advance, will not bring to an end these vexing leftovers from previous decades.

But apart from this omission, or lack of emphasis, on the origin of the problems, Dr Purcell's study of the conditions surrounding the overseas communities, their demography, resources, economic status, past histories and future prospects is excellent; he has also given a very good outline of the efforts jointly made by China and Indonesia in recent years to solve the dilemma of overseas communities. But much nonsense has been written about the overseas Chinese, as if they had been deliberately planted there, in the Nanyang, by China, to serve as "fifth columnists", to become infiltrators, and much is being done, today, to utilize them as tools for potential ill-feeling between Asians and Asians. It must be made clear, therefore, that their presence was not imposed by China, but due to the exigencies of Western powers. India faces the same problems with her overseas Indians in Burma, Ceylon, Africa and the Fiji Islands; it has led to mass repatriation, with great tragedies on both sides. The sooner both these communities, Chinese and Indian, are studied in their proper context, the sooner we realize that we are not dealing with *racial* traits and propensities, but with relics of an economic and social order in which the overseas are the victims, and not the perpetrators of injustice, the sooner shall we see the beginning of solution. Today the mess of the past is left for the new nationalisms of Asia to clear up; to hope it will be done with wisdom, and without taking up the artificial hatreds, the built-in complexes about each other which the past has created, is perhaps too optimistic. But we can at least try. For this the overseas communities need wise leadership, need the solidarity of working together, and not politicians who play up "racial" differences for their own benefit. But this cannot be done unless, at the same time, the economic and political fabric which maintains the old order is also replaced by something better.

(1965)

A Tale of Peacocks

SOMETIME ago a friend took me to a Shaohsing opera with a title cumbersome in English, *The Peacocks Fly One East, the Other South*, though in Chinese it sounds poetic. This opera was being performed at the City Hall Theatre of Hong Kong, and, as usual with the Shaohsing style, all the actors and singers were women. The leading male role was played by a tall, beautiful Cantonese actress, Hsiang Chun. Shaohsing opera is popular with women in Hong Kong, because the plays are always about love, and always sad. The denouement is tragic, and there is nothing that women love more than a good weep over a dead hero or heroine in drama or novel. This produces a cathartic soothing in the female emotional makeup, an effect which sometimes lasts for days.

The peacocks' separation also has a conventional tragic end. The story is of a young official, Sung Ching, who gets married. His mother, however, begins to dislike her daughter-in-law on the night of the wedding. Sung Ching, who is a magistrate, is called away that very evening to settle an official business, and, instead of first paying the ritual morning call to his mother on his return at dawn, rushes too eagerly to his new, still waiting bride instead. Mother-in-law's feelings are greatly hurt, and she begins to torment daughter-in-law, and continues to persecute her in all the ways which not so long ago were current in a Chinese family. The poor girl can do nothing right: she is made to work at weaving all day, sneered at in front of guests, rebuked and called unfilial, etc., etc. The truth is that Mother-in-law feels irritated because the dowry is very small, her son's wife coming from a relatively poor family. Finally Mother-in-law works herself up, goes into a raging tantrum, accuses the girl of the "seven sins", and obliges her son to give his wife a letter of divorce on the spot, and send her back to her own family.

The poor girl goes home, to be shouted at and beaten by her mother and elder brother, who are ashamed of her and furious at the breakup of a good match. Their one idea is to get rid of her as soon as possible.

86

The brother arranges another marriage for her, but the girl refuses the match, for she and her husband, Sung Ching, were deeply in love with each other; and still are. At the moment of parting, Sung Ching has promised to try to bring her back. They have pledged each other to eternal love, and will never marry anyone else. She intends to keep her promise. But her brother refuses to listen.

Sung Ching is told that his wife is marrying again, while at the same time his mother is arranging another wife for him. He rushes to a secret meeting with his erstwhile wife, and reproaches her with breaking her promise to him. An attendant maid, indignant at his selfishness, berates him. "You, under pressure from your mother, divorced your wife; she, under pressure from her brother, is forced to marry again; where is the fault?" Sung Ching realizes that it is his fault too, and husband and wife decide to escape together. But this plan is foiled; the girl is rushed into a bridal chair before her preparations for running away are complete, for her brother has arranged to marry her off against her will. On her way she drowns herself. Sung Ching discovers her shoes by the river edge, and hangs himself then and there.

This is a typical eternal "love-faithful-unto-death" tragedy. A Chinese Romeo and Juliet story, immortally affecting. And why peacocks in the title? Because peacocks are the most faithful of birds; once mated they never change, and if one dies, the other perishes of hunger and grief.

It was a fine opera, well acted, well sung, but in the middle of it I wanted to laugh, because I was reminded of something I had seen in Peking two years ago. Not an opera, but a real life scene.

I had gone that day to the divorce court, having waited a week to see a case, as divorce cases were few. There was quite a spate of divorces right after Liberation in 1949, when a lot of unhappy marriages could at last be dissolved; but this tailed off sharply, and in the last few years, marriage based on love is encouraged, although compatibility, the advice of group, organization, friends and relatives still count a lot ... perhaps that is a good thing. Divorce is not really encouraged. Hence the proportion of matches that actually come to court for dissolution is small, because all efforts to mediate, to patch up the couple and to effect reconciliation are attempted before such a decisive step as a divorce is undertaken.

In this case the "peacock pair" were a young man, a workman-technician in some factory, and his wife, also a factory worker. Both were between 24 and 26, both from peasant families, both had married for love, and now they wanted to divorce.

The "magistrate", a woman (it is often a woman, since women are reckoned more sensible and sympathetic than men), and two male assessors, or helpers, sat behind a table in an ordinary-size room in the district magistracy. The husband and his wife sat on chairs; there were a few benches for spectators such as myself. Some neighbours of the street committee from the street where the couple lived were also present.

The story was this: The young man had been sent to Mukden to another factory for a while, and there had met the girl. They had fallen in love and married. He was now back in Peking, where she had followed him, the factory obligingly transferring her to another factory there. They had a baby son aged six months, and all three lived with the husband's mother, who helped to look after the baby.

It appeared the Mother-in-law had, typically, taken a dislike to the girl; she felt her son could have "done better" for himself. She disapproved of women working outside the house. She disapproved of the girl not being at home to wait for her husband. She disapproved of the baby being given "Western" medicine. She said a marriage to a girl from another province could not work out. She started muttering, then grumbled. All this began to work on her son's nerves. He was a filial son, though a model worker, and a Communist Party member. He gave in to his old mother, and the young couple pretty soon found their own relationship strained and began to quarrel. Mother-in-law did her worst, and one day, accusing the girl of having been rude to her, she threw a tantrum and got her son to hit his wife, either, I think, with a wooden ladle or a saucepan lid, or some other domestic implement. Upon which the wife, knowing her rights under the Marriage Law, demanded a divorce on grounds of ill-treatment. The husband became quite worried; but the girl went to live with friends, and refused to return home.

Now they were in the divorce court. They appeared truly a well-matched pair, both young, round-cheeked, sturdily healthy; the magistrate obviously thought it a pity that they should separate. So did I. So did everyone else in the court. "You have married for love, haven't you?" asked the magistrate. "And you have such a nice baby. Why separate for matters which can be arranged?"

The witnesses then were called, and it developed that neighbours and the street committee had taken the matter in hand by getting at the source of the trouble, which was Mother-in-law. If anyone needed a bit of remoulding, it was the old lady; so they had gone to work on her. Mother-in-law was at first very stubborn; a couple of weeks of persuasion had some effect. Then the baby became ill and, with help of the street committee, was taken to a "Western" hospital for treatment and got well. Neighbours were still engaged in their work of persuasion. Wouldn't the girl give the old lady (and her husband) another chance?

The upshot of it was that the girl agreed to "give it a try". Mother-in-law was not present as she did not want to "lose face" openly, but apparently she had agreed to let the young ones work out their own problems without getting the benefit of too many of her own "old-time" opinions; the young husband was duly reminded several times by the magistrate that filial duty to one's mother did not mean beating one's wife; anyway beating people was not allowed under the constitution. He was obviously overjoyed to get his wife back and a grin spread on the girl's face as they shook hands with the magistrate, the helpers and the witnesses. Then everyone shook hands with me too and thanked me, as if I had had anything to do with it.

This pair of peacocks were thus re-united. And I hope they were happy for ever after.

In the middle of the opera, I remembered this true story and could not help laughing. The old tyrannies, so petty, yet capable of inflicting so much suffering, could also be done away with, but it took time, it took much time, and patience, and care.

Filial duty, respect to the mother-in-law, had done enough harm through the centuries. It was good that there should be less of it. I turned to my friend: "In all these hundreds of years before 1949, don't you think that there must have been many times where sons did *not* obey their mothers, and stayed with their wives, and were quite happy though unfilial?"

"There may have been, but we don't know. They were not held up as examples to be admired."

It is odd that in this modern age so many women all over the world still enjoy a tragedy where, Romeo and Juliet fashion, the lovers die for love's sake. However, if one stops to think about it, they do not die for love's sake; they die because of mothers-in-law, chastity, filial duty, property, family, vendettas, and so forth – props of the old family system, a whole paraphernalia of man-made concepts totally unrelated to love. Peacocks actually don't have mothers-in-law, Italian families with hereditary vendettas, dowries big and small, or filial virtue to cope with. And yet, though I felt it strange to be affected by a star-crossed love story, I too wept, as did hundreds of other women, at the opera's end, even though I had laughed in the middle.

(1965)

89

America, America...

LECTURE tours in the United States are a hot pursuit of the novelist, academician, or "person of merit". They are reputed exhausting, dangerous to mind and health, but financial manna. In English literary cliques tales circulate of writers who went on tour and died of heart attack, alcoholism, nervous breakdown, or – worse – became so addicted to lecturing that they never wrote another word. Half a dozen European publishers warned me that I would have tomatoes thrown at me, be roared off the platform, hooted by audiences both bigoted and ignorant. All this adorned with anecdotes of Dylan Thomas, Malcolm Muggeridge, Dame Edith Summerskill, and other intrepid venturers into US lecturedom.

I found America both wonderful and horrifying, the American people intelligent and deluded; the land magnificent and wasted; the audiences confused, earnest, occasionally violent, but never dull; the big cities more dangerous than jungles and the small towns most endearing. Anything one says about America, at first impression, consists of two contradictory adjectives, a collision of superlatives in irreconcilable conflict. I came back exhilarated and depressed; terror-stricken and enthusiastic; I thought I understood and I remain bemused. I made a thousand friends and possibly ten thousand enemies. No one threw tomatoes at me, or called me names, but I wonder whether I did not shake too much some paranoid complexes. Almost everywhere, I was treated with sincerity and given attention, but encountered walls of ignorance and battlements of hysterical fear. Like erratic ephemera, wind-driven, the minds I met were so subject to a constant battering of "new" things that it was difficult for them to keep on any one topic long enough really to think about it. The war conducted by America in Vietnam has, however, in spite of a bombardment of extraneous trivia, become a long-lasting anxiety, which is pinning down the volatile and the gullible, becoming a focus of awareness in America's public and private thinking. I returned with love in my heart for the American people, so intelligent, but with so little true application of their able minds to accept reality; possessed of so much desire to know, yet so steadily prevented from facing the basic facts of their own disequilibrium; subjected to such unremitting avalanches of pseudo-facts and non-facts, and still managing to attempt rationality. During my four months there, I saw the beginning of the Great Debate over Vietnam, derided and ridiculed by the administration, but still going on; and growing in extent and awareness. And I was glad that, in a small way, my lecture tour did contribute to what, in the end, will stir the great people of America into their maturity at last.

One aspect of the American information media particularly struck me from the very beginning, because it is inescapable. That is the equating of the important with the unimportant, the fusion of the trivial with the tragic. On the radio a commentator will announce: "Fourteen sorties were made yesterday by four hundred B-52 bombers on Vietcong hide-outs ... nineteen thousand pounds of bombs and four thousand pounds of napalm were dropped on strategic targets – an esimated 108 Vietcong were put out of action," and then, practically without drawing breath, "So you want to be SURE of yourself anywhere, everywhere? Then use Burn's new superdeodorant – so smooth, so flattering to your SKIN, with its whisper of spring violets...." On television, the most tragic programme, showing the beginning of a disembowelling of Vietcong prisoners by their captors, children and women weeping, huts being burnt, will be interrupted every few minutes by an advertisement boosting the sales of a yummy fruit-cake.... It is this constant assault upon the reasoning mind, the ceaseless dazing of rational intelligence by violent contrast, which induce a confused, dazed acceptance of the logical with the incoherent, the horrible with the delightful. The only valid comparison that comes to mind is the Roman circus, where delicious rose petals and perfumes were sprayed on the audience while the martyrs were being savaged by lions or trampled by elephants and gladiators slashed each other to ribbons. The continual violence on television is horrifying to a fresh viewer, but constant exposure to it induces a craving for *more*, not less, of the same kind, and particularly when coupled with whispers of violets, alluring tickle to taste-buds and other pleasurable feelings.

Any physiologist who has studied Pavlov's work on conditioned reflexes can understand the process which is warping the minds of millions in America. A dog can be conditioned or trained to respond in a certain way to a certain stimulus, say the sound of a bell. But a dog submitted to contradictory stimuli at the same time becomes confused, almost hysterical, and goes into either morbid rage or paralytic stupor. In the same way I contend that, submitted to the excessive and contradictory stimuli at all levels constantly showered upon him, the average American loses the power of discerning between issues; there is for him no differentiation in impulse left between napalming fifty children and sucking the latest sweet. The link between crime towards others and personal pleasure for self is achieved so many times in television and radio that it cannot be just fortuitous.

"It is absolutely frightening – I'm getting so I can't sleep any more," an English author, also on tour, said to me. But after a while one does get conditioned; the critical faculties diminish, one finds it increasingly easy to swallow the most confused, contradictory absurdities today, never remembering that precisely the opposite were the beliefs of the day before. Under such compelling brain-washing, the independent mind has either to resign, or to concentrate on those areas of activity which produce the least mental conflict – and that is money-making, sticking to what is called "facts", which is business, technical innovations and personal success.

In my contacts with American individuals, I found so much warm friendliness, yet also prompt forgetfulness. I never met so many wanting to be loved, yet hysterically contemplating destroying the whole world that doesn't love them as they *want* to be loved. Everywhere, in every place, I was asked the same question: *Tell me, why don't people love us when we give them so much money?* It became almost a refrain at my lectures.

Paradox, Ambivalence, Futility, Flatulence, Instability, Magnificence, Barbarity, and above all Confusion.... Psychologists know that the end result of confusion is *fear*. A state of constant fear, suppressed, unreasoning, almost impossible to relate to anything, virtually hits one in the face once the outer courtesies are over. And yet, under such strain, it is all to the credit of the Americans I met that a few, in spite of all this, were groping for reason, groping for coherence, for logic, for explanation. Perhaps the hyper-conditioning has begun to overreach itself? "I want to really know what it's all about," they said. But the walls of fear and hysteria were strong, and often, told a different view, they would perceptibly back away, flee from the painful deconditioning process, which would destroy so many cherished "beliefs".

My lecture tour began at Hawaii, and the reception at Honolulu airport was the typical Aloha one, orchid leis, photographers, TV.

The reporting in the newspapers was accurate, something true of almost any local small-town newspaper. Great-circulation papers and important weeklies may slant the news to the advertisers' demands, but the small-town paper concentrates on what "the folks here would like to know", and they are as honest as possible unless the subject becomes too controversial, in which case they ignore it, which after all is better than writing *Time* fantasy. Honolulu is in that respect a small town; the Press does its work well, when Big Business is not too involved. There was good reporting before, but not after, my lecture. Speaking on the concrete problems of the Asian people, without the mildew of reassurance, without the routine placebo phrasing, was like throwing firecrackers in the midst of a cathedral service. "Wait till you get to the mainland," said to me, uncomfortably, a Hawaiian Chinese girl who had studied at the same university as I had in Peking, and was now teaching in Hawaii, "they'll murder you there." Mentally isolated, ocean-claustrated folks in Hawaii, she told me, "don't like to think about unpleasant subjects, like poverty." They prefer to believe themselves an "island paradise", and the rest of the world a smiling area of potential tourists to be aloha'ed and lei'ed. And why not? Since from all the postcards the beautiful landscape stares, more real than real, deadly in its assurance that one must be happy here where it is so beautiful.

There was a big strike on while we were there, and several other Hawaiian Chinese told me they could not afford the entrance tickets to my lecture; they were only school teachers. The "social status" which differentiates those with houses built "on the hill" from those living downtown, and relegates native Hawaiians to "the back" of the island, was freely talked about, with a "well, it's human nature" acceptance. There was opulence on the hill, but a great dearth of books and bookstores in the midst of opulence. The wealthy had their own careful social ladder, each rung worth a million dollars. "So-and-so, he's the 20-million dollar man." His house was, correspondingly, on a midway level. I met a 14-million, a 20-million, a 49-million, a 68- and a 91-million millionaire, all at the same cocktail party. The 2-million man ("poor" millionaire) told me with awed satisfaction that it was "quite an honour" that the 91-million fellow deigned to come. Big Business is in the hands of the two-figure millionaires. The one-figure millionaires struggle bravely to carry on, under pressure of being swallowed by the larger ones. An Asian (one-figure) millionaire complained, "We Asians out here are still kept in our places by the Whites; they know how to unite and crush

us out of the picture, businesswise, because we're still disunited."
The main topics of conversation were money and business, and after
that, business and money. The words "the mainland" here mean the
USA. People came or went "to the mainland", but a trip "to the
mainland" was not within reach of everyone. Many girls, reception-
ists, hotel clerks, typists, teachers, dreamt of going "to the mainland"
at least once, but confessed they might feel lost, "away from home",
meaning Hawaii, and that they "couldn't leave home for long".

The half-dozen of my ex-schoolmates from Yenching University
whom I saw in Hawaii were eager to know what was happening in
Asia, but a positive statement numbed them into apprehensive
silence. Their eyes glazed and opacity settled between us. Like so
many other Americans, they wanted reassurance that they were
doing the right thing and were approved and loved, rather than facts.

Near the imposing University of Hawaii is the East–West
Center, a building which houses "cultural interchange", and under
whose roofs assemble scholars of repute from all over Asia. It is run
by a cheerful, rotund and intelligent ex-ambassador, knowledgeable
about Asian needs, and not hysterical when the words land reform
are used. The Center was beset by financial difficulties, he told me.
Every year it had to have funds voted to it by Congress; the
administrative staff had to come up with arguments to justify the
Center's existence as a bastion of free learning and to continue
receiving money. It was designed as a bulwark of psychological
warfare against communism; but running costs were high, and such
gifts as the Japanese garden, given to the Center by the Japanese
government, just ate into the money voted for hiring Asian scholars.
"It costs $5,000 a year for upkeep. We hope we won't be receiving
many gifts like that; it does cramp our scholarship projects a bit."
I wished him well, and hoped funds would become more generous
in the future.

San Francisco is reputed the most progressive place in the USA;
and certainly it is a city of surpassing beauty, with its great bridges
spanning the sea, its enormous multi-levelled flyover highways, and
the lovely, quiet little creeks and wooded hills that extend inland for
miles. It is the abode of liberal intellectuals; California has more
cults, cranks, morticians in the billion-dollar death business,
churches, banks, oranges and artists than any other state, and the
longest boulevards in the world are in Los Angeles. In Los Angeles,
the *New York Times* had to close down, the paper being too left-wing
for the city. There are more women's clubs in California than
anywhere else in the States. Besides Hollywood, health centres,

cemeteries like parks, banks with the architecture of churches, and churches that look like banks, it has businessmen clamouring for trade with China, and retired generals clamouring to bomb China. Here again, overall description is a mere kaleidoscope of contradictions, and we must leave it at that.

The night I arrived in a small California town, a meeting was being held in the hall of the hotel where I stayed. It was some society connected with either the Minute Men or the John Birch movement. It was being addressed by a general (retired) of the US Army, and a pastor, possibly of the Fundamental persuasion. The audience of about 300 were being warned against subversion by "Kamewnism". The general asked his audience to live with their finger on the trigger, and to man the beaches. He denounced artists, writers, painters, foreigners, as subverting American manhood. He exposed plots to poison the food of "our boys" in Saigon, who were defending the American way of life in far-off Vietnam. He denounced the State Department as riddled with Kamewnism; so was the FBI, the CIA, the White House, and the *New York Times*. He told of plots to throw impurities in American food supplies, and to liquidate upright American manhood with mixed marriages. I thought such a being, larger than life and stentorian, had been dreamt up by some satirical novelist or perhaps by Peter Sellers, but there he was. The clergyman's speech took me out of one trance to plunge me into another. He denounced the Beatles. The Beatles, he said, were "the vanguard of Kamewnism". He had evidence of this. Solemnly he lifted a hand while his voice dropped to a rolling whisper. The Beatles played "moosic", or so the innocent audience thought; but the beat of their moosic was ... 84 per minute! And 84 per minute was the beat of the unborn baby's heart! And in this way the Beatles hypnotized good, innocent American youngsters, so that "Kamewnist masterminds" could toone into their captive brains and make them do their will by sending them hypnotic commands! Beware of the Beatles, and other such Kamewnists, trying to soften up American youth through moosic for an eventual takeover of America!

And since then, perversely, I've liked the Beatles even more than I did before going to America.

(1966)

Computers and Horoscopes

"THE COMPUTERS have told us." This phrase, which like "in depth" and "sensitive" is delivered with the irrefutable solemnity of the undiscussed, began, after four months, to evoke giggles from my iconoclastic mind; alas, I seemed the only one to think it funny.

For today, like the oracle of Delphi in ancient Greece, the computer is Superman. All-Expert. The computer is "propositioned with data" or, in journalese, is "fed information", and, like Moloch devouring the children of his devotees, munches it all up and comes out with the answer, "delivers the goods", which I suppose means: the accurate, one hundred per cent solution to all the crises in which American foreign policy is landing America.

That computers can only be as reliable as the information fed to them is accurate, is something I never heard discussed. When I raised the query, I was told that the computer was "immunized against mistakes" by being fed "data at various levels". "You mean hors-d'oeuvres?" I asked flippantly. A stern look was the non-reply I got.

The hypnotic quality of such pseudoscientific phrases as "in depth", "expert evaluation of processed data" and other such gobbledegook have taken strong grip on the American mind; when this kind of polysyllabic nonsense is uttered, one can almost see the free minds of this big democracy perform the low, oriental obeisance of a kowtow. "The voice of the Computer shall be heard in the land." Amen. Against this new religion, no disbelief is possible.

This attitude illustrates what is perhaps the most obvious danger in America's thinking, an unwillingness to question the premises, the bases of the verbalizations and propositions upon which all calculations and subsequent deductions are founded. Even Big Business, so ruthlessly clear-minded about its profit, evades the final question: But what is the ultimate end to all these computerized activities? What is America's true objective? And it is this central core of insanity, wrapped in the most awe-inspiring paraphernalia of machinery and gadgets whose very non-humanity guarantees accuracy, which is profoundly disturbing. All the data fed to the computers are based upon premises or propositions that have not themselves been examined for their nearness to fact. All this magnificent build-up of computerized knowledge leaves one with an ungraspable nothing: Have the computers decided what was the ultimate End allowed by the means now pursued? Has there been adequate investigation as to whether the motivation behind the data propositioned corresponds to a working reality?

These questions have been worrying me for some time, ever since the Honolulu conference of summer 1964, when the Pentagon computers told America to escalate in Vietnam. The proposition then was: If we withdraw, we'll lose face in Asia, so what do we do not to lose face? And the answer was: escalate. Of course it was. And I did not need a computer to know that. I have a terrible feeling that, from the start, the computers were not supposed to give another answer.

The involvement of computers in decision-making, hailed as "an advance in forward-thinking processes", disquiets me. When President Kennedy was faced with the fiasco of the Bay of Pigs, he said, "I should have known better than to ask the experts." Well, I hope the Americans know better than to trust computers. But it seems as if the computer has increasingly displaced reason, logic, humanity, respect for any decent code of behaviour, and has egged on America to escalation. Has anyone checked the computer for its own motives, incidentally? How about some computer psychoanalysis to discover whether a Freudian death wish has not been built into the computer along with other capabilities?

In February this year, when the bombing of North Vietnam started, I was in a small city in Wisconsin, and was asked whether I thought bombing "would achieve our peace aims". I said I thought no bombing of any country would ever convince any population of American peace aims; it would, on the contrary, stiffen them into resistance to war aims. At a time when the White House was promising the American people a quick surrender and a short war with the boys home by Christmas, my views were too unorthodox. My reply was published, however, in the local newspaper, without comment. It was plain that most of my audiences, convinced that the bombing was actually a message to Hanoi for peace, felt it easier to agree with their government, and not with me; the President, brand new, must be trusted to know what he is doing. Asians, being Asians, are different from Americans; Asians knuckle under, and soon will understand the good intentions inherent in the bombing of a small country by a huge one, especially if we promise them money at the same time.

When the atomic bomb was dropped on Hiroshima, I was in England, and I became very upset; though I hated the Japanese for invading China, and the awful things they had done to the population in some cities, I could never have wished on them such a terrible retribution. But round me sensible, cheerful, kind English girls, medical students like myself, were all assuring me that it was actually a humane thing ... "because it will considerably shorten the war, and it is really a saving in human lives" – a saving in *what* human lives? European, or Japanese? That was never discussed. And afterwards it all came out that the Japanese government, *before* the bomb had been dropped, was already suing for peace, so that the bomb was quite unnecessary, simply an exercise in horror, wiping out 300,000 lives; admittedly, mere Japanese lives, not English or American lives. That was 1945, and now in 1965, 20 years later, when North Vietnam began to be bombed, I was faced with the same terrifying lack of imagination, the same assurance that actually it was an act of charity to bomb North Vietnam, that it would save lives in the end, because the war would end that much more quickly. When I said: "Put yourself in the same position – would you give in if you were bombed?", some replied: "But we *can't* lose face, *they* must understand that. We can do so much for them, once they give up."

Finally exasperated, I said, "They'll never give up. You are *creating* communism, not stamping it out."

"The computers have told us ..." was the answer. The Pentagon had calculated every possibility, fed it to the computer, "and that's what they've told us to do."

This was ten months ago. Since then I've read a lot about computers, and have subscribed to a computer magazine. I read about computers having temperature quirks, being put out of gear by a hot day: their capabilities boil down to an enormous saving of time for calculations, and the elimination of "human error" when a precise set of propositions is to be studied. But no one, so far, has been able to "proposition" to a computer the quality of doubt about the very propositions it is fed with, nor has that most outstanding factor of all in humanity, human fervour, the human will to resist, ever been measured by a computer. For we are not machines, at least not if one is a Christian; some part of us is *also* greater than mere cogs and wheels, the human spirit. It reminds me of a story about a certain warlord in Old China, who was told the people's spirits were rebellious. "Spirits," he barked, "how much money is worth a spirit? Tell me, how can spirit fight against guns?" This crassly mechanistic and definitely unchristian attitude seems accepted in America, that Christian country, today.

A new species of human beings is seen around Washington and the Pentagon: Homo computerensis, recognizable by a smooth-surfaced metallic sheen about his physique, and "tape utterance" formulation in his talk (sorry, I mean data evaluation exchange). Homo computerensis converses in dots and dashes, an even, monotonous delivery. He is always described by his friends as formidably efficient, "chewing up data" in less time and "logging'" more work hours per day than ordinary humans.

"Sir," a Press friend, addressing one of these new supermen, said: "I'm afraid I can't agree with some of our people about this bombing. A lot of us begin to feel the policy of bombing North Vietnam is a failure. I'd like to have your comments on that." Homo computerensis turns on the questioner the telescopic glint of Polaroid lenses. His strong jaw with its synthetic teeth receives the signal to commence formulation output. He starts decoding, "We proposition every day with all the available data, and every day the answer comes back: Bomb."

Before leaving the States, I met a man who had been working on a hush-hush experiment, known as Operation Last Judgement.

The end had come; earth was a nuclear volcano; 4,000 super-megaton bomb loads had been discharged upon the United States; in return 7,000 super-megaton bomb loads were at that moment being discharged upon "the unfriendly nation". Operation Last Judgement was devised to ascertain how, with a warning of only four minutes, one could organize "seed-bed survival".

It started with charts and graphs plotting the "priority ratings" of certain sections of the "biological material" in the country. It designated "values" to such material. The "values" were given to such agglomerations of vulnerable personnel as hospitals, banks, schools, etc., a "value factor" being assigned to each of these in terms of their usefulness in a future when, hostilities having ceased, the reorganization pickup would start on a priority basis. Obviously a high value factor would lead to a high priority rating, and such biological material would benefit from decontamination and survival privileges before others, reckoned "disposable", such as hospitals, old peoples' homes and "non-classified" residential areas, such as city slums. What this jargon (almost impossible to reproduce without nausea) cloaked in its euphemisms was this: Operation Last Judgement was designed to select those who would be allowed to survive, in case of nuclear attack. Businessmen, industries and military complexes such as the Pentagon received from the computer top-priority ratings for their survival values. Was I surprised? Not a bit.

A friend of mine, an American physicist, insists that computer-worship is a tremendous hoax played upon the credulous American people. He says that Americans are taught to believe that gadgets and gimmicks are supremely important, that machines are far more efficient than any man can be. Push a button, pull a lever, turn a knob; things run, leap, whirr, work.... "Americans will always argue about decisions taken by other human beings, but a scientific decision, taken by a computer, cannot be argued against." He thinks that this hoax is being pulled by the Pentagon since the military brass is in control of the data that is fed to the computers; only the brass knows which computers are *built* to answer what questions in certain ways, and in no other.

And this brings us back to the central nought, the blind core; few in America question the basic premises upon which rest the facts fed to the computers, or fed to the people through information media.

Facts are the things we know, but do not know how we know; and the more opinionated we become about facts, the less we know about their origin. Notions whose origin cannot be traced become all the more indisputable and emotion-rousing when questioned. The Catholic Inquisition felt that Galileo's discovery that the earth was round, and turned around the sun, was infernal heresy, disrupting the very foundations of Holy Church. Faith was in peril, and reacted by trying most assiduously to turn Galileo into ashes. In the same way, if one argues that the notions America believes indisputable are, on the contrary, very far from universal or even local truths, one finds a considerable amount of hysterical passion aroused; the foundations of reason quake, the blood pressures rise: how dare I question the flatness of the earth? How dare I question that America is doing a lot of good burning, bombing and napalming in Vietnam? Who can withstand the computer, revealed religion, Word of God? One look at its sublime hermetic visage, all gleaming steel and knobs and buttons and shiny panels, and lightning streaks across millions of wires, and that is enough. Our puny brains cannot compare with the super-knowledge filed in tubes, in rods of wonderful alloys, with their million electronic gadgets and their fabulous names.

But all is not well; the human being is so capriciously made that an accumulation of irrationality in him, like pent pus breeding a deep-seated abscess, gives birth to tension, a fever of insecurity which seeks outlet. In medieval times witchcraft rituals and astrology relieved man's spirit from the feeling of doom bred by the dreadful authority of the Unknown; today, the same undercurrent of insecurity finds relief in the same way.

The State Department, Washington, DC, is an imposing building; one is met and treated with the utmost courtesy and solicitude, everything being done to make things smooth and comfortable. The chair I sat on while I waited for a permit which I needed was so well padded I nearly fell asleep. It was cold outside; inside the State Department building an even temperature kept one's temper beautifully sunny.

I was told the permit would be issued late in the afternoon. I asked the official who was looking after me whether, in the meantime, we could get a map of Washington and start visiting a few places of interest. "Of course," he said with great urbanity. "Four doors down this very corridor there is a news-stand and stationery shop."

We proceeded to the news-stand, about thirty yards away. It sold newspapers, chewing-gum, but no maps of Washington, no maps at all. "Sorry, we never get anyone asking for maps here, but we've got horoscopes, if you wish," said the news-stand man, middle-aged and benign.

He then pointed to a rotating shelf, like those used to hold paperback bestsellers; there, lined up, were paperbacks labelled Gemini, Taurus, Aries, Your Zodiac sign; Your health, your wealth, your romances, Know them! Your luck every day of this month! On a shelf against the wall were thicker volumes: What the stars can tell you; Your character; Know yourself through scientific palmistry; Professor Shastri's handbook; Know your luck every day this year; The Hindu lore of the Zodiac....

"Why buys this stuff?" I asked.

"The people who work here, ma'am, they all do. And let me tell you, I'm always having more of them coming. There's been a run on them for the last month or so. I can never get too many. But no one's ever asked me for a map of Washington."

We chatted. Most people bought the slim monthly paperback. They wanted to know "what's going to happen tomorrow". On the last day of the month there was always a queue for the next month's supply. "I've noticed that the Scorpio people buy the most; Scorpio is always sold out." Next came Gemini and Taurus; Virgo people, on the whole, were not so eager to know what the stars had in store for them. "Virgo people are unusually sceptical. I always have a couple or so of Virgo booklets left over, but I never have enough of Scorpio." At Christmas and New Year there was always a big demand for the larger books, those containing a whole year of day-by-day fortune-telling with palmistry, physiognomy and other adjuncts thrown in. "They're much appreciated as presents."

We went round Washington without a map, only to find that nothing was open to the public before 2.30 p.m., and then only from 2.30 to 5.30 or 6 p.m. at the latest, which made sightseeing difficult. A black taxi driver drove us, pointing out things. We went into Abraham Lincoln's monument, gazed at the eternal flame and at Lincoln's solemn marble face. We were very cold, and soon returned to the State Department to keep warm: I bought my horoscope, under Virgo. "You will meet interesting people, who will enlarge your horizon" was my day's slogan. The very nice official turned up again with a "sorry to keep you waiting" and my passport beautifully stamped.

That night we had dinner with someone who, though not a computer man, talked like one. He was described as an executive. Inevitably, the talk stuck in the quagmire of Vietnam. "We can't pull out, we can't lose face, they've got to give in, like the president said," said the executive. "Besides, I don't see what we risk ... after all, we've given all the data to the computers. I know that for sure. The computers were working away for a whole week before we decided to bomb them." He waved his hand. "We had to take the risk, and the computers analysed it all for us and came up with the right answers. We can't lose."

"Have you also consulted the stars?" I asked.

"The stars? I don't quite get it," said our executive.

"Well, you know how it is. We in Asia still believe in the stars."

"Oh," he said, "I see. Well, how interesting." His face assumed a pleasant, benign indulgence. "Yes, I guess people in your country are rather traditional, still believe in fortune-telling ... wonder if there's anything to it...."

And now all I want to do is to proposition a computer with my horoscope, and start a new evaluation. I want a priority rating to be statistically assigned by the Zodiac, with extra survival values for Virgo, of course. It cannot be too impossible. I am sure that, when the Last Judgement of humanity is at hand, some great computer will be busy doing just that.

(1966)

The Neighbourhood Scene

PUBLIC schools in America are paid by public funds; in England public schools are private. Some of the sponsors of my lectures were also, as leaders of the community, members of school boards, but their schools were private, neighbourhood or community schools. In two places I lectured under their auspices, and was received with the breathless nervous stare of people who had committed a terrible *faux pas*. They were both good enough to tell me, after the lecture, the reason for their unease. In both these communities (one in California, one in an affluent exurbia near New York), the John Birchers had taken over the school boards. My sponsors were both badly frightened, and one of them was being voted out of the Board.

I shall start with the sponsor belonging to the affluent exurbia. She was so nervous that she kept twisting and turning her rings on her fingers; at the end of my lecture she looked like a wet bath towel. Before I began to speak, she tried to warn me, by hints and indications:

"We're a business community here, junior executives mostly, so we're rather quiet." She glanced at her husband. "We're quite well informed, quite well informed about ... ah ... other folks, but we've got our own ideas. We certainly don't like *disturbances*. We've got a lot of discussion groups here." She again paused. "I'd be rather careful not to hurt some feelings," she ended, desperately.

Unfortunately, I was not that night in a tactful mood, or, possibly, what I thought was moderate was to my audience and their delicate feelings like trampling their pet corns. It was the only audience that behaved like a charging bull. They snorted, they interrupted, they howled. This did not worry me too much (had I not been prepared for tomatoes?) but it surprised me. For Americans on the whole are a most courteous people: far more courteous and less arrogant than the ignorant young men in certain over-estimated British universities.

But perhaps, as "junior executives", they had to prove themselves "aggressive" (which, business-wise, is deemed essential to success).

In such an atmosphere, the empathy I had achieved in other places was not achieved. They were 100 per cent for "giving it to the commies", and the commies meant anyone who wasn't 100 per cent pro whatever the American policies abroad were. They felt the rest of the world should learn "to work hard, as we Americans do", and either "toe the line" or else be prepared to "get it". They were lurid, foul-mouthed, and as stuck full with prejudices as plum cakes are reputed to be with plums. The singular thing was that most of them were supposed to be "travelled"; in other words, they were executives sent out by their business companies for quick trips abroad, and they made no bones about the fact that "business is good in Vietnam as long as the Fleet are there to protect us".

A doctor got up and said that, instead of talking nonsense, I should tell the Asians to stop having children; otherwise, in twenty years, all of us in Asia "would be dying of hunger, and serve you right". He was loudly applauded.

Someone else rose and said they hadn't come to hear about what should be done by America, as America had done enough, and we Asians anyway couldn't pull together, and weren't grateful for what America was doing for us. "The only cause of your misery out there is that there are too many of you. Until you people start on that problem, I guess we Americans are suckers to help you."

After the lecture I was upbraided by some women who belonged, I believe, to the YWCA. "You *mustn't use* words like 'land reform' here ... we don't like that, it's Communistic."

"Well, we feel you did not give *us* the credit you oughtta...."

"We don't want Communism here; that's why we gotta fight in Vietnam. Otherwise we'd have to be fighting Communism right here."

I tried to expostulate, but was talked down. My sponsor was moaning: "I'll get it from my Board ... they didn't like your speech – they sure didn't." She told me, as her grimly silent husband drove me back to the station: "You see, I'm new here. I'm on the School Board. We've got a different policy now. You were invited last year, under the other sponsor, so I couldn't cancel you...."

"Thank you," I said.

When we got to the station where I would catch the train, her husband unclenched at last: "Well, I guess that's that. If I were you, I'd talk a bit more about what *we've done*, not so much about what's to be done ... that's *your* problem."

"I thought I had come to lecture on the problems of Asia," I replied.

"Yep, we've got our own problems," he snapped.

I liked my sponsor and her husband. I felt so sorry for the poor woman; she'd take a long time to live me down in her community. But the full explanation of her fear was not known to me until a few days later, when I received a letter from a well-wisher from that community, explaining that the school board had now been "taken over" by the John Birchers. And among the audience had been the very wealthy Mrs So and So, who every year went to India, where she had founded a school with funds from American private persons, who were giving money for that school and nobody liked to hear that it wasn't any good giving money; they wanted to be told how *grateful* everybody was to the Americans, to them, for all they were trying to do.

Well, I had learnt two things. That the inroads of the extreme Right Wing concentrate in exurbias, in capturing school boards and getting rid of liberal elements. The exurbanite, being in a tight-knit small community, was particularly vulnerable. His job, as "junior executive", and his prospects of advancement were threatened by rumours, and the faintest whiff of suspicion would decide his future career; his children's education also, was at stake: for the school boards might feel the children were as unco-operative as their parents. The more "travelled" these junior executives were (which meant that they flew to Hong Kong, Manila or Tokyo for "aggressive selling" and "business contacts"), the more they felt emotionally involved in America's spread overseas, in expanding US investment abroad. "Returns from direct investment abroad have consistently been greater than capital outlay," they said. One firm, in twelve years, had chalked up a 14-billion-dollar *surplus* in profits. Who was I to tell them that "doing good" didn't mean doing well profit-wise? As one of them rightly said, "We're making good money in South Vietnam; the longer the war goes on, and the more of our troops out there, the more protection for us – suits me down to the ground to have the bombing go on...." This was the voice of Big Business, Monopoly, in the shape of the junior executive, the up-and-coming but still vulnerable employee who has to prove himself rabidly loyal to the organization that hires him. Monopoly reaches out everywhere, for control of talent, ideas and raw materials, and everything for Big Business is defined in terms of markets and profits.

Very succinctly, in the next few days, another executive was to put it to me. "One of our problems, as an international outfit, is that we have different goals from a nation state – from *any* nation state. We simply cannot have any curb from the nationalistic policies of the nation state. That's outmoded."

"In other words," I said, "your kind of internationalism means profit for you, and everyone else has to give up everything, including the needs of their own nation?"

"Now, now, now," he said, "that's a Communist idea, nationalism."

In the other place where I lectured, a community near Los Angeles, the sponsor was explicit. "I am getting out; the school board has been taken over by the John Birchers, and they don't want me. They said I brought too many foreign lecturers in, and not enough Americans." How can the Right Wing get so much influence, I wondered, "there are so few of them." "Yes, they are few," said my sponsor, "but they are active, aggressive, and they've got plenty of money – they forge ahead. And they smear everybody who doesn't agree with them. They hint that there's something un-American about one, and out you go. There is one of them among the eight of us, but somehow she got me out. I pointed out to the board that out of nine lecturers I had only invited two foreigners; you were the second. 'That's two too many,' the John Bircher said. 'Good Americans shouldn't listen to foreigner's guff.'"

"So I'm getting out," my sponsor continued. "You see, my children go to our neighbourhood school. I couldn't have them suffer." For these women, that was the heart of their fear: that their children would suffer, in that invisible but so damningly effective way, in the "neighbourhood schools". I spent a whole afternoon listening to some of these women's stories about the schools, the neighbourhood schools, to beat the problem of integration, to keep the community's "way of life". Everyone I met assured me that they were not racialists, not at all; on the contrary, they would welcome "Negroes" to their school and their community, *provided* these "coloured people" knew how to behave and "didn't bring our standards down". And that was the telling phrase. Insidiously they were being persuaded that the standards would be lowered; "so our community is paying for its own neighbourhood schooling; we want to give our children the best". They were evading integration by taking their children out of integrated schools, into neighbourhood schools. Of course, I am speaking of the more affluent; when it came to less affluent neighbourhoods, there was resentment on the whole subject. "Of course I'm not against integration in principle, but it just doesn't work." On the other hand, it would be unfair not to point out that I also found many individuals deliberately going out of their way to help integration, to fight against the insidious, creeping racialism. "We've got to do something to prove that we are a democracy, we can't let that problem grow on us and grow on us." But by and large, there was a withdrawal of the children of the more affluent into "private" or "neighbourhood" schools, and "we've now got the best teachers, because we can afford them". And in their private schools, John Birchers were active.

The question of racial discrimination is not easy to answer; in my case, there was none at all. We were never refused service, ill-treated, or in any way made to feel unwelcome, even in Richmond and Charleston; everywhere people were most courteous. But it was only too obvious that there were two economic layers, white on top, coloured and black below. In all the airports, the menial work was done by Blacks; also in all the hotels. I travelled by air back and forth across the States and in more than fifty airplane trips, I saw only one Black and he was an army man, going to Vietnam; otherwise I never met any Black travelling by plane. That of course does not mean that there are none, but the statistical infrequency points to an economic scale of differentiation, which is the true problem, rather than "colour".

This economic ghettoism is again very obvious in all the big cities, with their Black slums; some of them extending block after block, with the ravaged look which wilts the spirit. I did, however, see some affluent Blacks; it was in a San Francisco restaurant, where nine women, all Black, were eating together; they dripped with feathers and furs and diamonds. "It's the Negro who's climbed on top who won't do anything for his fellow men," said to me one of my sponsors who was with me. "Look at these women. They wouldn't dream of doing anything for their own people." And of course it is true that, irrespective of race, those who are, or imagine themselves to be, belonging to an "upper class" will exploit their own people just as cheerfully as a "White" would.

I met other Blacks in Harlem, in the slums, clear-minded and vocal. "No, this can't go on; and they say integration now, but what does it mean? They say I can send my son to a white school now, and I say thank you, but it is going to cost me more, not less. The bus fares have gone up, and it's quite a way out."

The American, white factory girl I met on a ferry in Seattle was one of the many working people (taximen, factory girls, farm-hands, newspaper sellers) who in that superbly direct American way came up to me and started talking, talking with that frankness and sincerity which makes one admire and respect the American people.

"Look, everything's going up in price, and you should see where I live: rats as big as that running around ... and it's a white neighbourhood, the niggers are worse off, a couple blocks down...."

She was vehement. "All the girls where I work, we're the same: I've got no way to look after my baby; everything is so expensive; we're in debt up to the neck. Why can't we just stay home instead of spending all that money in Vietnam fighting? We need more hospitals: you should see what the hospitals are like when you can't pay."

"What the hell are we fighting for? Can you tell me why we've got to go way out there to fight?" This was a taximan. "I say, why don't you let those guys do what they want with their country, and why don't we improve things here? I'm making eighty dollars a week, I can't make ends meet...."

Some workmen I met (they were welders) had been in Korea. "We don't want any more wars. Live and let live. My kid is running around with a bad gang where I live. Dope addicts, delinquents. I say let's clean up our own house first; let's have good schools, good teachers. Why, where I live the teachers have all resigned; they're scared of being beaten up."

(1966)

Come Laugh with Me...

ONE OF the nicest discoveries about America is the sense of humour of the "ordinary people": taximen, waiters, salesgirls, gas station attendants, black sweepers and porters, road workers, busmen, factory girls ... a variegation of kindly astringent wit, an Easter-bonnet fun in contrast with the utter dreariness of nightclubs (expensive variety), computermen and executives, all three of them one category; much sound to deafen reason is emitted by them.

But then, I always found it easy to chuckle with American humorists; easier than with *Punch*, or Searle; as for Malcolm Muggeridge, his "funny" professional pieces on "The American Woman and Sex in America" (after his most lucrative lecture tour, complete with a BBC team), I found neither funny, nor altogether in good taste. Early in my young days I fell under the spell of Mark Twain; from thence proceeded, via *The Little King*, to Thurber; I miss something when I do not see Fernando Krahn's magnificent cartoons; and Roger Angell's ironical deft essays tickle with delicate delight. Art Buchwald consoles me for a lot of things I don't like about what America does; and my favourite book is *Dreams of Glory* by Steig. As for Peter Arno, Jules Feiffer, so many others, life would be poorer deprived of their appreciation of life's tragic absurdities. And it is this gift of laughter that one finds, easy to breathe as air, in many situations in America.

So let me praise them; let me praise the waiter, alarmed at my alarm at the size of my steak, and his wonderful monologue on steaks; let me praise the porters and the stevedores, the New York taximen and the motel-keeper in Arizona, the traffic officers who did not arrest us for speeding, and the rescue squad who rescued us in a blizzard; the four-o'clock-in-the-morning coffee-stand attendants and the bulky bus-drivers ploughing us safely through a snowstorm night; the income-tax man, who, when it came to paying my income tax, was most concerned that my claims for expenses were too small.

"Well, now, we aren't used to people eating so little ... I'll give you another 800 for meals expenses and take 20 off your long-distance phones – that'll make it about even."

Let me praise the courtesy, the sincerity, the earnestness of my audiences, sitting patient, listening to the unpalatable. Let me say how much I could vision the potential of America for doing good; and let me also say that it made me all the more frightened, all the more sad, to see what is being done, in the name of the people of America, to turn all that good into an international evil as well as a national catastrophe. And it is precisely *because* one becomes attached to America, *because* one is enchanted by the people of America, that one tries, all the more, to save America despite herself from suicide in dishonour and shame.

Only yesterday I received a letter. The writer is an American woman doctor, a psychologist. "We are suffering from wholesale paranoia," she writes. "We make assumptions about people; assumptions based upon our own wishful thinking; these grow into delusions; we imagine that what we think *must* be true because *we* think it so. When things don't turn out as *we* think, we get terribly disappointed and immediately turn from love to hatred; in a frenzy, we want to batter down what we built up, not realizing that all the time what we built up only existed in our own minds ... and it's all part of our own insanity, which is wreaking havoc upon others, as well as upon ourselves.

"Ten years ago we were crazily worried about Russia; worked ourselves into frenzies about Moscow, had witch-hunts for 'commies', but now we've switched. We're rapidly building up the Russians *in our minds* as the nicest, the most honest, the best guys in the world, forgetting that they cheated us more than once and that with them, as with us, self-interest comes first. Now it's China that's The Bad Guy and we see Chin-coms everywhere, even in Alabama. Maybe one day we'll discover we've made a mistake again. Then we'll have to find someone else to *hate*, someone else to *love*...."

I don't know whether my psychologist friend (who has been to China as a missionary and claims that American missionaries suffer from a love-hate complex about China, and that too many of these ex-missionaries are now in the China Lobby, trying to make policy for the United States) is entirely correct in her psychological analysis; however, I have seen it elsewhere, in other words. Historian Hofstadter claims that the American policy has always been haunted by the terror of a *great conspiracy against America*. Whether this has to do with the guilt complex generated by the massacre of many American Indians I would not know. But apparently, always, America has seen a Devil, a Bogeyman, in the Darkness Beyond. And the Devil must be made Flesh, in order to be exorcised, destroyed, to keep America safe. At first it was a secret society called the Illuminati, attacking the United States with such secret weapons as stink-in-the-toilets, to produce foul diseases; then it became the Pope and the Jesuits, practising free love, and prowling in disguise to lure the young. Later it became Communism; the Russian brand first, and now the Chinese, with Senator McCarthy and the witch-hunters. Always, somewhere, haunting the unquiet soul of America, the Bogeyman, Devil with smell of sulphur and concealed cloven hoof. This almost permanent hallucination throughout America's history, contends Hofstadter, this strong myth-making, distorts reality to an extent that can be called psychopathic for the makers of policy; for he calls his book *The Paranoid Style in American Politics*.

Dr Tang Tsou, a Chinese historian long resident in the USA, puts it in a different way. He thinks that Americans "misunderstand" the world around them. Because they assume that certain facts of history and geography, peculiar to America, are universal truths, God-given premises, and that whoever does not comply with them is anti-God and therefore anti-America (which almost amounts to the same thing). "The moral unity and uniformity in American life," says Tang Tsou, "accentuates the tendency to view alien things in terms of an *image* of one's self, and to judge foreign life in terms of one's own assumptions."

In various ways, all three of these opinions emphasize the same thing. I, too, was to become aware of it in America; the propensity to mythomania, and beyond mythomania, even more dangerous, as Fullbright says, "gap between fact and perception becomes a chasm, and action becomes irrelevant and irrational". For what characterizes every delusion when it has extended beyond the threshold of neurosis to psychopathology is the inability to accept that the delusion is a mistake. In old parlance, this lack of insight used to be called *the mortal sin of pride*. Today it is called: "We mustn't lose face."

"We can never accept that we've made a mistake. The British, the French, they can withdraw, admit an error, be defeated. But not *us*. Not the USA. Our *image* would suffer; and the *image* we have built up of ourselves is something quite tremendous. In fact all our communication media are haunted by *image building*. Reality, whether the person, the book, or product we sell, comes second; what

111

is important is the advertising, the *image*. We talk of people as 'projecting a favourable image', as if we had become incapable of seeing them as anything else but appearances on a screen." Again and again, all over America, I was met with this wall of shadows; and only a few days ago, I was to receive a letter from a fan: "All you told us last year about our bombing North Vietnam has come to pass," he wrote. "But I am sure you must understand that we *must* have face ... you, as an oriental can appreciate that...." I as an oriental replied that the more bombing, the less face; in fact I did not think America had any face left....

Another dangerous reaction, also part of what Hofstadter calls the paranoid tendency, and my doctor friend plain paranoia, is the *scapegoat* complex. "When we are jolted," said a radio commentator who had come to talk out with me his own private perturbation over America's actions in Vietnam, "we always turn round to blame the other guy. Same with our policies. Not only we can't admit a mistake; but we must always then denounce the other guy, who deceived us. We've been misled, we've been fooled; we are always the good guys, the suckers, taken for a ride, but never never doing anything unkind. We're always full of good intentions. The creation of the scapegoat, the scapegoat being a projection of guilt, but cut away from the ego which cannot admit to being wrong, is part of the delusion, and it leads to witch-hunt, looking for the guilty to clean up the community." One university professor told me, in rather frightened tones, that if ever it was found out that America had made "one hell of a mistake getting into this Vietnam business" there would immediately be such a colossal witch-hunt that a lot of officials would rather carry on with the war than contemplate the result of withdrawal while they were still in office.

I had a small taste of this process at one of my lectures. I had talked about Vietnam; everyone always asked about Vietnam. One of the women in the audience came up to grip my hand. "I knew it. It's our State Department. It's full of Reds." "I beg your pardon?" I said, not understanding. "They're purposely giving us the wrong advice, making us escalate; they want us in a mess, so the Russians will win ... I always thought State was full of Commies." Off she went, and left me wondering.

Out of the mouths, out of the troubled hearts of some Americans themselves, come these analyses, this insight into their system's disease.

In keeping with the myth-making has grown up a whole new vocabulary, the semantics of liquidation, smuggling a bland, pseudoscientific jargon, to perpetuate this delusive mania. A scientist working on a space project told me: "It's the gigantic projects, going to the moon, conquering space and the new words for all this. They dwarf the human being; quite honestly I don't feel a thing if I'm told a million beings must be killed off; not a thing." Obviously, the methods now employed condition the death-dealers: bombing or napalming from on high must dispense a feeling almost of godliness, Zeus letting the lightning fall; far less repugnant than hand-to-hand combat, where one has to come to close grip with "reality" in the person of The Other Human Being. This added dimension of impersonality, odiousness at machine distance, superpower, sucks meaning out of description, terror out of numbers, humanity out of the suffering inflicted. The new sarcophagus vocabulary, wrapping the putrefaction within in sterile, stench-proof syllables, talks of the "spraying of weed killer", which means destroying the crops of a population; and "area neutralization" to mean carpet bombing and genocide. One encounter I had with this new aspect of words was at a dinner party. I sat next to an eminent gentleman, whose handsome looks, marvellous suit, and official position, bespoke wealth, power, and good taste. He spoke in calm, matter-of-fact tones. I mentioned to him an article I had read in a magazine, which had appalled me. I had been about ten days in America, and was jittery with the verbiage of slaughter I encountered. The morning paper presented scientists from a "research foundation" boasting of America's nuclear arsenal "enough to blast all life on earth seventy-five times over". The TV report, after the weather forecast, presented a panel discussing shelters against radiation, and calculating (offhandedly) in tens of millions the human beings America could nuclearize out of existence. In the afternoon an interview by some experts on "Communist aggression" would be followed by a pep talk by some senator on how "deterrent action" should be instituted immediately; this was followed by a gruesome fantasy on death rays dealt out by super robots, and some sadistic shrieks with implied tortures. After a few days of such single-minded concentration on death, annihilation, slaughter, cruelty, I was forever hearing, off stage, a huge vacuum cleaner clearing up large tracts of the earth's surface of all life. Now I knew what anxiety neurosis meant; never, even during the bombings in Chungking, had I felt so tense. Then I had read in this magazine the report of an expert (and a doctor too!) stating that the use of gas in warfare was *humane*; that the "spraying" of villages with various gases would be the best way to tackle the Vietcong. He particularly recommended the use of vomiting gas upon the population; while everyone was vomiting (babies, invalids, women not excluded) the GIs would safely "wade in" and be able to pick out the Vietcong from the "friendly natives".

I mentioned to Mr Palmer (this is not his real name) my reaction to this article: indignation, stupefaction that a doctor (a doctor!) could preach this inhumanity. I said that possibly a man could survive an hour or two of vomiting, but no baby could outlive the vomiting gas, and it would be, therefore, the babies who would die; and, anyway, how would they be able to tell the Vietcong from the others, when everyone knew that the Vietcong were the population, the people themselves? Mr Palmer, between scoops of his silver spoon at the dessert, told me I was incorrect in my evaluation. "We think on the contrary that these gases will have great value, great value. Not only the nerve gas and the vomiting gas but other gases. In fact they will have a function even when the world is at peace again."

"At peace again?" I queried, almost hopefully (the bombing of North Vietnam had just begun).

"Well, of course. Eventually, when peace comes. In certain areas, such as Africa, for example, or certain parts of Asia, we might still have to deal with problems there, occasionally."

"Such as what?"

"Well, demonstrations, that sort of thing. Some of these people are quite inflammable; they might need a bit of checking; that's where gases are so useful. Our scientists should be working on tranquillizing gases. Spray and people calm down."

"But don't you think," I said, "that people riot because they are hungry? Look at the recent hunger riots in India: it's the women who led the crowds to storm the hoarders' shops and get some rice. Don't you think they are justified?"

Mr Palmer did not think so. "No, I don't thing they are really." He shook his head with elegant weariness. "It's so destructive. If they were *really* starving, they wouldn't have the *strength* to riot, to . . . er, destroy things. It's all quite exaggerated, you know, these reports of hunger – these people are being incited, they're not really starving."

Two elegant ladies at our table, who had followed the conversation, nodded sagely, in full agreement. They were not having dessert, of course. Too fattening.

"People who are hungry *don't* go out in the street to demonstrate; they stay at home," said one.

"I don't think these women accomplished *anything* by this sort of behaviour," said another.

"When I'm hungry I just feel sleepy," a man added, smiling wittily.

"That's where tranquillizing gases might become quite useful," concluded Mr Palmer, "quite useful. Spray around, tranquillize the mobs; no harm done, off they go, and no destruction...."

I felt a minor dose of vomiting gas had been wafted my way and was glad when we rose from the table. Since then I've pondered over Mr Palmer's tranquil words. Mr Palmer's peace – what did *he* mean by peace ... the peace of death? Was he really serious when he thought the great unsolved injustices, the growing gap between haves and have-nots, the hunger and misery, could be dealt with by spraying "tranquillizer gases"? Or was this a macabre sense of humour I had not yet encountered? And I've wondered too whether, next time there is an eruption such as the one which occurred at Los Angeles when the frustrated come storming out of their slums, tranquillizer gases will be used, experimentally, upon America's own have-nots?

Mr Palmer was not an isolated event; I met other elegant men, just as calmly contemplating the art of massive elimination, or tranquil suppression; as if this was the answer to all the world's problems. And the way they murmured these solutions, meditatively sipping a Manhattan, patiently explaining, in the extraordinary language of annihilation, the advantages of such a peace, was a new dimension in horror comics ... or comic horror.

I also met two scientists working in a research foundation involving the study of world population. "The single cause of poverty, misery, delinquency in the world," they intoned, "is the population explosion." They had found no other; and already, they said, a point of no return had been reached in certain areas, such as Latin America, Africa, and Asia. There, humanity was suffocating itself; soon an enormous wave of people from these overpopulated areas would wash in one gigantic tide, over the USA, swamping civilization, honour, decency, and the standard of living. In the research foundation, intensive work was urged, to develop sterilizing materials which, thrown in water, sprayed over crops, would automatically render whole populations sterile. In this way the world population explosion would be curbed, and "art, civilization, thought, knowledge flourish again as man would reach his highest self-development".

The two scientists differed as to whether the consent of the nations to be sterilized should be obtained prior to action; one averred that "co-operation" was all to the good; the other said that such populations were emotionally and intellectually retarded, suffering from taboos, and the best thing would be an agency, supra-governmental, composed of the world's chief Brains, scientists, and experts (like himself) who had studied the problem and knew best. This agency would decide what was to be done, and which nations should thus be temporarily sterilized. Another scientist suggested that no one should be allowed to reproduce without first obtaining a certificate. Overpopulation led to Communism, the scientists added as I tried to dispute their theories; China was Communist, wasn't it? That's because it was overpopulated. Experiments had proved that overcrowded rats became neurotic, belligerent, and riddled with abnormal behaviour; in the same way China would only be a civilized and peaceful nation when her overpopulation was done away with.

I bought a book on population. I found out that the Netherlands, Japan, and Britain, had 885, 650 and 550 persons per square mile respectively, while Switzerland and Belgium had about 900. India had 368, and China 170 per square mile. Therefore, it appeared to me, the Netherlands, Britain, and Japan should be sterilized imme-diately, otherwise they would certainly go wildly Communistic, as compared with underpopulated China. I also found out that the average population per square mile was 167 in Europe, 108 in Asia, 49 in the USA, 31 in Latin America, and 26 in Africa. Obviously the USA was ready to pour uncivilized hordes to swamp out civilization in Latin America, and qualified for spraying too. Yet such gobblede-gook was being uttered by these "scientists" on lecture tours, up and down the country, to university audiences. ... There was the fat, brilliantly clever opinion-maker, who between two vodka martinis told me that he was participating in the work of a research foundation devoted to the study of undersea living for humans, when the land areas on the globe would have become unlivable. "Why unlivable?" I asked. "Radiation," he answered, surprised that I should ask. I said: "But, instead of preparing for a nuclear holocaust, for armageddon, and going on piling up megaton warheads, don't you think it would be more sane to do something about the world's real problems, equalizing the world's resources, solving the food situa-tion; there are so many areas in the world which, if properly developed, could support two or three times the population they now have...." But I was met with the glazed, entranced stare of the paranoiac, that gaze into emptiness, which rejects all vision but the fixed *image* set up as its own, all attempts to question its reality.

Gigantism, the monster death-wish, inhabited these high-level brains; it seemed to me they were sick, sick, and I longed to be away from them. It seemed appalling that out there in the street could be so many *other* Americans, who did not have these monstrous dreams, who were quite unaware of them, and I prayed that perhaps it wasn't true, perhaps it was all just a few crackpots....

But then gas *was* used in Vietnam, quite soon after the article; and nuclear warheads *have* kept on piling up; and just to keep one's eyes and ears tightly closed and say: "This cannot happen," is just not good enough any more....

America, America, the Devil that haunts you is not abroad, but within you; it inhabits your own head, it is coiled in your own heart; you must exorcise it from your own body: and no one can do this for you, but yourself, your own people.

I want to believe that somehow America will save herself; that common sense, the sanity of protest, will save this beautiful country. I like to think of the many in America, candid-eyed, earnest, wanting to know the truth. America is the country of McCarthy, but also of I. F. Stone; of General Le May who wants to bomb us all back into the stone age, but also of the young students who protest against the Vietnam shame. If there are sick dreams and sick people in America, driving her to her doom, there are also others, striving to know the truth and the cure.

I want to remember the little American woman I met in Hong Kong, going to China. "China," I said, "why go to China?" "Because my life has to be a witness to truth. I am a Christian," she said. "As a Christian I would rather be in a country that is going to be bombed, than in a country that is doing the bombing."

So I keep hoping, hoping that one day America the beautiful will recover from her paranoid dream, and we shall all laugh together, humanity regained....

(1966)

117

The Fruit of Their Loins

FEAR is not merely physical circumstance corresponding to an objective event: it is a subjective emotion based on assumption or previous experience and sometimes unrelated to the situation faced. Fear occurred to me in Los Angeles; half past ten at night, and fine. I strolled as Asians do, along the streets, ambling in the soft night air. My companion stopped. "Have you noticed, we two are the only people walking?" I looked. No one, up and down the wide wide boulevard; an asphalt desert, nothing but a car whizzing by, hounded by its own shadow. Suddenly I was afraid, afraid because of the unknown. Later I was told by a resident that people could be arrested for walking about, which in Los Angeles is called loitering.

Through our weeks in America, there was this strange hiatus between an impalpable climate of terror, for which I could find no adequate reason, and the pragmatic, fearless attitude which we adopted, taking people for granted, things for well-intentioned, refusing hostility. I did not lock my hotel door nor my suitcases; I went to Harlem; I walked in Central Park; all things which I had been told not to do. And I left America without having encountered any of these dreary episodes so often told, of rudeness, discrimination, or being robbed. Maybe I was lucky. But all the time, I did have to fight: to fight against fear, not a real fear, but the word-bred fear of the communication media and the tenseness of the atmosphere. Hysteria escalated in the raucous blare of radio and television; the phraseology of war ripened as exculpatory speeches promising more war in the name of peace descended upon us with their camouflage of half-truths. The TV screen blossomed with scenes of tortured prisoners and burnt houses and disgusted GIs and maimed children ... after a time, almost ghoulishly relished, made normal by repetition. All the time one's nerve kept on the raw with expectation of dreadfulness, thus fulfilling President Roosevelt's famous sentence: *We in America have nothing to fear but fear itself.*

Some lines kept going through my mind:

I never heard the monster roar
But sensed a bull-horned shadow near.
Can that reflection be my own?
Into this labyrinth of fear ...

This labyrinth of fear ... but we ignored the corridors of panic, and one of the great reliefs, issues out from this shadow tenseness gripping more horribly than any hands could do at my throat, was lecturing at the women's clubs.

"I think the women's clubs are terrible, so boring," said a prominent lecturer to me. After twenty-eight lectures in as many clubs, I do not agree. I am a women's club lover. I have never enjoyed myself so much as lecturing to women's clubs in America.

There is a simple explanation for this almost natural sympathy: I am a woman who likes other women, even prefers them, collectively, to men. I think men are more catty, and of course far more vindictive (especially when one is a brainy woman, or a successful one). I have always been interested in the emancipation of woman, and in America I found a woman *not yet* emancipated, in spite of an abundance of material affluence, and an immense potential strength. This is because man, being an astute brute, always devises new ways of keeping her down; and it all boils down to one thing: making her loath to think for herself; making her accept a man's evaluation of the world, and especially, a man's evaluation of herself as a Woman, Object, Adjunct to his own ego.

I was startled when, at three colleges, I was approached by anxious young girls who told me that they wanted to study medicine, but were not going to do so because then they would never "get a date". Men, apparently, hated the "brainy" or "serious" type of girl; and they would quit if they knew the girl they partnered was studying such a serious subject. The girls were astounded when I told them that in Asia we felt that medicine was a woman's career. Perhaps that is why in America today there is only a small percentage of women studying subjects like engineering or law or medicine.

Nevertheless, in spite of that undertow of male hostility, woman in America is potentially a great force; she has more of the money in her hands (and economic emancipation goes hand in hand with spiritual and physical emancipation) than anywhere else in the world. She could do a lot more than she is doing; she even has the organization through which she can express herself as a shaping force: the women's club.

The women's club is the Social Being of the American woman; it is fountainhead of reassurance, chaperon, guardian of the *mores*, mentor and guide; it is the acceptor and rejector, establisher of a woman's "image", hub of social life, relief from loneliness, testing ground and educator. It forms, moulds and conditions her various activities and is also a reflection of them. It is also a way of spending money and time. Through it she is spoken of as "well-adjusted", becomes a "desirable" neighbour, her children benefit in school, her husband benefits in his organization. I have a theory that the club is an offshoot of the old Puritan Society, that most tightly regimented, sternly disciplinarian group ever devised by mankind, whose residual moral dogmatism still regiments American society today.

But besides this status-seeking, brainwashing aspect of the group, club or community, with its fascinating intermeshing of financial standing, "image building", and the subtle pressures constantly inflicted and being inflicted, there is another and more likable aspect to the club: it is also disseminator of information, gatherer of opinion, and as such, it can wield an extraordinary, and I hope salutary influence in bringing America to its senses. The women's clubs did it before, and may do it again.

That is why I found the women's clubs with their constant shimmer of social innuendo, their interplay of nuances, pressures, allusions, and their programmes of activities, absolutely fascinating as a tribal manifestation of the American ethos.

In the women's clubs, in America today, the great issues facing America are being debated; and they begin, as did my lecture tour, with Vietnam: Vietnam, two syllables that like a mighty peal of bells toll and thunder throughout the length and breadth of America today. Vietnam, by which America stands or falls, in honour or in shame, and in which her future is being decided.

And it is this issue which the women's clubs, the conscience of America, *are* taking up; it is with this that I was faced, almost from the first day that I was in America.

"What would you like me to talk about particularly?" I would ask my sponsors.

Invariably the answer would be: "We want to hear about Vietnam ... we're so confused about it."

This was last year, February and March; *before* the teach-ins, the sit-ins, and the demonstrations; it was in the women's clubs; the very conservative women's clubs. The only exception was in Texas, where the club president asked me *not* to talk of anything controversial, political, "because we don't like it ... we've had a lot of trouble here".

Not one women's club wanted me to talk about love, literature or writing; and even my agent was nonplussed.

Thus, willy-nilly, I was brought to speak of Vietnam. I had not had the intention of doing so when I went to America; it is the American women themselves who precipitated me into facing the issue squarely.

I could not avoid, therefore, telling them what my attitude was, or the way I saw American action. Much of what I said must have been very unpalatable; I always warned them that it would be; and they braced themselves for it, took it straight between the eyes, *and clapped*. "It's your sincerity we like; you gave it to us straight."

For this I shall always be grateful to them.

Some questions, some attitudes, kept on recurring during these lectures.

"Why don't people love us when we give them so much money?"

The women's clubs, and the women who compose it, are persons, organizations, full of "good" intentions; but we must define the word *good*. In the vocabulary of the system, it means: doing charity, giving money. Maternalistic moneyism is expressed in manifold charity drives, fund-raising, and other worthy actions; giving money is the greatest goodwill, and substance of *good* itself; to refuse money, or to be ungrateful about it, is not only un-American, it is nearly ungodly. "We've always got the best intentions," say the women, almost defensively, when it is pointed out to them that *aid* is *not* really all that it is meant to be; and that it actually impoverishes the nations which get it, because at the same time American policy does not permit these countries to stand upon their own feet. But the image of a generous USA ladling out great amounts of money, and getting only spit in the eye as a result, persists; and bitterness and irritation that it should be so. In a good many places, people felt that *aid* should be entirely cut off. "Let the rest of the world sink or swim as they like." With which I agreed. "If you *would* only leave other countries alone, but you don't." "Well, perhaps we aren't such angels as we think we are."

When told that the Vietnam war was a shame and a blot on America, that the bombing of North Vietnam would *not* bring a speedy end to the war, in fact it would do the precise opposite (which today, a year later, is recognized), they listened with disbelief. "How could anyone stand up against such mighty machinery as the USA had?" "Of course you can kill us all, then you wil reign over an empire of corpses; is that the peace you want?" I quoted the rates of desertion of the Saigon troops (which have vastly increased, so that

121

it is the Americans who do nearly all the fighting nowadays); I explained the terms of the 1954 Geneva Conference, which most of them knew nothing about; then they would say: "But we can't go away ... we can't lose *face*."

I have never heard so much talk of *face* as in America. One would think America a despotic Asiatic state, officialed by corrupt mandarins, intent only on keeping face, irrespective of what the face is on. I let fly and told them the only face they had was the face of the Bully. One newspaper printed that and still no one threw tomatoes, or called me names. I think they were wonderful. That was in March 1965.

And in after-lecture talks I came to realize that in every women's club, whether in Virginia or Iowa, California or Texas, there was not only deep unease, but a proportion of the audience actually against the war in Vietnam.

It is impossible to give figures; how could I ascertain, except by making them raise their hands? But from the number of people asking questions, voicing doubts, or just coming up to talk after the lecture, it was my guess, last spring (a guess I committed to paper, as a memorandum), that about 40 per cent of these staid, affluent, reasonable, conservative women were not with the policy as expounded and not convinced by the reasons given. I was gratified when a month later some poll did give pretty much the same figure for the whole country.

Time and again, when the lecture was over, someone would come up: "You ought to talk to our President," or "I'm going to write to my congressman."

"You do say things that are hard for us to take, but we feel you mean them and they certainly make us think." Now, a year later, I am getting letters, showing that some of them did think.

It is true that it was for *their* sake that I spoke; I felt that my duty, as a woman, was to promote *their own good*. I am just as concerned as they are that America should play a great role in the world – why not, when she is such a great and mighty nation? But my view of her role and her greatness is *not* the view of the Pentagon: I do not think that dropping millions of tons of bombs on other people, massive genocide of a small, brave people of 31 million, smaller than the state of California, enhances America's image; I do not think it helps to promote democracy; I do not believe that America is going to win anything but disgrace and shame; I think the course she is pursuing is a total disaster and a total danger to all of us; I think America is burying "democracy" and *promoting* Communism by her behaviour for which words seem inadequate. I feel it only fair and just to tell the American people so.

In certain cases of insanity, the patient not only does not wish to be cured; he beats any doctor who attempts to help him. Time and again in the world's history, a country's greatest patriots have been those who went against the current myth, the day's frenzy; it is my conviction that men like Emmett Hughes and I. F. Stone are better Americans than General Le May and the late McCarthy.

In the same way the greatest service any friend of America could render to America was to tell the truth; and if that is called "anti-American", or "un-American", then God help America. No one else can.

And so this Great Debate started last year for me in the women's clubs of America.

And those women who then said to me: "We are not satisfied and convinced by the explanations given by the policy makers; we would like to know what you think we should do ..." those, although in the minority, are, I feel, going to increase, in numbers and in strength.

And although the majority wanted, above all, reassurance that America's policies were right, reassurance that they were doing right, how can one be reassured by lies? After all it was Abraham Lincoln who pointed out that you can't fool all the people all the time.

A final argument was produced: "But if we don't fight Communism *there*, we'll have to fight it *here*, in our very homes. You don't know how *near* to Communism we are, right here in our big cities...." Well, the answer to that is obvious.

I also heard a variety of highly fanciful explanations. "The Chinese will bomb us as *they did Pearl Harbour*" (by a lady who got the Chinese and the Japanese mixed up). "The Chinese are already here; look how they're stirring up trouble in Alabama (sic!)". "But we must fight Communism, because the Communists do the most terrible things ... they torture people...." When pointing to the TV programmes showing these things being done by Saigon troops, they retort: "Well, that's not *our* boys; that's the South Vietnamese ... everyone knows Asians are naturally cruel ... and we can't stop them; they're on our side...." One even came up with a beauty: "But Asians don't feel pain as we do." These confabulations are part of the great *fear*, the disease of America today.

While we were there, the protest against the Vietnam war began to grow; in the *New York Times*, almost daily, large full-page advertisements appeared, condemning the bombing, condemning the war. "But it's no use, they can't reach the President," someone said to me. The rumour was that the President had become inaccessible save to a small conclave of advisers.

"We all know that it's been decided to escalate, but where do we go from there?"

I ended my lecture tour before any of the demonstrations now occurring in America took place; and all I could report, from my own direct experience, was that a proportion of women, in the women's clubs, were genuinely worried and uneasy about the fate of their own country in its pelting course to war.

But not before I had met an intelligent and very high-up official who said to me: "We've *got* to make war. We can't stop. We shall go on making war. Too much of our industrial system is based on *war*; peace would worry us; we'd have to cut down the profits of so many of our Big Business monopolies."

Just before leaving America I received a letter from a woman who at the time was having a nervous breakdown and was under psychological care.

"I know you will say, as so many, that I'm not well in the head," she wrote. "I got this worrying over Gene [her son] being drafted. But I want you to know that I think I am more sane than all those generals who send our sons to die in the mud of Vietnam, and what for, I ask you? What for? I am more sane than those greedy and foolish women who call themselves mothers, who are so damn scared of losing their status symbols and their affluence that they would rather see the fruit of their loins butchered in Vietnam, than get together and ask that the madness stop...."

But I hope the day will come when in a great outburst of common sense, in a shattering clamour *for* life and *against* death, American women will find it not good enough that their sons should be sacrificed, for doomed dreams of empire and domination. I like them too much not to hope that it will be so.

(1966)

124

Looking for a Platypus, and Meeting the Australians

WHEN I was a child, I was fascinated by a book on animals which showed, among others, the platypus. With a duck's bill, the body of an otter, webbed feet and a tail, the platypus is a shy, retiring animal, completely inoffensive, and a genuine Australian. It lays eggs, and is about ten million years old. In its makeup, it seems to have remained an undecided mixture of bird and mammal. It swims and is playful in water. It is devoted to its family. It also ambles on land. Going to Australia this April, I wanted to meet the platypus. The platypus, to me, meant Australia, but there was much more to see besides.

Arriving in Sydney in late April, I fell upon a Sydney full of sun and full of stir; for the Queen of England was there, visiting; and it was also the bicentenary of Cook's discovery of Australia. It was my good fortune to meet a lot of Australians, not only in Sydney, but in other cities; and to take little trips, in between my lectures. The best way to meet people and to see things is lecturing, provided one remains conscious of the fact that lecturing is a two-way gesture, a means of contact with people and what they are interested in. In this manner, I was more than satisfied; for the crowds at every lecture were a lecturer's dream. Moreover, they were, like the platypus, a cross-section of Australia; there was something of everything among them. I had been told, previously, that Australians were not concerned about anything except beer, football and the races, and that they would not come to listen to a lecturer, especially a lecturer on such "solid" subjects as Asia, China, the Vietnam (now the Indochina) war. Even some very able people told me so; and the worst disbelievers were of course the academic circles, what Asians call "intellectuals" of high calibre, and also students. "We never never have more than one hundred people come to our lectures," said a young and energetic student who had arranged one of my lectures at the university. When 1,500 turned up and 300 had to be turned away because they simply could not be squashed in, he said: "You win." That is because I had asked them to take a larger hall, which they had done, a little reluctantly. This process was repeated everywhere in Australia. Like the platypus, the Australian was startling and unexpected: I took the opportunity to meet as many as possible. He was truly a composite, and fascinating, being!

The vastness of Australia (as large an area as the United States, or China) has to be flown, travelled in, to be realized; suddenly I understood what the word "walkabout" meant. Before such distances, such wide expanses, bare and looming with a terrible vitality of their own, the irrepressible urge is to *walk*, walk and walk, as if to reach that distant horizon with the blue hills lifting their promise, under a sky so steady and silent, it makes one talk to oneself. The map does not convey this enormity: its emptiness, which Australians talk about and are very proud of, is an ambiguousness which I was conscious of before being able to explain to myself; but drives and walks through bush and forest made me realize it; it is due to the native vegetation; one sees trees that are trees, but look somehow odd; grass that is tinged with strangeness; and the sunsets due to the reflection of the desert are truly extraordinary. The trees and the plants of Australia, the native ones, are disappearing before the onslaught of imported trees; I was told of many suburbs where people hack down or burn the magnificent native trees, in order to plant trees from England; this occurs and has occurred wildly. Round Perth one still finds untouched areas, sanctuaries, as they are now called, preserves for the plants and trees of Australian origin; among them the black boy, a wonderful and weird half-grass half-tree half-palm which, like the platypus, was still after millions of years trying to make up its mind what category it belonged to.

But so many of the new Australians, buying one of those new bungalows which, for square miles around, make up the vast expanse of "residential districts" of each city or town, were cutting down the native trees and planting "English trees" instead: and the weirdness of the landscape's clothing was due to this; it was also due to the fact, which any visitor to the botanical gardens would notice, that even the imported trees grew in a different way. The climate, the abundant sunlight, did something to them. They were touched with this difference which was the undertang of all I was looking at; and so Australia had its platypus touch, at least where vegetation was concerned ... but what of the people?

"You think Australians are kind, warm-hearted, intelligent, interested, concerned ... how wrong you are." This was said to me at least fifty times. Yet seeing the vast throngs congregating to hear a difficult lecture on "China's role in the world" and "The Asian Revolution", throngs composed of workers, housewives, secretaries, ordinary people, as well as students (high-class intellectuals were in a minority: many eminent professors did not attend, though of course a few did), I could not but repeat, tenaciously: "*Trust the people.*" There were hundreds and hundreds of questions asked at every lecture, and also over the radio. I could not but feel that people must be trusted: that Australians, at least where my lecturing was concerned, were no different from Filipinos, Frenchmen, or others: that they were uneasy and worried about what was really happening in the world and wanted to know; and that although they had been thoroughly brainwashed in the most absurd manner, against China, they were really trying to find out where they stood in a changing world.

Perhaps this optimistic view of mine is subjective; it is due to the singular warmheartedness, kindness and welcome we received everywhere. After a session on television, the next day, the hotel waiters, people on the street, saleswomen, all came to tell me they had enjoyed it. "It isn't the kind of thing we hear all the time," they said. "Keep on giving us something new." Now to read the newspapers, supposedly opinion formers, or to listen to the government pronunciamentos, one would not get at all this impression of a wide-awake willingness to learn, to hear "the other side". Yet this impression was not confined merely to people who might call themselves "friendly to China" or knowledgeable about Asia; it truly came from the street, from ordinary people, from workers, especially, some of whom came 200 miles or so from other cities to listen to some of my lectures. It came from a wide variety of women, who wrote in after television or radio programmes. The newspapers only published the adverse letters: although they themselves acknowledged (a friend was told by one of the editors about this) that the favourable mail had been overwhelming, and only a minority unfavourable; yet they chose to print only the attacks and the more objectionable comments (some of them very personal) on the lectures and the lecturer; whereas the vast mass of favourable mail was not aired in the Press!

Thus I stick to my ideas that like the platypus (whom I never saw) the Australians I did meet were hardworking, honest, shrewd and shy, just awakening and becoming aware that the issues in Asia did concern them very much; they wanted to know more. But alas, here comes the rub. Like the platypus, kept so safe and away (for literally he has been almost wiped out, and only few survive, in zoos) in a cage, and only exhibited at certain times (so that I never did meet one), the Australian is subjected, mostly through intensive utilization of the Press, to a most thorough indoctrination of fear of the "red hordes of Chinese who will come to invade Australia" and who are only prevented from doing so by the American and "allied" presence in Vietnam!

This fear is all-pervasive; it is in some cases impervious to reason; it is backed by what one might call the "three hoary old chestnuts" always brought up in the audience when some of the hearers are at a loss to find *something* to say against China: China's aggressiveness and bellicosity is proved, so run the chestnuts, by her "aggression in Korea, invasion and occupation of Tibet, a neutral [sic] and democratic [!!] independent [!!!!] country, and her invasion of India." Apart from these three "convictions", which seemed to be the tripod upon which "fear of China" was being built, there was little else to pinpoint a reason for this fear, except the other sometimes mentioned point of "an exploding population" and "need for more territory because of the population explosion." Yet in spite of this built-in habit of mind, sedulously kept up by official speeches, the reaction of the vast majority, whenever they heard something different, was refreshing, spontaneous and warm; I therefore cannot but stick to my opinion, that pessimists should read Chairman Mao: "*Trust the people*", and should realize that there is a fundamental desire, not only among the young, but among many people in Australia, to "hear something different".

The television and radio were fair, even if they bent backwards to counter some parts. The TV brought many letters, queries and questions; people rang up the hotel to ask what book they should read about China; people rang up to say: "Well done"; and asked for more. Many discussed frankly their fear, then added: "But in the past it was Japan we fought, now we're giving all our minerals to Japan. They've even got their fishing fleets on our coast."

The cities of Australia contain 65 per cent of the population of about 12 million; the rest is outback, sheep runs and wheat and other farms, and of course desert; and the desert is growing because sheep who crop grass close tend to turn more land arid; due to the fact that there is a wheat glut in the world today, wheat growing will be cut 40 per cent. The enormous area and the small population encourage waste, profligacy, a spread of the cities so that Perth, which only has about 200,000 inhabitants, occupies as large an area as Greater London; most of the cities are of a pattern: a centre with tall buildings, most of them belonging to some American or Japanese monopoly (IBM, National, etc.) and then an enormous spread of small bungalows, rows and rows of them, miles upon miles of them. It is this spread of bungalows which makes cities so large. Everyone has to own a car as public transport is almost non-existent. Sydney the oldest city has some older quarters and houses, but these are being destroyed and the spread outward continues. There is an enormous amount of cutting down of trees which goes on; in the past a great deal of harm was thus done by destroying the most beautiful forests; indeed this quality of sheer waste and "hacking down" goes on in the elimination of kangaroos: they will soon become almost extinct, I am told; at the moment, a million a year are killed for meat and because they are reckoned "a pest" and the land is needed for more sheep runs. A law will soon, I hope, stop this massacre.

The USA and Japan

The most curious argument I had in Australia with some Australians was about population. This, together with "fear of the Chinese red hordes", is another intense and morbid preoccupation. A surgeon told me, in all seriousness, that twelve million people was all that Australia could support; because "so much is desert".

However, with its vast mineral wealth, with its enormous fertile areas (and these are large, larger than all England), with the possibility, were irrigation undertaken, for development, and especially with a larger population, Australia could be an immensely productive, rich land. The middle of Australia, its desert, is below sea level; I was told that a plan had been put forward to create an inland sea; the cutting of a canal 500 miles long from the sea into the interior would throughly alter the climate. There is an enormous amount of water available underground; artesian wells, the damming of the rivers (instead of allowing the water to be lost in the central desert) can extend greatly the amount of land to be used for pastures; and sheep runs are not, in the final analysis, the only thing Australians can do. But sheep farming is a lazy way of making money; the sheep look after themselves; sheep shearers, many of them immigrants, others called half-bloods (namely half Aborigines), are only required for seasonal work; and thus sheep farming goes on. But there could be a much greater extension of all kinds of crops. The soil is excellent and many of these pastures could be used for other things. An increase in the production of cattle would be a great asset. But the curious fact is that in this, as in the new industries and mineral extraction, Australia plays the part of an object of the foreign monopolies and businesses, rather than of an independent country. Even the Press is occasionally bitter about some scandal or another, which reveals the extent to which Australia is really a "colony", not of the British Empire (r.i.p.) but of the United States and Japan.

The extraction of iron ore is one of the features of this hold on the Australian economy; the Australian government has signed contracts with Japan to supply this iron ore to Japan, and almost 30 per cent of the Japanese steel industry relies on Australian ore (which is of very high calibre). Salt is also being shipped to Japan, and there are other minerals, bauxite, tin, nickel, copper, in which foreign capital plays an outstanding part. The deposits of nickel, actually, are now the subject of much discussion: it will mean another penetration by US and Japanese capital in the country.

There is a lot of talk and discontent about the policies of the government in regard to the disposal of these resources; in the past, it is said, some Prime Minister or another almost sold the top half of Australia to Japan and the United States; and it is feared that the same process is being repeated, through certain members of the government, who seem to concern themselves more in pleasing the USA (and Japan) than in looking after the interests of the Australian people. A recent scandal which found much echo in the Press was about the purchase of F111 airplanes; these were pressed upon the Australian government and it now appears that they are unusable, and Australia will be mulcted to the tune of something like 150 or 200 million dollars if she returns the planes because they are unusable. Seventy per cent of all Australian industry is owned by non-Australians (USA, Japan, at the head). Recently another scandal, over terms of a contract with Japan, was in the offing. Meanwhile propaganda against student demonstrations in favour of Vietnam occupied the time of quite a few official figures. The amount of querulous malice poured over students, or anyone who questions what is being done, is really startling. Another startling thing was to find, when I returned to India, that some Australian diplomats abroad send to people, free of charge, the weekly magazine put out by the most extreme right-wing party, an outright fascist publication! To find the diplomats of a government gladly dispensing this kind of magazine (which is not even that of the ruling Party) was surprising. It was also an eye-opener to find that the government policies were so thoroughly aligned to the United States, a few sounded much like Spiro Agnew, and one at least was heard to threaten, sometimes with physical coercion, people who did not believe in the same things as he did.

However, these were a minority; but an active minority. Some of them made statements which to me appeared hair-raising in their inaccuracy and unabashed provocativeness. It was clear that the Australian people could still be intimidated and frightened when such statements, accompanied by what were obviously threats, were pronounced. But there was a growing resistance, and this was clear.

White Australia

The "white Australia" policy is still a main pillar of foreign policy. The Immigration Department encourages the entry of immigrants from "white" European countries; especially those with skills and crafts. Doctors from the United Kingdom, engineers, builders, carpenters and others, even from Yugoslavia, are found here; but this open door is found closed to "coloured" immigrants, for whom language tests are devised and all sorts of rules too abstruse to detail are set up. Thus a certain immigrant from a "coloured" country, having successfully passed the test in English, French, and Italian, now found himself questioned ... in Swahili, which he did not know, and thus refused entry. But a certain latitude seems to have been extended recently to Anglo-Indians. Many of this minority (chiefly the more skilled ones, such as engineers and accountants) are now leaving India, because they are in fear of the future there. "There's going to be a revolution in India, so I came here," an Anglo-Indian told me frankly . He happens to be so fair that he can pass as an Englishman, and he had no trouble. Many of the new immigrants from Ireland, Spain and Italy, and the Anglo-Indians, are Catholic, and this has much reinforced the Catholic church and its power in Australia. As for academics and intellectuals, there are a few, but very few, Asians in universities as lecturers and research workers; there are a great many students from Malaya and Singapore who owing to the recent racial riots have continued their studies here. They are very disturbed in mind; they cannot stay in Australia, yet at the same time they are unwilling to return to Malaya. As in England, there is a nursing shortage, which is not compensated by an influx, as in England, of "coloured personnel". Indeed, the medical services in England would probably collapse without the Indian and Pakistani nurses and doctors there. In Australia the shortage will probably be made up by immigrants from Europe.

This regrettable racialism, which appears even in public speeches, is nowhere so evident as in the treatment still meted out to the Old Australians, called the Aborigines.

These are the original inhabitants: numbering at one time, it is said, almost 3 million; now reduced in number to about 400,000, of whom more than 340,000 are of mixed origin, and only 60,000 can be reckoned full-blooded Old Australians.

Today, the Old Australian, the Aborigine, still does not have Australian citizenship as others have it. Any "white" immigrant coming in has more rights, privileges and freedom than an Aborigine born in Australia, whose race was in Australia thousands of years before the white man came in.

The Aborigines are treated as wards of the governments of the states; and a thick curtain of hypocrisy and silence surrounds their treatment, which differs in each state. This difficulty makes it imperative for them to unite all through Australia in order to achieve something. But until now, the odds against them are heavy. Not only do they have no proper citizenship; they have no land of their own; they cannot obtain passports; they cannot even move about without a whole apparatus of police permits and licences; they cannot settle where they please; they cannot leave the special "missions" or reserves where they are. A few, a very few, mixed bloods have broken through the barrers and been educated; they form a voice for their people. I met some of them, including Kath Walker, the poet.

In Sydney, as the bicentenary of Cook's "discovery" of Australia was being celebrated, the Aborigines, and also many progressive white people, demonstrated silently in protest, yet the Press gave them scarcely a line; all the space in the papers was devoted to the hat Princess Anne wore, the Queen's smile, and such mundanities. To the Aborigines it was a bitter commemoration of the beginning of their wholesale massacre.

"But we are simply not part of the story," said Kath Walker bitterly. "They would like to just forget that we exist; mention Aborigines to the average Australian, and he shirks the question." I did mention; and indeed this is the point where the warmheartedness, the friendliness, stiffen into something like disapproval, and very soon tension. Then comes defensiveness. A very important academic personage told me, in all seriousness, that Aborigines, being Stone Age people, needed care and were quite "incapable" of doing anything more than what they were doing. Mostly the answer is that the brain content of the Aborigine is not equal to that of the white man. That the Aborigine is lazy, dirty, shiftless, gets drunk, does not know the value of money, has no family life, etc., etc. There is a startling similarity with what was being said about the Afro-American (and is still being said in certain areas of the USA) only a few years ago.

A race against genocide

Today, the survival of the Aborigine is still a race against genocide. I spent an afternoon with Kath Walker and other representatives of this national minority. They were keenly aware that they had been singled out and privileged: held up as a shining example of the white man's goodness and liberality; they were "assimilated" and "integrated"; but they pointed out that it was their part-white origin that had given them rights which the others, the full-blooded, could not enjoy; although in other respects, they shared the same disadvantages, yet they could move about, they were not confined to tribal "reserves or missions".

Genocide of the Aborigine has a long story in Australia. The *Daily News* (Melbourne) published some stories of the past which fill one with horror. The systematic slaughter of the Aborigines right up till the late 1930s, hunted as today the kangaroo is hunted and pitilessly killed, was a common feature of life in the outback; on Sundays, holidays, or any day, people would go hunting the Aborigine, on horseback and later by jeep, running him exhausted and then killing him. Necklaces of ears and hands were made, as trophies of the chase. Women and children were not spared, of course; the *Daily News* tells of a mother and baby climbing a tree in front of a hunter: he pointed his gun to shoot: another man intervened. "Let her go." Later this second man was abused by his fellows for being a "nigger lover". Strychnine was mixed with flour and given to the Aborigines to eat; Kath Walker told me how their wise men found out they were poisoned, and directed their tribe to mud holes, where they ate mud, in order to counteract the strychnine. But many died. Their numbers decreased appallingly. In other areas, Aborigines were driven to the sea, given the choice to drown or "face the guns". In Tasmania, nearly all the original inhabitants were slaughtered. There is a painting in the museum in Melbourne, depicting a scene of slaughter; the native Tasmanians huddled round a fire, unconscious of danger; from the forest round them the white men, in a circle, with guns, creep stealthily up, to shoot them. "A night's work."

Today the policies towards Aborigines are still unsatisfactory; the Old Australian cannot really call any portion of the land his own. At one time guaranteed tracts of land, he had these removed from him as soon as minerals were discovered; thus the Woomera range was established; thus the deposits of nickel, and bauxite, have led to further destitution of the Aborigines. "Missions" are set up; similar to those for the Eskimos; there a kind of minimum programme of welfare exists. Even then, some people argue that this is doing "too much" for them. In some cases Aborigine children were taken away to be reared in mission schools; white people then "adopted" them, without even consulting or telling the parents, who were waiting for them. These missions suffer from a constant lack of money: medical services are primitive, though no doubt much of the personnel is hardworking and devoted. But all is simply in control of the "state authorities", and this in the final analysis means the police. The police issue permits which allow an Aborigine to have a drink: they used to have these permits in the form of collars, hung round the neck of the Aborigines. "Dog collars", Kath Walker called them. This proved the Aborigine a "good" fellow. In the missions the Aborigine simply vegetates; he cannot be instructed, the teaching of skills is frighteningly limited; he can subsist by doing "tourist" bark paintings, which are sold for him; he cannot leave the mission without police control. Visitors have to have permits to visit such places.

The situation is much worse in North Australia where about 20 million acres of land belong to one British nobleman. The workers on these lands are Aborigines; they work on the sheep runs and are paid around 7 dollars a week where the average white man would get 50; all of this land was taken away from the Aborigines. Those who refuse to enter into this slavery, or into the mission, are driven into the desert, where they live on grubs, and dig in mud holes. They used to hunt the kangaroo but the latter is being exterminated too and so there is no meat for the Aborigine to eat. The photographs I saw of some of these Aborigines show their pitiable condition of health. There is leprosy among them. And now, through the white man, venereal disease is ravaging them. Many Aborigine women were raped in the past; many more, today, especially those of mixed race, drift to the brothels of the cities. Prostitution is open in the Australian cities, though this is not admitted. The Aborigine woman has no protection against the exploitation of society. Yet some glib professor would explain to me that the Aborigines "have no sense of family life" or are "unable to take responsibility".

Everywhere where deposits of metals were found, the Aborigine lands were taken away from them. The salaries that should be paid to Aborigines working on sheep runs are not paid in their entirety to them: ostensibly this is because "they don't know what to do with their money"! The royalties which should come to them from the exploitation, on their lands, of minerals, does not go to them. It is utilized for other purposes.

Yet in the past two or three years there has been a remarkable awakening: and this is what the "white Australian" will talk about with disquiet (until it is pointed out to him that he is indulging in racialism). "There is a population explosion among the Aborigines," he announces. Their number, which was dwindling, is now maintaining itself, and it may increase; for although the child death rate is horrifying, yet still there is a small increase, and this very small increase is enough to panic some people – so wicked, and profoundly racialist has the indoctrination been so far. But against this must be set the fact that many white men, workers, progressive people, and students, are aware now of this great wrong; the Aborigines have joined in strikes in the past ten years. The proportion of mixed-bloods (many are illegitimate) in the city slums is what makes the increase of the Aborigines today; and many of these "half-bloods" are deeply aware that they want their own culture, and their rights, as a national minority, with full equality with their "white" counterparts.

The creative talent, intelligence, and awareness of the Old Australian was the subject of my conversation with one of Australia's most interesting artists, John J. Jones.

I met John J. Jones at a Writers Club social gathering in Perth. I was glad to meet him, as he had been a contributor to *Eastern Horizon*. He was now engaged on a project which was, to me, most interesting; in the hills outside Perth, he was building a theatre where plays and other creations by Australian writers and musicians could be produced; it would be an open-air theatre. He asked me to see it.

Together with some Australian writer friends I went there one day; and was very much impressed. In a valley with a small rivulet (which turns to a torrent when in full spate) John Jones had built a theatre which actually was five open-air stages, using the natural beauty and setting of Australia: the trees were mostly native trees; and he had done this in a remarkable manner.

"This is the Seddon Vincent Memorial Theatre for Australian playwrights," he said. "The idea is to produce here the people's plays, the plays and the music of Australia itself; so that the people can enjoy it."

The project would not have been possible, John Jones told me, if he had not had the help of some private companies, who donated to him a quantity of the material needed. "And all the work was done by prisoners," said John Jones.

It must be said here that in this area of Western Australia, out of the prison population, almost 25 per cent are Aborigines, although the proportion of Aborigines to the total population is only 2 per cent. This is because an Aborigine can be arrested so easily: for "vagrancy and loitering"; for "causing an obstruction"; for being "drunk and disorderly" – the police vocabulary can be so definitely vague, and so imperatively efficient, in the case of Aborigines!

The theatre was built by 800 prisoners, and out of this number 70 per cent were Aborigines. Not all worked at the same time, but in lots of 25 or so; the continuous component of 70 per cent was maintained.... "It is their ideas, their creativeness, which is in this theatre, for we discussed everything together and they suggested so many beautiful and interesting things," said John Jones.

And by working at something their own, by being treated as men, in a very short time they were full of initiative, creativeness; "dignity they always had," said Jones. "But they were deprived of this human dignity, treated like beasts. Suddenly, they felt they were no longer beasts. I felt humbled by them. I saw so many possibilities in them, perhaps they also realized that they could be much more than they were."

In the building 1,000 tons of *jarrah* wood, 800 tons of *marri* wood, 7,000 old railway sleepers (made of *jarrah* and *mandoo* wood) were utilized. All these are old Australian trees, good timber, now being fearfully cut down in that waste and vandalism characteristic of so much of Australian "development". Jones obtained a truck on loan and saws from the jail, and some supervising officers. The work was begun in August 1967 and the expected opening is September 1970.

Afterwards we met some of the Aborigines working there: tall men, with great dignity, and natural. One of them was returning next day to his work on the sheep run where he had been arrested; two brothers had painted landscapes on the walls of the orchestra pit, all the Aborigines had contributed ideas; it was my hope, and that of Jones, that one day they would stand here, masters of their own land, and sing and create the tales and the plays and the music of their own culture.

Afterwards John Jones sang for us; the acoustics were remarkable, and this singing in the sun, under the trees, with the running brook, was truly a wonderful moment. He sang the song of the whalers, and then he sang a song called "Monsoon", which I reproduce in full:*

> There is a monsoon blowing out of Asia
> and who knows where it will blow?
> There is a hot wind blowing out of Asia
> for the people there want to grow....
> There is a monsoon blowing out of Asia,
> and the season's wrong but the reason's right,
> for the name of the wind is man-be-equal,
> white man and yellow man, black man and brown, be equal.
> There is a monsoon blowing out of Asia
> and the whole world will know
> that the hot wind blowing out of Asia
> has a mighty long way to go!
> There is a monsoon blowing out of Asia
> and it's blowing a freedom song.
> And the name of the wind is man-be-equal,
> white man and yellow man, black man and brown, be equal.
> And the monsoon blowing out of Asia
> will burn like a torch in the sky,
> and the hot wind blowing out of Asia
> will tell you the reason why!

This song was composed and sung by Jones in 1964, and "after that," said Jones, "I could not get any more engagements on television." Previously he had been well known as a singer and composer, and his records of folk songs were very popular.

All too soon the day came to depart. I had not seen the platypus; he was on show only between 2 and 4 p.m. in Melbourne sanctuary. But I had seen many Australians and found with them a common bond, for now so many knew that they too were in Asia, and the hideous old ways, the rotten old ideas, were being blown out of their minds by the wind of tomorrow.

(1971)

---

* Copyright by John Jesse Jones.

Algeria – Profile of a Nation

TO STAY in France, even for a short while, is to become imbued with some erroneous notions about Algeria. Why about Algeria more than any other country? Certainly due to the ex-colonial relationship between the two countries, and the bitter war of national liberation, which only ended in 1962. Even the "Left" intellectuals and Press in France seem to lack a correct perspective on the Algerian people and nation. There is a great lesson to learn on the unconscious relics, in behaviour and outlook, of a colonial past even among people who call themselves "Left".

I must confess that I too was infected with some erroneous notions about Algeria, so persistent and undenied is the image projected in Europe. I know a good many progressive European writers who prefer to go to Morocco or Tunisia to escape the bitter winter. They bypass Algeria; when, on my return, I asked them why, they replied, in a surprised manner: "We never thought of going there."

I blame myself for not having gone earlier to Algeria. It was more than a fascinating experience, a voyage of discovery. The discovery of a magnificent country and a great people, hardened by a bitter war of national liberation. And I had no idea how exciting, how beautiful Algeria was, with its astonishing variety which neither of its small neighbours can offer. The reason tourists do not come in droves is that propaganda about Algeria abroad is not the kind to entice those in search of the exotic; Algeria is not "exotic" in the sense that there is no special exotic gear or craft for tourists. The Algerian people are a proud people; they have fought and won a great war against a strong enemy, and because they continue to fight for total independence, their pride and their independence sticks out of them; they look one straight in the eye and are neither fawning nor servile. Many Algerians to whom I spoke are not so sure that they would *like* a flood of tourists upon them. "They harm people morally.... they will teach our children to beg. We do not want to be a nation of tailors and shoemakers and quaint curio and carpet sellers. We want our minds to get rid of colonial servility...."

When we took the plane in February to visit Algeria, it was with the firm determination *not* to be tourists, a resolve difficult to keep, because the land is so beautiful, so exciting. One is almost obliged to go round, in a perfect enchantment, and nothing less than a month will do, to visit the oases of the Sahara, Oran and its beautiful surroundings, Constantine, the Aures, the Hoggar, the fantastic M'Zab, the mountains and villages of Kabylia.... There is enough and to spare, in a land four times the size of France, to discover for many weeks. We were lucky to have Algerian friends as well as the most competent, cultivated charming and unobtrusive official from the Ministry of Information that one could imagine. Bouchenne (that was his name) was the most perfect public relations officer one could have. Algerian courtesy and hospitality is genuine, but Bouchenne was more; he discussed ideas and gave us his country to see with its greatness and weaknesses, its good points and its defects and omissions. There was no attempt to hide the problems of the country. Indeed we saw them, heard them everywhere. The Algerians have a reputation for being touchy about criticism. I do not think they are. But there is one exception: they do not appreciate people who tell them: "Ah, but all was much better when you were French Algeria!" Incredibly, some people still say this to them ... it is part of a myth still cultivated in France that Algeria "cannot do" without the French. But it was clear to me that the main thing Algerians want is to be *completely* independent, mentally, culturally, politically and economically. They can do it - they know it and they have already done much in the short eight years since the war ended in 1962.

Yet the first thing that strikes one as the jet from Paris (two hours from airport to airport) lands is that there are still a good many French people around. They are the *coopérants*, cadres sent to teach in the universities, engineers and medical personnel. Algeria was left with the usual post-colonial heritage of ignorance, poverty, mono-culture and monetary dependence after the war. Out of ten million people a million died in the fighting; many of those killed were intellectuals and they were very few. The lack in trained personnel, in cadres, is felt very starkly. The problems are enormous. And the Accords which ended the war provided for French aid.

But of the million and more Europeans who had established themselves in Algeria, a good many of them Corsicans, Sicilians, as well as French, called *pieds noirs*, few are left. Most returned to

France, and their estates have been nationalized, for they owned the most fertile parts of the country. There are now about 15,000 French *coopérants*, mostly teachers, some engineers, doctors. They are on contract and they do not plan to remain in Algeria. The younger ones are often enthusiastic, impressed with the achievements of Algeria in the last eight years since the war ended. I know at least one who took up Algerian nationality and plans to stay in Algeria where he was born.

We stayed at the Hotel St George, in Algiers. The capital has some excellent hotels, with beautiful views of the bay. The St George Hotel is high on a hill, and a magnificent view of the whole city was ours. But many of Algeria's best hotels, both in Algiers and other cities, have one defect: their restaurants, almost without exception, serve only French food. True, the cooking is very good. But why is it that one cannot get Algerian food in a "good" hotel, unless one asks for it specially? This reminded me of the hotels in India, where English type curries are served. Even the new tourist complex built near the sea a few kilometres from Algiers, with the best scenery, beaches, small apartments for tourists, restaurant, swimming-pool, etc., does not offer good Algerian food. The couscous I ate there was not a patch on what one gets in the small, but perfectly clean little restaurants of the Kasbah, the old city, or for that matter, in many places as soon as one gets out of the "good" hotels.

As a result I ate few meals at the St George, but we roamed the city and found tiny food shops where the most delicious mutton, couscous and vegetables were to be had, and very cheap. Algeria's wonderful fruit and vegetables come from the rich valley of the Mitjina (once almost entirely French-owned), and supply not only the local inhabitants but are exported to many European Common Market countries.

Another thing which at the St George Hotel appeared odd was the marble statue of a naked woman in the hall. It was so much out of place, in a land where women still go about veiled, and any way covered up, that what would not have affected me in Paris or London affected me almost as an indecency in Algiers. But perhaps the management had decided to remain "international"; tourists do prefer to find what they are accustomed to, and to them the "exotic" must not affect comfort. Certainly the hotels in Algiers are most comfortable.

Algeria's people, in spite of colonial "deculturization", remain profoundly attached to their cultural roots, and those are not Arab alone, but the old cultures of the Maghreb, before the Arabs came, as well. I was to discover that there are many Algerias, a mosaic of peoples, all bound in national identity. But one of the Algerias is still the "French Algeria", what France had left behind, and the other Algerias, of the Algerian people, grappling with all the difficulties of post-colonization, are hampered by this leftover of colonialism, which even today breeds many problems, economic, social, cultural, political. I shall say little of the French Algeria except that I have to mention it because it still impinges upon one, and perhaps, oddly enough, in circles called "intellectual" and in the cities. Among Algerian intellectuals the "colonized mind" still exists, more than among the working people. This is a problem in a country with such an ardent desire for independence as Algeria today, and such a need for cadres, for professional talent, but it is a problem shared with many other countries in Africa and Asia, who also have this need and also have the problem of changing their own intellectuals so that they may serve their own people.

The heart of Algiers is the Kasbah. The Kasbah is the old Algerian city, before the French came; it is now surrounded by the bigger Algiers, but it has retained its tortuous narrow streets, shaded against the summer heat; the small white houses with their flat roofs, the many lanes like tunnels, and all of it so clean, in the morning freshness, that it is a pleasure to walk its up and down ways. Here the doors are narrow, the houses dark; here are crowds of children, children swarming everywhere; women veiled in thin white from head to foot and half the face. The tourist usually likes the Kasbah, its fruit stalls, its exotic look, but the Kasbah is far more than all that; more than the industrious common people; more than its children and veiled women and its ancient traditions. The Kasbah is enormously vital; it is the teeming prolific belly of the Algerian people. The Kasbah produced, for years, the heroes of the Algerian national liberation movement in Algiers city. The Kasbah was blockaded, bombed, mined, saturated with searches; every street, every house suffered; many were tortured to death. It was here that the resistance, including the women, went on. And the Kasbah was one of many other such foci in Algeria, but its extent, situation, and proximity to the colonial army's headquarters made its resistance epic.

And this indomitable spirit has remained, not only a feel in the air, but an air about the people, a pride and a sureness. "We Algerians know what we want," said my Algerian friend Salah to me. There are many men and women here who walk unnoticed, unobtrusively do their work, and who were heroes during the war. There are children of martyrs, too, girls and boys whose parents were tortured and killed. There are special schools for them, though not always enough. The majority in Algiers come from the Kasbah. Here one can see plainly, all within the compass of a couple of square kilometres, that when Mao Tsetung said: "The masses are the real heroes", he was stating a fact. Here on the walls are chalked the words: "There is only one hero, the people."

The Kasbah, symbol of defiance within Algiers, is not the only one: every city, every village, of Algeria has its martyrs, its dead, its memories, its Kasbahs. As we walked the Kasbah with Bouchenne, he told us many of the stories of the war. That night we went to see the film *The Battle of Algiers*.

The Battle of Algiers was made by Italian and Algerian film producers; it is technically excellent, but not entirely satisfying. As President Houari Boumedienne, who gave me an audience at the end of my stay, said in a very matter-of-fact way: "The film is not good. It was not so civilized, that war. In the film they tried to be what they call 'fair', and so they betrayed the people of Algiers, they tried to show the French commander as 'good'. But it was a most brutal and horrible war, and they softened that." Then I could see what he meant. I had indeed praised the film, because it had many good points. But it is true that it insisted that colonizers were "innocent" too. And for a man who fought in that war, as did President Boumedienne, this was not the real story. The real story was that of the people in the countryside and in the cities, their suffering and their courage, and though this was depicted, it is true that reality was not entirely conveyed by the film. President Boumedienne also deplored that the film only showed city resistance and not what happened in the villages. "What happened in the Aures, in Kabylia, everywhere the real battles were waged in the countryside, whole villages were wiped out." Yet the film *The Battle of Algiers* is still forbidden in France. It is curious that a democratic country like France should refuse permission to see even a part of what colonialism meant to the Algerians; yet the film would help the French people to understand what had happened. It is curious that there should still be a refusal to face the truth of the war in Algeria.

And the reason is the *pieds noirs*, the ex-colons back from Algeria, and the extreme right-wing organizations which still curse de Gaulle for making peace with Algeria ... they wanted to continue the war until not one Algerian remained alive (so they said).

Yet there is no hatred of the French in Algeria. I am not speaking here of the French-inclined intellectuals, but of the ordinary people.

Right after the war, when victory came, there were many French people still resident in Algeria, a million or so; though they were going by the thousands every week, a large portion had believed in the victory of French weapons until the last moment. "For three days they stayed at home when independence came, locking and bolting doors and windows, expecting a general massacre. Outside in the streets the Algerians rejoiced; there was dancing and singing and triumphant parades, but no Frenchman was hurt or molested. Nothing was done to them. No houses broken into. Nothing."

The Algerian likes to communicate; to talk, to discuss; it is the Arab tradition, and every village, every small city, has its many places in the sun where people sit and talk. In Algiers there is a wide broad square; in the cool of evening people walk about it, and it was in this square that the Med-el-disouk, the popular poets, accompanying themselves on the flute, sang tales of the old days; or sang their new poems. Often the poet would sing or recite one line of verse and round him the listeners would reply, inventing the next line for him; they would applaud or criticize, and argue with him as he spun his verses. This popular literature, the poetry of the street in a complete merging with the people, is a very strong feature of Algerian tradition. "All of Algeria's history continued, under colonialism, only through the oral tradition of these ambulant poets," said my Algerian friends. On the square facing the sea, as we too ambled, it looked peaceful enough today, but I could imagine, in years gone by, how people came, eager to hear the poet sing, about themselves, about their own country. And how they went home, and hope and anger and the need for justice was a great fire in them burning out the night of servitude and despair. The songs the poets sang, created by the people themselves, became the battle hymns of the war.

"The Algerian theatre was born in confrontation with imperialism," the director of the new theatre school said to me. We had driven to the theatre and art school, located near the seashore, simple buildings designed to house about 60 or more inmates. Priority among the admissions is given to "the children of the martyrs", youngsters whose parents died in the war of national liberation. I saw eight or nine girls; tall, fresh-faced. "What do you want to do when you have finished your course here?" I asked. "I want to go on playing, for the people," said one girl, Fatimah. She was nineteen years old, and studying acting. Algeria's film industry is developing, and talent is needed.

There are very few such art schools in Africa; one in Algeria, six in the rest of the continent, far too few. The programme is interesting; in its achievements as well as in what I considered its defects. To begin with, there was an entrance examination; out of 500 candidates, only 30 were admitted, far too few, I thought. All were interns. "It is easier for the children of martyrs, who are used to a collective life," said the director. Other children did not always like the discipline, whereas the orphans have had to be cared for in institutions and are used to collective living. We spoke about the problem of employment, one which the Algerian government is trying to tackle in all seriousness, but it remains a great problem, and so is the problem of vocational training for young people. I felt that an admission of 30 interns was insufficient. Why not broaden the scope? "We only started six years ago," was the answer.

The course is of four years for an actor and six for a dancer; only two ballet troupes have been formed so far but more will be forming. Because Algeria has various ethnic groups, the scope and variety of dancing is rich and diversified; Alger, Oran, Kabylia, Constantine, all have their own style. And there is plenty to choose from.

During the French colonial period, there was no Algerian training in dancing in the cities. All traces of Arab culture were suppressed. Children were not allowed to speak Arabic; hence there is a great dearth of Arabic scholars today. And Algerian artists and writers are only beginning to grapple with the problems of language and audience. The same goes for dancing and the theatre. No theatrical plays were allowed by the French. It was only 1964 that the Algerian government began recording the dances and music of Algeria, which provided the material for basic study. In the past, the tradition of dancing, especially in the cities, was of the single dancer, rather than the group, although this is not true in certain parts of Algeria such as Kabylia. Now the school was trying to transform this individual type into group dancing, ten dancers or more forming a group. There were some Bulgarian teachers at the school to teach ballet and choreography, and a classical ballet troupe was being formed to dance *Swan Lake*. This last endeavour I felt was a mistake. I said I thought that *Swan Lake* was not going to promote Algerian dancing, music, or the theatre. Why choose *Swan Lake*? "Because we feel we also want to learn from other sources," said the director. But I was not convinced. neither was he. On 5 July there had been some representations of "great national themes", such as industrialization, etc., all done by the school. But it had been done too hastily and not too well. The director was very frank about it; all Algerians are frank about their failures or defects. "The peasant dancing groups who came straight from the villages danced very much better than we did." There followed a long discussion. I opined that if the young were sent to the villages, perhaps they would learn better dancing, create new dances, and the people would be more interested.

The first theatre troupe was organized during the war of national liberation; "our theatre began with anti-colonialism". The oral tradition of the theatre was uprooted because of the uprooting of Arabic culture; from 1832 to 1962 only three schools of Arabic, in Tlemcen, Alger and Constantine, were allowed, and then only to train religious teachers (*Kadis*) and interpreters for the law courts. The judges were French, and the people could not understand them. In 1945 Arabic free schools were started, but in 1954 they were suppressed because the war started.

We visited the various studying groups, those who studied mime, scripts, theatre techniques, dancing, etc. It was an interesting and courageous experiment, and the enthusiasm of the young students was touching. I did tell the director that too much reliance on cadres, professors, etc. would not really achieve the aim, which was of a widespread dissemination of art, of the theatre, among the people. "Let the people themselves create, as they used to give the poet his lines on the market place." On the other hand, it was true that some basic discipline and coaching was needed, but perhaps not quite the way it was being done. The director told me that the best theatre play that had been created, the most popular, was *El Roula*, created by Ruished, an illiterate peasant. Algerians are a very vital, inventive, hard-working people. They will one day create a new art and literature, but it will come from the Arab-speaking, the working people, the Kasbah, and the clamour for books to read, and songs and poems, in Arabic, is very strong.

Algiers is a pleasant and beautiful city of white buildings, cradled in trees and flower bushes and groves of orange, lemon and persimmon trees. The sea, the blue and wine-coloured Mediterranean, gives it a perpetual holiday look. The "chic" quarter has large stores, and there are European imports still; but imports are being cut, as Algeria makes its own clothes, textiles and shoes, and is already self-sufficient in a good many of these, such as men's shirts and shoes. There is a "night life", as in all capitals, but it is mostly for tourists and the Algerian élite; Algerians are frugal and abstemious on the whole, though an occasional drunk is seen. Their real passion seems to be football. Every village, every small town, even the suburbs of Algiers, teem with adolescents, children, grown men, playing football.

I admire the many hard-working and devoted Algerians I met, the workers in the agricultural estates, in the factories, the hard-working officials, but in a city one is apt to meet the "élite", and of course Algeria is also burdened with a small "élite", few but lethal, whose example is poisonous, and who really are the implants of colonialism among their own people. I meet the same in India, and I know the type. They look down with contempt on their own people, and doubt that their country can do without the West. They grumble that there is no "freedom", meaning the freedom for them to go abroad, to enrich themselves. The government is well aware that these are foci of danger, people who would like a "more flexible government", meaning a more servile one, which would sell out the interests of the country and its working people for the comforts of a small, egoistical bourgeoisie.

I was told by an Algerian official, young (35) but already in high position (and in Algeria all the leaders are young), that in his own office three years ago he was looked upon as odd because he said good morning in Arabic instead of in French! This is the kind of mentality which persists in some groups, fortunately small, unfortunately at times in positions where they can have much influence. In the universities the alliance between such a bourgeoisie, intellectuals, and certain French experts had a bad influence on the young. Some are convinced that, unless they imitate all that is being done in Europe, they are not up to date. Hence a big problem, known as "the problem of the successors".

Efforts are being made to eradicate this, which again is not peculiar to Algeria, but found in all ex-colonies. However every time the Algerian government wants to take matters in hand, it is accused of being "arbitrary"; words about "freedom of expression" are bandied about, and much more, in the Western press, and in Algeria by some pro-Western journalists. It is the same with bookstores; some of them stock Western books, thrillers, crime and sex stories, magazines of the most inane type; the quality of Western books supplied to Algeria so far is not of high level, and steps are taken to control this inflow of trash, paid for in foreign exchange. But this means a policy of producing good books in Algeria itself; of importing necessary books and cutting off magazines and books which are of no value except negative. But then the few who think of themselves as the élite will scream "censorship", forgetting that there is censorship (for instance over the film *The Battle of Algiers*) in Europe too. Yet the Algerian government is keenly aware of the manipulation of public opinion through books, the Press, the news media.

"The biggest defect we have ... is that we are too near to Europe," said to me my friend Salah, a hardy, tough Algerian revolutionary, honest, devoted worker for Algerian independence. "If only we could be 2,000 kilometres away, many of our problems would vanish – especially where the younger generation is concerned."

But nothing can be done about geography. However something *can* be done about a positive policy for national identity and a national culture. The year 1971 has been proclaimed the year of Arabization, and it indicates a definite policy. I interviewed the Minister of Information and Culture, Mr Ahmed Taleb, formerly Minister of Education, on these matters. For information, public opinion and education are related policies, and this Mr Taleb stressed. They could not be dissociated, for "the preparation of the future is the work of the present, and for this there must be a total, conscious and effective mobilization of all the people," said Mr Taleb. The Minister is a tall, remarkably handsome, extremely gifted man; he writes very well in Arabic (he is one of the few Arabic scholars), in French, in English. He was five years in jail for his political activities during the war, and is an unflinching patriot. When in jail he wrote some excellent critical essays and a collection of letters. They are most interesting and reflect great firmness and clearness of mind in distressing circumstances. One essay which I found extremely interesting was Taleb's exposure and condemnation of the French writer Marcel Camus, winner of the Nobel Prize and always called a "humanist". Camus always claimed he was "Algerian" because he was born in Algeria of French parentage. When the struggle for independence developed, Camus did not stand on the side of the Algerian patriots; he even condemned their heroic defiance as "violence". Though the myth persists in France that he described "Algeria", because he wrote of the Algerian sun, the beauty of the country, its mountains and fertile plains, the Algerians refuse to recognize him as one of theirs because he was against their war of independence, against the liberation of the Algerian people. He never did, in fact, belong in heart or mind to the country. Bouchenne also told me how, educated in a Swiss school, he had written against Camus's "humanism", and been "failed" for it in literature! Taleb's essays on Camus really made the point, refusing and refuting the "humanism" of a writer who refused to incur any risk by condemning the atrocities then perpetrated by some French paratroops on the Algerian people. Yet the myth of an "Algerian" Camus, who "understood" the "Algerian soul" and was gifted with "humanism", persists. The claim that Camus represented Algeria, when he merely represented an intellectual who had abdicated his responsibility to speak for justice and for the freedom of his own people, was vigorously attacked by Ahmed Taleb.

In 1962, said Taleb to me, after 130 years of occupation, there were in all Algeria 300,000 children in school out of 11 million people. Eight years later in 1970 there were 2,200,000. In 1973, 75 per cent of all school-age children would be at school and in 1980, 100 per cent of the school-age population would be at school. In 1962 there were only 2,000 Algerian university students for the total population, the University of Algiers had "5,000 students" enrolled, but 4,300 were French *pieds noirs*! By 1970 there were 15,000 Algerian students in the universities.

There is not an engineer over 50 years old in Algeria; the colonial power did not encourage them; and *no* engineers were allowed till 1962! Some Algerians did go to France to study engineering, but many remained in France. A school of engineering was established in 1963. This year 70 engineers will be produced in Algeria, the first 70. They are all young, of course, under 30 years old. There are about the same number of older engineers (under 50 years old), and the demand is enormous.

Where medical personnel was concerned it was even worse. In 1962, *10 doctors a year* were being formed; in 1970, 100 doctors graduated from the University of Algiers.

As a result all the officials, the prefects, mayors, Ministers, etc., in leadership positions are young and most of them have been active fighters in the war. There is an enormous lack of specialized and professional personnel and a fantastic need for them. There is especially need of technical people, for industry, agriculture, building. As a result, it happens that, due to the type of higher education, still French-influenced, the graduates are demanding, asking many privileges, as this is a market where education and training is highly valued. Of course one does find unselfish, patriotic, sincere and devoted young people. But the values inculcated in these universities are still bourgeois values, and the government is trying to solve the dilemma: How to train quickly these young people (for which French teachers, professors, etc., are necessary still as there are not enough Algerian trained experts), and yet avoid the young being influenced by their teachers in thinking themselves a superior intelligentsia, requiring special privileges.

The whole education system has to be rethought, in terms of

Arabization, in terms of aims, motivation. "We'll solve the problem, but it will take a little while," says Minister Taleb. The cultural situation of Algeria was very different from that of other Arab countries; in Tunisia and in Morocco foci of Arab culture were left; but in Algeria an almost total uprooting occurred, since Algeria was considered a district of France. It is this which makes the Algerians determined to recreate their own culture, not on the past structures, but "on new, revolutionary, socialist bases". They immediately understood what a *cultural revolution* meant: "the most profound necessity for a people to move forward in its own history," said Taleb.

From 1830 onwards, never did the Algerian people really stay "quiet"; every few years there were revolts. The years 1930 to 1954 especially were a time of preparation of minds for armed struggle, and many leaders, including President Boumedienne, grew up in this "preparation for independence" and took active part in it. November 1954 saw the end of the first phase of struggle. Underground circulated the slogans, repeated by each child: "Algeria is my country. Arabic is my language. Islam is my religion." These three assertions represented all that had been taken away and which the Algerian people wanted to regain. Before 1962, Arabic had even been named a "foreign language", on a par with German or English, and French made *the* language of Algeria.

Arabization would take eight years to be completed. In primary school the first three years would be totally in Arabic, the second three in Arabic plus French (because we need a window on technical civilization, the Minister explained). Eighty per cent of the children now wanted to study English, and so French would no longer be obligatory.

The rewriting of history was also very important. I was delighted to see, in that connection, my old friend Lacheraf, who had been a fighter in the national liberation and later became ambassador in Latin America. Lacheraf was back in Algiers, taking an active part in a long-term well-thought-out decision-making strategy of revolution in education and all the media of information. It was also essential to rewrite and reassess all the past, rewrite history, and create conditions in which there would be full emancipation for the minds of Algerian people to work out a *socialist* system. History must have its own aspects, and not be merely the history of the ancient Muslim empires, or a *religion-based* history. Algeria, though an Arab State, has its differences with other parts of the Arabic world. This is the Maghreb; it has components different from that of

Arabia proper. Hence the national identity and history must be seen in the context of a new, socialist Algeria.

(1971)

Kabylia – Villages on the Crests

SALAH, who is a Kabyle, "and all Kabyles are revolutionaries", he told us with a big smile, took us to his
native village in Kabylia to see his mother and sisters
and his native hamlet. Piled with the children in the car,
we drove on to Tizi Ouzou, a charming little town, chief
city of the region. Kabylia begins there, and after that the road goes
on and up, winding into the mountains of Kabylia. It was the day of
voting in each commune, and 87 per cent of the electorate turned out
to vote, including many women; Tizi Ouzou was full of cyclists,
footballers and voters.

The beauty of Kabylia is something breath-taking. It cannot
really be described adequately; all around us suddenly were the
mountains; sharp-crested, the ranges running a living line, the line
of their summits which seemed to romp, to fling itself like a rope of
dancers, like a daisy chain, under the sun-dazzled sky. And on this
line of crests, high up, are the Kabyle villages, strung like agate
stones, pink and red, on the long necklace of the mountain range. The
villages look down upon the valleys and there are no habitations
down where the stream runs; an attempt to make the villagers come
down and live in pleasant little houses in the valley failed utterly.
The houses stand as they were built; not a pane of glass, not a door,
not a brick has been taken from them, yet the people are not wealthy.
"Kabyles are like that," says Salah.

The villages of Kabylia can only be reached by climbing; so climb
we did, until we were at Salah's native hamlet.

All of Kabylia was guerrilla-war region; for years my friend Salah
had gone by night, talking of independence, organizing cells, walking
the crests of the mountains. The uprising had started in this area
and in the Aures, another region of Algeria. And now the tales of
these war days were told; each village had its own. Many songs of the
war were first sung here, in the oral tradition of singing and poetry
which the Kabyles have kept.

The houses of the Kabyles are fantastic. They are made of stone and plaster, and they are white and orange, burnt orange. The doors are reached by stone steps. Within, the walls are smoothed by hand; like a tent's inside, there are no sharp-edged corners. Little slits of windows let in the light, and there is a place for goats under a raised platform which is the bedroom. The women weave on extraordinary handlooms. There is no shuttle; but they produce marvellous blankets and rugs; the process is very slow. They also make pottery and many kinds of jars, decorated in the colours of sienna and ochre they love. Even the fields here are aslant, and appear precipitous to a non-Kabyle. The population is clear-skinned, with big round eyes, and a great love of colourful clothes. The women are unveiled, and there were many women fighters from Kabylia in the war.

The loveliness of Kabylia, the sheer excitement of these villages, like nests in high trees, stuck on the sheer summits, the tales of their long resistance, would inspire an Algerian writer, it seemed to me. I felt a great urge to walk that loping crest line, studded with its sienna and white clusters, collecting the stories of these gay, lively Kabyles. What a wealth of material there is to collect, to make known, in this transformation, which even now was reaching them, as the government built schools and factories. And then there was the war, with all its stories – such a project had begun, Salah told me, and in fact it was an Algerian woman who had lived here, and written a doctoral thesis on the Kabyles, but there was need for much more in that line "because some of our writers still yearn to copy the French"; they did not leave the comfortable cities – they saw nothing of value in Kabylia.

Everywhere the story is the same. In China too, for so many years, a good many writers and intellectuals had resisted change; had preferred to cut themselves off from their own people, rather than to change themselves; had been blind to the wealth of life of their own people. Just as in China, too, *Swan Lake* had been performed. The mind can remain servile after the body is freed....

Returning from that marvellous day in Kabylia, I was to meet such a writer. He was Algerian, tall, handsome, glib. He preferred to speak French; when we ordered mutton and couscous (Algerian dishes), he ordered steak and chips. He talked of the latest novels in Paris, which I had not read.

And when I enthused about Kabylia, his eyes, full of perplexity, stared at me. He froze into something like disdain; his sentences shortened. It was not the first time "intellectuals" had found me "simple". Perhaps I was not complex and confused enough.

But I could not get out of my eye the vision of those sharp and lovely mountain people; the women with their multi-coloured blouses and skirts, the smooth gloss of their skin and hair, their singing voices, going with their water jars upon their backs by the stone paths, perpetual laughter pouring from them like the stream water. The men, so handsome and grave; the hand-turned houses, and far beyond looming right above us, the further ranges of the Magnificent Djurdjura, the contorted peaks, snow clad, of Algeria's great Alps, and as far as one could stretch the arm the stark white and orange villages clasping the summits.

"But what is there really of art in all this?" said the writer, somewhat exasperated. "It is only primary material." And how could I explain? That it was the writer's business to catch this radiance and its hope; that the children now went to school, that the women voted; that there were difficulties because life was changing, the young going into new factories; but that this also had its romance. That it was finding such sturdy and vigorous independence of mind, finding this potential wealth, which was so exalting. That the discussion with the women about the communes of Algeria, and seeing the great number of women, even if veiled, go down to vote at Tizi Ouzou, that was the beginning of tomorrow.

"You are a romantic," he said, and declaimed some French poet of the nineteenth century and sighed: "France is the land of my exile," because he felt more at home in Europe than in his own country. The revolution in Algeria, the difficulties, the tough and hard work which I saw the people do, their faith in spite of suffering, setbacks, their shining hope, meant little to him. He only saw the bad things, the things not done, the bureaucracy, expanding as it does any time there is a bureaucracy, the omissions, the defects. I told him that the people of his country were marvellous and had fought a great war. He looked quizzical. I knew then once again, it would be among the élite, the bourgeoisie, that the old enemy would implant itself anew.

The women of Algeria fought alongside the men; they unveiled, cut off their hair, carried bombs in their handbags, did guerrilla war. I met one of them, Dr Halimi. She was a guerrilla in the mountains of Kabylia. The villages gave asylum; their children used to go with bread to feed the hidden guerrillas. No child, no woman, betrayed.

My friend Salah himself carried bread to an insurgent when he was a child, all of 30 years ago, before the war of independence. "Our mothers used to teach us how to take the bread; we would go out to play; and then we would cover up for one of us, who would take the bread. This lasted for years."

The Kabyles fought from their villages; they liquidated the

officials who collaborated, the Harkis. Dr Halimi was caught and then was in jail for seven years. "I read your book when I was hiding in a Kabyle village," she told me. She is now running a hospital for obstetrics and gynaecology in Algiers. "This hospital started in 1968." Like so many other things in Algeria, it is new; and there are not enough doctors and not enough nurses; though a nursing school and a midwifery school have started.

"There is no bar at all to family planning in the Islamic religion here," Dr Halimi said. She is now married, with children. A vivid, extraordinarily graceful and young-looking woman; one would not think, seeing her carefully dressed hair and her fine hands, that she held a gun and was a guerrilla. "In the villages of Kabylia, there is no false shame, no reticence about having or not having children. But there must be much education; we do not have enough doctors willing to go to the countryside and to the villages. We are now offering special privileges for these doctors."

The population increase is about 3 per cent a year in Algeria; but they are less than 12 million, for a territory which is four times the size of France. Much of it is desert. The fertile valleys such as the Mititja, which once belonged to the French, run along the edge of the sea; beyond the desert starts. However the desert is not poor. Underneath the Sahara is the biggest table of fresh water in the world. It only needs to be tapped.... The Algerian government is thinking about it, but it is an arduous and difficult job; it requires an immense amount of capital.

Off to the desert we went, to the famous valley of the Mzab.

Bassa, secretary general of the Red Cross, put us in touch with the inhabitants of Mzab.

Algeria is not one land but many regions of great diversity put together, yet cohesive through the common war in a deep national unity. From the high mountains with perpetual snow, and ski resorts; from the fertile valleys bigger and better than the best in Europe; from the 600 miles of coastline and sea, and modern cities; one drops plumb into the world of the desert, and its oases. The desert itself is not one. It houses several large main groups of people: the Hoggar, the Touaregs, who live there where the women are the poets, unveiled, presiding over culture and property, and the men serve them and are veiled. But the Mozabites are just the opposite. The women are bundled in a vast white sheet, and peer out from only one eye; the other is also covered. Yet it all makes one thing: Algeria. But it means that every 200 kilometres you fall into a different land

and have to readjust. All of Europe is far more monotonously the same than 200 kilometres in any direction in Algeria.

Mzab land is the desert edge, our energetic Mozabite host, Hadji Mohammed Bafdel, told me. "We are not the deep south of the desert, only the fringe." But it is desert all right.

A big sand wind blowing as we landed at Ghardaia; and for a first acquaintance with the desert, nothing is more perfect than a sandstorm. For the storm cleared and there it was: the land of the Mzab, with its five cities, like dreams, like abstract paintings, pink and pale blue and white with hand-made minarets like fingers, with their hand-made walls just a little crooked, swaying to the wind and beautiful as all things conceived in faith and passion. The most perfect dreams of cities; scoured bone stark by the sand, five mirages in the desert. I was spellbound. Never had I seen anything so beautiful and so extraordinary. We gazed for hours from a promontory rich in clean boulders stark as bones.

The cities' names: Ghardaia, Melika, Benis Ghen, Bounoura, and El Ateuf. Together these five make the Mzab; each of them is shaped like a small pyramid, rising to the centre the highest point, crowned by the minaret. The colours, white and pink and blue, all melting into each other, stand out like modern conceptions of art in the vast ochre of the desert, quite unreal. Built in the eleventh century, they remain as they were, kept up by an extraordinary human endurance. Perhaps that is why one cannot believe they are real; as my memory's eye sees them again, it is an unsubstantial, "floating" feeling I recapture as if they might disappear on awakening. Yet the inhabitants are among the most practical, the most in touch with modern life, of all in Algeria; it is they who run all the shops in the big cities of Algiers and Oran and Constantine. The Mzab is their home, their heart; they return here and bring their money back to this strange, monastic, puritan and frugal valley. For that is what they chose; to remain hardly as a community they eschew all luxury.

They have kept the oldest and most conservative customs of all in Algeria, yet at the same time they are completely in touch with all that goes on in the world. But they see no reason to "imitate" any one else. Two hundred kilometres further south, the Touareg tribes, entirely different, where the man veils his face against the desert storm, where the woman is the poet, the writer, the singer, and the man serves her; this does not incite them to change. And they explained to me why they did not want to give up their way of life.

Ghardaia is the largest and perhaps the most colourful of the five cities, with a population of 70,000 people. The streets are narrow corridors between white, pink and blue walls; there are no cars, no cars at all, only people walking, an occasional ambling goat. Sometimes a biblical figure on a donkey comes by and speaks a greeting, and time goes back a thousand years. It is a profoundly puritan and strict society which the Mozabites run. There are no cinemas or dance halls; five times a day much of the male population climbs the steep streets up to the mosque for prayers. There are no beggars. The tight-knit community sees to it that everyone is provided for.

The Mozabites are a sect of Islam, the Ibadites. The Ibadites apply the Koran to the absolute letter, even today. They sought the arid desert to build their beautiful austere cities, in order to be far from temptation. Here all is flat straight lines; no ornament is permitted. No advertising posters, no statues, no carvings defile the plain and stark beauty of an idea expressed in all the gestures of living.

When voting for an administrator, a governor, etc., the Ibadites say that the man who is voted into power must "practise the Koran" in all its details. Also they hold it permissible to revolt against a ruler who misbehaves and depose him.

The first Ibadite state was founded in what is now Libya, near Tripoli. In the eleventh century the Ibadites, hunted and persecuted, came here and have stayed here, as their "heart base". They are only half a million, scattered all over the Middle East, but there are even some in Poland, so they told me. They have a history of grandeur and decay; the decay, due to wealth and ostentation, made for the decision to practise abstemiousness and frugality, so they deliberately sought out the desert, and settled in the valley of Mzab in order to remain pure and therefore strong, nine centuries ago. They had a kind of autonomy under the French, but they were proud of not taking any money for their religious schools. The head of their State, they recall, was a stone cutter, and they believe in working hard and in manual labour. The Mzab communities teach their children to work and refuse to give them luxuries, for fear of spoiling them. Yet being a commercial community they are very wealthy.

Out of 70,000 inhabitants, 10,000 are children aged 7 to 14; 100 per cent of the male child population is at school but only 20 per cent of the girls. This the Mozabites will tell one quite frankly. The subject of woman's emancipation is a delicate one with them. The Mozabites are afraid of corruption coming with women's emancipation and education and it is difficult to argue with them on this point. Mozabites are one and all with the revolution and none was with the French and against the revolution; "there are no traitors here, unlike

what happened in some cities," said Hadji Bafdel to me. Through
their commercial connections, since most of the shops in Algiers are
owned by them, they were active in supplying the resistance with
food and with equipment. "This is because we have great solidarity
- we do not want to lose our customs."

As we were talking about the condition of women, the Hadjis of
the mosque, intelligent and able men, who had come to dinner and to
talk with me, pointed out: "Our dowries are very low, so that even the
poor can get married." But they conceded that things would change.
At the moment there were only four doctors in the whole of the
Mzab. "There are as yet no Algerian doctors in the Sahara desert
except in Ghardaia." They were, however, keenly aware of change
and greatly interested in the rest of the world, especially in China,
the communes, education.

The problem of the young "being corrupted" worried them very
much. They were also very intent on promoting the Arabization of
education. And one and all were for an end to any kind of foreign
control of resources. "Algeria is our country. We can be the strongest
industrial state in North Africa, with our mineral resources."

The Mayor of Ghardaia, whom I saw the next day, is an ex-officer
of the revolutionary army. He was in "Wilaya 5", each wilaya being
a well-defined region of Algeria. Wilaya 5 was under the command
of Boumedienne. "We had 90 per cent of the people with us, and
though we had limited material means, they helped us all they could.
We had a well-established net of the National Liberation Front
although the French were militarily very strong."

"The fighting in the Sahara was most difficult, because there is no
cover, but we learned to dig holes. The French were never sure
whether the sand dune in front of them, with some very sparse
clumps, was or was not crawling with men. People, even the poorest
nomads, shared their food with us." Afterwards to prevent food
being passed the nomads of the desert had been regrouped. The
women had done intelligence for the guerrillas, but the most difficult
was munitions. Sometimes just to obtain ammunition and guns an
attack would be launched.

Thus all over Algeria, in each region, the last war is still a lesson
for the future, an encouragement to continue, not to stagnate. The
turning towards building, towards industrial and agricultural
progress, is an essential preoccupation, and the people of Algeria are
ready for any sacrifice to ensure economic independence.

First of all, of course, there is petrol, the energy of nations.
Algerian petrol is excellent petrol, without sulphur component; and

this makes it a particularly precious commodity. Even the Japanese are eager to step into the Algerian petrol market, for in Japan the petrol used has some sulphur component, and that is why the pollution due to motor-car traffic is so dangerous in Japanese cities.

Algeria is the tenth oil-producing country in the world with 60 million tons in 1970; it has also reserves of natural gas estimated at 2,000 billion cubic metres. Natural gas is to be exported this year, and will ensure a good income to the country. But the Algerians also want to pipe it to their own homes.

It was in 1962 that, the war over, Algeria could look forward to taking its own wealth in its own hands. But there were many difficulties. How does a country with new independence control its own resources in Africa? So many African and Asian countries still do not. Under Houari Boumedienne, in 1968 the state made a bid to nationalize all the foreign oil companies; because for all these years the price paid to the producing countries has remained low, but the consuming countries have doubled and trebled the prices of goods sold to the producers and the petrol price to their own populations. The present large-scale and determined effort by the producing countries, with Algeria at the head, to stop this exploitation, is a turning point in the history of the relations between the "industrialized" and the so-called "undeveloped"; it is a sign and herald of this world change which we are living through today.

The Algerian people support the moves of the government to become master of its own resources; never has the government been more popular.

In France, which was much affected by this determination of the Algerian government, it is surprising how many of the French people sympathized *with* the Algerians. The price of oil in France had risen even *before* there had been any nationalization or rise in price of the oil produced in Algeria; and the French people were all aware that it was not the fault of the Algerian government, but the profit-making by super-greedy oil companies. "They are quite right to want to be masters in their own land," many of the French say. Only a few right-wing newspapers and one fascist magazine incite the French people and the French government to "take counter-measures", notably about wine, or to throw out Algerian workers in France.

More than 45 per cent of the wine used in France was actually grown in Algeria, by the French *pieds-noirs*. Since their departure the Algerians took over the big wine plantations. And they have started to tear up the vineyards, and grow wheat, fruit, vegetables instead. But it is difficult to change the pattern of a colonial monoculture right away; how can one retrain and at the same time procure a livelihood for the agricultural workers? So for a while the pattern continued; but all over Algeria the agricultural policy is to cut down vine growing and replace it with other agricultural produce; already nearly 50 per cent of the vineyards have been turned to other agricultural produce. The problem of Algerian workers is a double-edged one. There are 250,000 to 300,000 of them in France, and French industry, the building trade, needs them for jobs the French won't do themselves.

The fundamental problem of oil is not only its extraction to furnish Europe with its energy; oil is also the basis of most synthetic industries, plastics, detergent, synthetic fibres, petro-chemicals. Almost 300,000 products of industry are derivatives of oil; fertilizers also are based on oil: hence agriculture is linked to industry and to the production of oil. It is only in the last ten years that North Africa has become one of the wealthiest oil-producing sites (Libya and Algeria). But the oil market and production has been dominated, from the first, wherever produced, by a few international monopolies. Eighty per cent of the world market is controlled by them. It is already many years since the oil-producing countries have demanded fairer rates of payment than the royalties they draw; but the question is not only a rate of royalties, it is that oil is the basis of national industrialization, the basis of self-reliance for Algeria. This oil is taken away from Algeria and therefore no other industries based on oil are started unless Algeria controls her own oil and establishes a petro-chemical industry of her own.

We went to Oran and thence by car to Arzew, which, with Annaba, is one of the two main industrial sites of Algeria. Seeing that it is only eight years since Algeria emerged from colonialism, both sites are impressive. More interesting still is the fact that as soon as possible the Algerians replace the foreign experts with their own technical people, but they still have far too few, especially engineers, as we have seen from the figures.

Speaking at the UNCTAD conference, in 1968 in New Delhi, the Algerian Minister for Industry and Energy had said: "it is no coincidence that the economies of developing countries ... should be ignorant of industrialization, forced into monoculture ... coercion, conquest and domination still continue 'arresting the evolution of these countries ...'"

Algeria's determination to master its own industrialization plans is very plain at Arzew and Annaba, but this is fraught with difficulties. The Algerian engineers we spoke to were all eager to be truly independent. One project had been "stalled' for two years; the Algerian engineers believed that this was deliberate. They themselves had, in one case, taken repairs in hand and their section had been efficiently working within a month; the other section, under "foreign control", was still "under repair" 18 months later....

"There is little one can do at the moment. But the determination to get rid as soon as possible of all such help and to be truly independent is very strong among us," said one engineer. The awareness of neo-colonial "milking" is intense. "Of course we need cadres, we need help, we need so much, but we want to be on our own feet as soon as possible."

The willingness is there, and the government does all it can to encourage engineers; but the rub is that at the same time the problem remains of the selfishness of the privileged élite. The sacrifice necessary for pioneering and for the development of national resources in its own countries is compensated by high pay, but the élite is tempted to "export" itself abroad for a higher living standard.

With steel works at Annaba, a nitrogen fertilizer plant, the liquefaction and transport of natural gas at Arzew, refineries, a petro-chemical complex, Algeria is trying to develop its industry as quickly as possibly; the potential is there as regards raw material, the potential in man still lacks, and every step the Algerian government takes is not made easier by pressures from outside as well as by what might be called the enemy within, a type of education inherited from the past, which emphasizes individualism, selfish complacency, and privilege for the educated.

The Algerian effort is hampered by these neutral and social structures which still remain, and of which they are much aware. President Boumedienne, however, told me that it is a firm decision to press on towards socialism, that the problem is seen with clarity and determination.

President Houari Boumedienne is a very quiet, soft-spoken man, with keen eyes, and a great intelligence and sense of reality. He is a man who grows and learns with responsibility, a very modest and sincere man. He insists on speaking Arabic in his speeches, so that certain Europeans, who think that anyone must speak a European dialect to be civilized, asked me ironically: "How good is President Boumedienne's French?" after the audience. "Far better than mine," I replied. And it is true that President Boumedienne speaks a pure, precise French when and if he wants to. But he is keen on the

development of Arabic, single-minded in the pursuit of the independence of his nation, and it is clear to him that the national
liberation of Algeria is only beginning; he is very much aware and
absolutely determined that Algeria must pursue a socialist course.
"We are only at the beginning, but determination is very important."
The greatest problem was the problem of education of the next
generation, the young. Will they drift back? Will they be brainwashed with hankerings for ease, luxury, the lazy shiftless kind of
spurious happiness which is only intense selfishness, or will they
learn to serve their own people? This is a very great problem, a
problem connected also to that of bureaucracy. With the great
demand for cadres, for administrative trained personnel, there is also
the contradiction that education immediately removes the young
people from wanting to do manual labour jobs. And how does one
cope with this?

It was an impressive hour that President Boumedienne gave us,
when he spoke so frankly of the situation confronting his country,
and like all truly great men did not try to make out that all was well.
"But we know the world is changing; we do not want to slide back.
We have fought colonialism and we fight imperialism in all its
forms." Algeria had remained true to itself; in the Middle East, in
Africa, on the barbarous war in Vietnam, its positions were always
on the side of the just wars of the revolutionary people. "We have the
best relations with the Democratic Republic of North Vietnam." The
President also praised China, and what it was doing, which was an
example and an inspiration to the whole world. "It is the future of the
world which is now being built, and China has seen it very clearly,"
said the president. I left feeling that Algeria was luckier than many
other nations emergent from colonialism in its leadership; for
certainly Boumedienne, who fought throughout the war for
Algerian independence, is a true patriot, a self-sacrificing and
intensely dedicated man. His popularity among the people is great
and is growing precisely because of his staunch determination not to
fall back, but to go forward. That is why Algeria does not have a good
Press in the West, where many would prefer a "more flexible" and
less revolutionary-minded leadership, one that could be pressured
and made to serve the interests of monopoly capital.

In agriculture, the difficulties are frankly faced, and there are
difficulties. To begin with, the vast estates of the French colons were
nationalized; and a system of self-management installed. But there
also last year a thorough revamping was started. There is much that
has been done, but much remains.

We visited one such estate, which once grew vineyards, and now is planting fruit, vegetables, and getting early produce by putting plastic covers which keep the heat in, and thus makes it possible to export large quantities of fruit and vegetables of all kinds to Europe in the winter, when Europe has none.

The peasants of these nationalized farms are salaried in part, which means that the profits from their collective farms are equally distributed among them. But there are quite a number of difficulties in operating this system, not the least being that once again the cadres to work it are very few and among those that do run the estates not all are experienced. There is also the fact that bad habits of bureaucracy constantly have to be checked. Roughly, it can be said that Algeria has two kinds of agriculture systems going; one is the modern, collectivized one. This applies especially in the valley of the Mititja, where the old French estates were. There the self-management farms employ agricultural workers, who have a fixed income, and who have a voice in the running of the estate (but this varies; in certain areas, they really do have a lot to say, but in others the bureaucratic cadres are not so keen in listening to them). Algeria has the wine problem; she wants to pass from this culture which was dependent on French buying to large wheat farms; but once again cereal growing is not so profitable as are, for instance, fruit and vegetable farms; these farms will be mainly for export of produce and they have a very quick turnover. But at other times the markets for this produce are uncertain, or flooded from other sources. Then there is the problem of secondary occupations in these self-managed farms.

The other kind of agriculture is in the more remote regions, where there are still landlords, and poor peasants, and a great economic disparity. About 3 million hectares are nationalized, and jobs have been created for the soldiers of the army among these collective farms. There remain about 6 million hectares which are not yet nationalized. In October 1970 President Boumedienne announced the intention to proceed to put an end to rural poverty, and "the evil conditions of life" of the feudal system operated in Algeria. The big landlords, though a minority, resist the agrarian reform with all their might. It seemed to me that in that sector, perhaps the most difficult of all, the Algerian government was in search of a model, at the same time desirous of finding its own formulae for solving the problem. The peasants and the managers of the collective farms were immensely interested in the communes of China. It is difficult, however, in one visit to make up one's mind. I do not agree with the pessimism and the vilification one finds in most of Europe about Algerian agricultural management; so much of it is due to jealousy and resentment. I think it has been a bold, imaginative and necessary effort. And it has needed courage, and dedication. A great deal of positive action has taken place.

One thing is certain. All those I met agreed that "we must go forward, for to stagnate is to fall back". Remembering the problems encountered in China in agriculture, one is not surprised there should be problems still in Algeria. But certainly something has been attempted here which has not been done in many other ex-colonial countries, and one can only hope for its success, and try to help.

(1971)

Water Too Pure...

SPRING into summer late June, and noon sultry with balked rain. Expectation of rain is the talk on trolley buses, among the walkers under the tree-lined ways, within the bicycle clusters coursing the avenues. There was a drought last year and 400,000 people from the city went to the surrounding communes to help the peasant brothers carry water to the fields. Will the pranky Old Man in Heaven again be parsimonious?

I am not surprised when the girl on a bicycle coasting by the sidewalk addresses me. There are no strangers in China's Big Family, and her timid spectacled eyes have been staring at me for a while. At the red light of the Eastern Peace crossroads we stop and she says:

"The radio announces rain tomorrow but I think it may be too early."

We peer at the grey cellophane lid holding back the blessed water.

"My ancestors are from the south but I have been in Peking many years. I recognized you by your grey hair."

Her deference pleases me, though in Europe, where elderliness is slightly obscene, I would feel a trifle put out.

"I am Jade Magnolia. I would like to talk with you about writing."

We decide to eat noon rice together and she walks her bicycle with me to the restaurant in the East Wind market, and secures it under the care of the grandma who hitches the iron donkeys in neat rows along the building's red brick wall. We manage a table and order bean curd and peppered chicken.

Jade Magnolia is now politely nervous. "Forgive me ... I do want to write but do not know how to start."

She looks at me with such hope, such faith, such candour (but this is a candid, frank country) that I nearly tell her: It is you who help me: a writer depends so much on such encounters, unexpected light ... I too have much to write about the Revolution, what it has done

164

to me...I too do not know how to begin. But assuming judiciousness I say: "You must start with yourself."

"That is difficult. I may not be representative. We must write *about* workers and peasants, *for* workers and peasants. I am an intellectual, my father is an engineer in America. I came back to the Old Country twenty years ago. I want to tell what I felt, how I have changed...."

She is asking for a recipe and I am taking her life from her, bounteous rain for my own small drought. Jade Magnolia was born in America and aged 19, twenty years ago, she felt the pull of the Old Ancestral Country stirring and shaking itself and the world. She abandoned university "and also a boyfriend whom I thought I loved".

"I had then all sorts of romantic ideas – to live the great revolution ... to live nobly every hour, a passionate, continuous throb. Then for years I thought: Is this Revolution? I was bewildered, bored and depressed until the Cultural Revolution happened."

On her return in 1950 Jade Magnolia had been given a well paid teaching job, a nice flat. She married and had two children. And the great adventure became a daily stint of small, routine and mediocre things, sometimes boring, sometimes mean and petty; gap between humdrum reality and exclamatory entrancing slogans, often an absence of surging conviction, a shadow emptiness replete with small frustrations. Bureaucracy, rules and regulations. "Just do your work well. Why do more? All that is required of you is to obey the rules." There was total security. No one could ever be fired. And there was this yawn within her. Was this the wonderful revolution?

She moved her chopsticks in eager, earnest small stabs. "That was before the Cultural Revolution. I had lost a sense of purpose. I attended study meetings and I could always explain things, politically I mean, to myself. And so many things happened. China was changing, but it did not touch nor affect me. I went down to visit communes and factories, with others of my Institute. We wrote reports about our 'profound experience', we interviewed peasants and workers. It was like looking at flowers on horseback, no touch, no real feel. Then came the Cultural Revolution and I was totally involved, body and soul."

"I hadn't understood before when people said: 'Revolution means changing one's very bones, every bone in the body.' Now I know what it means, I've lived it. And I never want to go back to the non-being of what was."

"So you'd like to write it down, write it like it is, remember it for always, but you are also afraid ... because some things were highly unpleasant, and you also have to relive them. But you're afraid that if you do write these unpleasant things some people will not like it. It would show them up. You are afraid of being criticized...."

Jade Magnolia coloured and gulped. "I suppose so ... but I still want to write."

"Then you must. Whatever happens. Does not the Chairman say: 'Dare to think, to speak, to act'?"

"The Chairman says it. But there are still bureaucrats about, whose only justification is their ability to find fault. They're wonderful at stopping others from doing, in the name of 'political correctness'."

The Cultural Revolution had meant a battle against stagnation, against freezing, against bureaucracy, but more battles were to come. "We all knew it, it was said openly. 'Bureaucracy is a hydra-headed monster, ingrained in us for two millennia, the refuge of those who don't want revolution but pretend to be revolutionaries. Slogan-mouthing. Hierarchy. Rules and regulations.' They did it every time."

"That's why the Cultural Revolution was ... so wonderful. And also working and living with the peasants for three years. I really belonged then, to this earth and sky, to this people my people."

I could give her no advice which she did not already know, inside herself. "Begin with one day, any day that sticks and that you live again and shoo off, that you can't get away from."

Her face was suddenly docile, withdrawn. "I left America because I wanted to join the revolution."

"Now you're dehydrating the stuff, ironing words like white napkins in order. Say to yourself what is in you that you're afraid of wording and yet which stops you from beginning to word it all."

I thought she would leave me, but then she closed her eyes, and looked much less than her 39 years. "Be a peasant, seize that minute which sticks somewhere like a fishbone in your throat."

Eyes closed, she said: "I see them come for me. I look through the window, it is June, so many leaves on the trees, and I see the group walking without hurry towards my flat. I know them all, they are my colleagues in the Institute, and they are coming for me."

"They?"

"Red Guards, but not my group. I was a Red Guard of the 'Always Revolution' group. They belonged to the other group, 'Uphold Forever'. We had all started together, we the people, to criticize the leadership, the administration in our Institute. We really worked hard; we held meetings, we debated everything. We were so enthusiastic, so brimful of new ideas ... we wanted to sweep the place clean of stupidity and silliness, pull down the bureaucrats, change the many rules and regulations which suffocated the teaching. Then I knew what Revolution meant. I would have died for it. Everything had meaning again."

"Then we split. We *were* split. They are clever, the mandarins masquerading as Party members. They launched us against each other to save themselves, faction against faction, person against person. At one time six groups in my school all fought each other – even with knives and stones and firearms."

She was describing what was common knowledge, the emergence of extremist groups, like the "May 16", manipulated by someone who wanted to take power by promoting violence and chaos and sabotage. And although the Cultural Revolution proclaimed that all must be done by debate and *not* violence; even though the Chairman had said, "It is impermissible to ill-treat anyone", yet by June 1967 the May 16 group had terrorized the city and there had been beatings and torturing and even murders. The world outside had seen only this evil, not what the Cultural Revolution was meant to be.

"I knew they were coming for me. I wanted to run away, hide in a friend's flat, upstairs; but I could not move. I sat and waited for them and when they knocked on my door I said, 'Come in, please.' The door opened. 'We want to talk to you.'"

It had lasted six weeks. They had mounted guard over her even while she slept, afraid that she might kill herself. "The leader was a man I knew, my colleague, my age. He had always been amiable, witty, we had often chatted, eaten together ... strange how people reveal themselves in new circumstances. He was now leading the 'Uphold Forever' faction, making a reputation unmasking what he called hidden counter-revolutionaries. His group praised him for his thoroughness in 'finding out' things."

For six weeks he had questioned her, to make her admit she was counter-revolutionary "with illicit relations with foreigners". During that time they had fed her, purchasing whatever food she liked, called a doctor when she had been ill. The man led the questioning, day after day. "I did not admit." Her eyes gleamed with reminiscent victory. They had tired and left her, and she had gone to a commune to labour. "And that is when everything came clear at last."

"What's become of the man?"

"He's back at his job, as I am back at mine. We don't talk much to him, no one does. We know him too well. We all know each other, now, all the small hidden shameful things ... and he knows we think he's an opportunist who will try to start again, but next time we won't let him. He keeps quiet."

"But it's when I was working in the commune that I understood the Revolution. I saw it with all its ups and downs and twists and turns, like an enormous slow river, relentless. I had never really thought of it as a sum of all things, but the peasants did. Their day-after-day, year-after-year lives of work and long patience and planting and harvest and and coping with drought and slowly changing the earth with their hands and hoping, hoping. What I had endured which seemed so tragic became so ridiculously small, dwindled into nothing much, before them. One freezing night I remember the frost swooped down and they went in the dark to light fires, smoke to keep frost from the wheat, bringing their household charcoal, and all the winter through they went cold in their own houses. I thought I could never bear that life when I arrived; no toilets, no running water, and the peasants said: 'Look how good are our lives now.' I do not want to forget all this, I want to write it down ... but shall I be criticized?"

Small Fortitude was not only famed and read before Liberation, but of a scholarly family, educated abroad, doing translations of Western authors: Virginia Woolf and Chaucer. Now at 70 she was most beautiful, with sleek black hair, oval unwrinkled face. I had known her for almost 30 years and at the Cultural Revolution she had been reported dead, but here she was, in her booklined study, making small cakes for me. Her granddaughter a Red Guard, nurse in the Army Medical Corps, brought in the tea tray and Small Fortitude chatted on tea picking, for she had gone to a commune in the south, and planted vegetables and picked tea; "We also built our own houses. I was very proud of the wall I built." Though old people and the sick were not to be sent to labour, she had volunteered.

I knew that Fortitude and a woman doctor, also in her seventies, had been paraded in the streets early in the Cultural Revolution, wearing dunce's paper caps, exhibited as "serpent spirits" and "bourgeois authorities" to be overthrown.

"It must have been an awful ordeal for you," I said.

"It was a trifle uncomfortable," said Fortitude, "loss of face, all that. But in some ways ... a good thing. Hadn't I perhaps deserved it?"

The woman doctor had since been rehabilitated, highly honoured, now held a most important position. "We always said we were ready to die for the Revolution, for the people. So what is a little thing like wearing a cap for a few hours? And somehow we thought ourselves revolutionaries. Being in China, in the Revolution, we always thought the enemy was The Other, was outside. We learnt it was here, among us, within us, it was ourselves, too, dragging along with us all our old desires of élitism and superiority, our Confucian arrogance. We learned that Revolution has to have new beginnings within itself, again and again, that nothing can be taken for granted."

The Cultural Revolution had been for her a vindication of all she had believed in but somehow assumed had already been achieved: the transformation of Man himself; "It isn't done ... it will need so much more self-awareness. We've only just begun the process." What had happened to her had shocked her into a new conscious- ness, and she blamed herself for having so long kept up her privileges as a "superior person", and intending to remain so. "We all became bureaucrats, members of the Ministry of Culture, of the Writers Federation. In a land of illiterates, we were precious and knew it too well. We occupied the seats of influence, and though we were told we should write for the labouring masses, we really tried to re-create, consciously or not, our own autocratism. We quoted the classics and considered uncouth the young writers and judged all works by our own classical standards. Then came the Cultural Revolution and 'there was no way out but to explore my own heart, look really into myself'. For the first time I was submerged, totally submerged in the maelstrom ... but the glass wall between the working people and myself disappeared, and now I am afraid to lose this new, life-giving touch. I'm writing poetry as when I was 25 years old."

She told me, as I left, the story of the radio comedian, who had been so popular before the Cultural Revolution. They had come for him too, the righteous cohorts, and he said to them: "I have my dunce's cap all ready" and placed a tall paper hat on his head. But the young investigators were not satisfied. "Ah, I see the cap is not high enough, I've got another one." And he fetched a preposterous three- foot-high confection and put it on his head. "Shall we parade now?" and all the way he told stories and made people laugh, and he was now back on the radio, more popular than ever.

But was it really a matter of personal endurance and faith alone? And was it really necessary to do the Cultural Revolution the way it was done? Were there not many innocent victims in this stimulated tornado rousing the millions to revolt against the administration? Almost inconceivable that the head of a Party should rouse the ordinary people against his own hierarchy, against his own Establishment. It had never been done before, yet the Chairman had done it. But was it needful to do it just like that?

Stalwart Autumn and his wife Peony were back in their old house, with its midget courtyard inhabited by a peach tree. Many autumns had we sat under it, at the Moon Festival, toasting the planet, Stalwart Autumn reciting poetry, talking of writing and revolution and cooking and almost everything under Heaven. The peach tree had endured; "We shall have another crop of sweet fruit this year," said Peony. She had put on weight in her two years as a factory worker. Her fine round eyes now exuded a busy firmness, where they had been doe-like and hesitant. Her once puzzled hands fingering many things were determined. Dedication was written all over her. "Our relations with the other families in our street are so much better. Before the Cultural Revolution we were a cut above them; they did not approach us." She had stayed at home, feeling out of things.

As I had reached their doorstep that day the policeman in charge of the district was leaving; a neat round-faced country boy, bursting with zeal, who had come to ask Stalwart Autumn and Peony their advice about some small problems of the street. "People do come now, drop in at any time to discuss matters with us," said Stalwart Autumn, surprised and gratified. "The barriers are down."

Stalwart Autumn had been through a gruelling ordeal, and was nursing an ulcer at home on long rest with full pay. All the writers coming back had massive bank accounts; paid full salaries during their years away in the countryside, or when made to "stand aside" on probation, or at the May 7 schools in the communes, to be re-educated through labour and study and by intimate contact with the labouring people. Stalwart Autumn spoke of his own transformation; how unwilling he had been to admit new forms in art. "Often without knowing it. Like classic painters condemning ... oh, Picasso say, or Braque. We had the blinkers of our own classical upbringing and we did not really want to change, deep in our hearts."

But I wanted to talk about the victims, and asked the fate of Young Domain, an old writer best known abroad, a book of his having been translated three decades ago. Young Domain had a corrosive wit, a satirical turn of phrase. He had been reported killed at the onset of the Cultural Revolution. An English friend of his, distressed by this news, had begged me to find out. Now this Englishman was himself dead, and it was too late to tell him, but I still wanted to know.

Stalwart Autumn said he had killed himself. Young Domain wrote tongue-in-cheek stories about bureaucrats who lorded it above the people. He was acidulous and bland, the hierarchy said he "attacked the Party", when he was denouncing the bureaucracy.

"And now we know bureaucracy should not be the Party apparatus." Stalwart Autumn's eyes twinkled. But what more exquisite revenge for the bureaucrats who were to be "overthrown by the masses" than to direct the latter's ire upon Young Domain? "Everything was so confused in the early stages, no one knew who was really to be the target, so we all went through ... unpleasantness." Young Domain was pointed out to some Red Guard group as a "typical bourgeois". He had chrysanthemums and goldfish, proof of an unregenerate nature. "Though he laughed at others, he could not endure mockery or personal attacks." When they had come for him, instead of submitting to the silliness, and trusting in the ultimate justice of the people, he had thrown himself into the pond in front of his house, perhaps from his flowered veranda. "There was a short space in time when having flowers was considered bourgeois; my wife had to discard her flower pots and plant castor oil and spinach."

And another writer, though coming from a peasant family, had also been hounded to death. "It was ugly," said Stalwart Autumn. "These things did happen. And there were murders disguised as suicides, too." But now all this was being investigated, to find the culprits. "But it was a war, a civil war with no definite battle lines, war in the mind but physically too. And we had to dig deep within ourselves, our own motivations, everything."

The "ultra-left" extremists, who had done so much harm, had a head "high up in the Party". Someone who wanted to take power. In the end everything came out; but during the first three years there was so much confusion ... all that was good and all that was rotten, everything boiled up...."

But what about the mental wreckage, even admitting that the physical casualties were few? In the last two years I had met hundreds of people reported dead, but alive and well; back into their posts, even promoted. Even some who had "committed mistakes", for this was the Chairman's policy: "Rally the largest number."

Stalwart Autumn thought a little when I asked about writers whose mental equilibrium might be disturbed.

"I don't know of any, personally. Artists are tough, as a whole, tougher than ordinary people under mental stress."

He himself thought that he had been buoyed up by his ability to laugh at himself. He split himself into observer and actor, one side of him endured; the other went home to burst into peals of laughter. "I am full of good feeling for those who inflicted petty humiliations upon me. They were so sincere, so righteous. And they did a good job, because in the end they did pull down the top bad ones, the corrupt and the traitors. Such a lesson for our whole society."

But the main thing, said Peony, was this: "The Cultural Revolution has given the ordinary people the right to criticize, to denounce Party members who misbehave, to protest. The whole Party is under the supervision of the masses. In China today it is the right and duty of every citizen to point out what is wrong, not to shut up. For 2,500 years our people have been taught to shut up. Only the Cultural Revolution, such a tremendous earthquake, could shake this terrible docility. Do you think the price we had to pay was too large for creating this decisive break in China's long history of autocratic power?"

Well of Literature, about whom I had often enquired during the years, was back. He came in at ten at night, muscled and bronzed and younger with thick black hair straight as toothbrush bristles upon his head.

"I've come back from the countryside, didn't have time for a haircut." He now wore shorts, which he had never done.

"I look like a boyscout, don't I?"

In his department, the "ultra-left" had taken over, and he as well as other top officials of the Ministry of Culture, had been made to clean the offices. At their trial they had stood together in the "jet plane" position, arms extended backwards, chin upon their chest. "Whenever my arms fell they pulled them back." After two weeks this had been stopped. "Physical ill-treatment is impermissible." They were all given chairs to sit on.

"The result is that I fell asleep, and snored. I was awakened by people laughing because I was sleeping at my own trial."

Often it was the ordinary people who stopped the extremist young. "Our people don't like violence. In one city they had enough of it and rose and rounded up the 'May 16' group in three days, and stopped the nastiness."

I said that, however, the abuse heaped upon some writers had been wholesale condemnation rather than exact political or artistic analysis, and some were still on passive strike. Given back their positions, exhorted to write, they said with bland faces masking rancour: "Please tell us what to write. We don't want to commit political mistakes. Please point out what sentences, what chapters, were wrong in our previous 'poisonous weeds'." And there was an underground whisper campaign: "To write is dangerous ... leave it alone."

"Yes, some haven't come to terms with the whole thing. It's a dilemma. We can only settle it by writing, then see what happens, but of course it is not easy." To slough off the old, to identify with workers and peasants, to really be absorbed in their lives and write truthfully – "The Chairman himself said, in 1942, that it would take many years for us."

"Yet, I do not want to forget this valuable great storm. Only now I feel I shall never be frightened of anything again. But how do I renew myself? It's like peeling an onion, layer by layer by layer...."

I could see that he too must first write down about himself, slough off himself in words, before knowing truly what had happened to his very core, digging endlessly to whatever change he had undergone and which he felt so precious. "Only the written word is proof against time and forgetfulness and death," I said, pompous.

Well of Literature looked at me with shut-in wisdom: "Thank you for your encouragement," he said.

Now in charge of a printing press, he received thousands of manuscripts from factories and communes. In his two years in the countryside he had found peasants writing at night, after work. Sometimes they did not know the words and drew pictures instead. The commune had built its own hydroelectric station, and with electric light the peasants wanted evening schools, and books; they made up poems about their own achievements; they played comic sketches about their own lives.

"When I left they said to me: 'Old Well, don't forget us, when you sit in a high chair again. Read what we send you ... there's as much sweat in it as in rice-planting.'"

Well of Literature was positive that nothing else could have worked except the Cultural Revolution. "We had so much of Confucius still in us ... high up in the Communist Party. The old mandarinocracy all over again. If it hadn't been pulled down we would have lost the revolution."

He now read all the scripts he received. When he found promising material, he would travel to the factory or commune to see the writer. "I never did that before."

I told him: "I hear that the Chairman has said: 'Water too pure breeds no fish; too harsh a teacher finds no pupils.' Do you think too harsh criteria of political correctness will discourage future writing?"

"Water too pure. . . ." Well of Literature looked a little uncertain. "I think we have learnt to be much more careful in criticizing and condemning. But I am 58, getting old. The young must take over, and they must find their own way. And now our people are no longer illiterate, we the old writers are no longer an élite. We shall still make mistakes, but we have learnt so much."

"Well, then down with Confucius," I said.

"Water too pure ... that was also Confucius. The Supreme Master. He even codified music," said Well of Literature, laughing.

He turned to wave again as he walked under the trees. A tentative small rain had come, making the air kind with new freshness. I heard the smooth whirr of many cycles, the hum of voices, and laughter.

(1972)

Population Growth and Birth Control in China

THE CHINESE government is often accused of a deliberate policy of evading or avoiding population questions and birth-control questions. This impression is not accurate. The fact is that the government does not have entirely accurate figures at its disposal, or rather, as I was told frankly, it has two sets of figures with a discrepancy of about 30 million people. This may seem a large "error margin", but even in the USA, with all technological facilities and computerization, there is a 2.5 per cent error margin which brings the error to round 5 million people. Assuming an 800 million (or near) population, the margin of error in China would be under 4 per cent. Present estimates vary round 750 million including national minorities, which tallies with what Chairman Mao told Edgar Snow in 1966 (a population round 680 to 690 million, allowing for a 12 million increase of thereabouts per year). Premier Chou En-lai spoke in April 1972 of a total population "well over the 700 million mark".

This error margin of almost 4 per cent in China arises from the differences, at any time, between registration of births and deaths figures and registration of grain ration cards. Everyone in China is registered and everyone owns a ration card, necessary for the equitable distribution and the total stability of prices of essential foodstuffs. But what happens in the communes is that people tend to lag in reporting the deaths of old people and of babies. Since in rural areas grain distribution is done twice a year, this lag in reporting causes sometimes over-distribution up to a year in time.

In the year 1800 the estimated population of China was 300 million, but only 340 million in 1910. This slow growth was explained by staggering losses in war, floods and famine. Demographers have worked out that, up till 1949, population growth in China was round 0.3 to 0.4 per cent per year, a very low figure indeed, and this is borne out by my own investigations. Thus in North-west Kansu the population actually declined by almost 20 per cent during the years

1920 to 1950, and even in privileged areas such as the Peking area the increase in population in 1949 was 0.4 per cent.

In 1949, total population in China was reckoned by European observers at 540 million, but this is probably far too much. The census in 1953 showed a population over 583 million, with 15 per cent of the total composed of children under 4 years of age. This tremendous and sudden increase was the result of the success of Chinese communist measures in preventive inoculations and sanitation (smallpox inoculation performed on 180 million between 1949 and mid-1952; eradication of flies and rats and mosquitoes and hence of malaria, bubonic plague and many other diseases; eradication of cholera by 1957; child inoculation against infectious diseases – every child in China today gets automatically six preventive inoculations by the time he is 3 years old. The lowered death rate and especially the lowered infant mortality rate sent the population soaring. Whereas the longevity figure was under 40 before 1949, it is now between 55 and 60. The infant mortality rate, up to 250 per 1,000 in rural areas, reckoned as an average to be 100 per thousand in the cities, has dropped to the low 20s in the cities and is probably between 40 and 50 in rural areas. (In Malaysia it was 80 per thousand in the early 1960s in rural areas.) With increased food consumption, lowered mortality, increased longevity, no famines, sanitation, medical care and internal peace, population soared. China today has as a result a very young population with a high birth rate and a low death rate. In the cities such as Shanghai and Peking, where there is industrial development and hence a young population, the death rate is only between 6 and 7 per thousand (11 to 13 per thousand as an average for the country is an estimate).

Some guesstimates of the composition of the population, from doctors in hospitals, and street committees and commune committees, is that probably 40 per cent of the population is under 15 and that 50 per cent is under 30.

Prosperity and plenty do not lead, in China, to lowered production of children. In the past, it was among the wealthy that the highest number of children were found. This is due to the traditional and deep love for children of the Chinese Han people as a whole. No one in China thinks of children as a burden, quite the contrary. This great traditional love for children is reflected in an anecdote that I heard recently. A young couple (both under 24) had already two children. They were both working, with a grandmother at home to look after the two children. Both got a recent increase in salaries, and their first reaction was: "How splendid, we can now have a third baby."

The present government has always shown itself both aware and intensely considerate and human in dealing with problems of tradition. Thus it is freely acknowledged that there are still traditional ideas which are very strongly against birth control. One is the fact that families are protected and are together, and by that is meant three generations, especially in the countryside (rural population is still 80 per cent of the total, only 20 per cent live in cities). The love for children is increased by the older people, grandparents, wanting their sons to bring brides home early, to have grandchildren soon, and to produce many sons and grandsons. With security, stability and assured food (equitable grain distribution to all), and a child-care programme perhaps the best in any developing country, there is no pressure towards restricting births from the economic point of view. On the contrary, in Szechwan province which I investigated in 1971, commune peasants used to sing a ballad: "Better produce a little flesh dumpling [a baby] than produce workpoints." The fact that each baby born received an adult share of grain (500 to 600 lb per annum, or even more in certain provinces, going up to 1,400 lb per annum in some national minority areas rich in rice, as in Yunnan) testifies both to the Chinese success in food production and its humane handling of the people, but it also made peasants feel that a large family was no handicap. On the contrary, they benefited by it and in the long run, with the children grown up, and all working, the family profited from having more labour power and therefore the greater income too.

"We have actually been concerned with population growth ever since 1949," Madame Lee, an important official of the Ministry of Health, told me. "But this problem cannot be treated as in capitalist countries, by economic pressure, threats, stringency. It must be part of socialist planning and the socialist system. This means it must be a thorough political education, stimulating the collective consciousness of the people."

This, even if more difficult to achieve, appears to the Chinese both humane and possible, and in the long term more successful. The objectives of birth control are tied in with the liberation of woman: with her participation in production and her economic and political equality; with her own raised intellectual level and consciousness; with better health for all, smaller families, and healthy ones, in a society where public spiritedness and a sense of sharing enmeshes everyone. In this true liberation of woman she has to be freed of biological weaknesses, and birth control becomes part of the total programme of her own total equality.

At no time, it is asserted, has there been a change in the long-term policy of planning population in the socialist society which China is building.

Chairman Mao's words in 1958, "It is a very good thing that China has a big population," are often quoted out of context, as meaning that birth control policies were reversed. But this is a shallow and inaccurate interpretation, since in 1957 Chairman Mao wrote: "In drawing up plans ... or thinking of problems, we must proceed from the fact that China has a population of 600 million people." The reference to a big population was to emphasize that China had a huge capital of manpower to achieve self-reliance, in place of machinery, for a long time; it was never meant to stop birth control, but to promote self-reliance.

But the first birth-control experiments were not done well, I was told. In 1954 a hasty propaganda had no effect. In 1956 I personally investigated the first instance of birth control drives in the cities. In Peking, in Canton, in Shanghai, people queued up in parks and other places to hear lectures, see films, and contraceptives were freely shown and distributed in pharmacies. This technique was acceptable to intellectuals and people with some notion of science, but when these methods were taken to rural areas the results were bad. Peasants became horrified, indignant, their traditional modesty was "shocked", and they were also literally panicked by the brusque approach. The reason is obvious. Death of children, infanticide, small families, were emotionally related to famines and wars; infanticide, chiefly female, was commonly practised in the past when peasants starved. Hence the exhortation to "have fewer children" seemed indicative of impending disaster. This drive, therefore, was stopped.

Birth control education was somewhat muted during the three bad years, 1959 to 1961, when poor harvests, due to natural disasters, the hectic disorders and stoppages in industrial production due to over-haste during the Leap Forward of 1958 and to Russian sabotage, produced especially in the cities a situation of stringent shortage. Birth control however went on in the cities and was most acceptable, abortions being performed on demand. But in the rural areas the peasants were much better fed, on the whole, for they ate whatever they produced and therefore the shortages were more obvious in the cities, relieved by vast purchases of grain abroad. By 1962–63, however, there was some recovery. The teaching of birth control techniques was being done through medical personnel and members of the women's federation, trade unions, etc., and pamphlets printed for distribution and issued.

It was in 1963, with good harvests and a general recovery, that the birth control drive acquired a new impetus. "Our first programme was to attain a rate of 1 per cent population growth in cities, 2 per cent in the countryside." But at the time, due to the health measures taken, never had the overall population increase been so high, and an overall rate of 2.5 per cent per year was freely mentioned. I duly reported this new drive in Singapore in 1963. Once again, it was successful in the cities, as the following figures will show.

In 1949, in the Peking area (population then round 3 million):

birth rate   18.7 per thousand

death rate   14.1 per thousand

increase: 4.6 per thousand (or 0.46 per cent, the low pre-Liberation figure for a privileged area: the overall China figure round 0.3 per cent).

In 1963, with 7,300,000 people in the enlarged Peking area (an additional 9 rural areas were included), the figures were:

birth rate   43.4 per thousand (2.5 times pre-Liberation)

death rate   8.1 per thousand

increase: 35.3 per thousand or 3.5 per per cent.

In 1965, with the drive for birth control in process, and a population of 7,700,000 in the Peking area (same as 1963):

birth rate   23 per thousand

death rate   6.7 per thousand

increase: 16.3 per thousand or 1.6 per cent, under half of 1963.

In 1972, after the next birth control drive starting in 1971, the figures for the same area, and a population of 7,890,000 are:

birth rate   17.8 per thousand

death rate   6.1 per thousand

increase: 11.7 per thousand or near 1.2 per cent.

Here two cautionary notes must be added: The death rate is very low in Peking and in other industrial cities, because of the high preponderance of young people due to industrial development, hence the death rate is down to between 6 and 8 per cent. The same holds good for Shanghai. In Chengtu, in Szechwan Province, due to industrial development since 1957–58 with the influx of young workers' families and security, fully half the population was made up of children under 12 years old, but figures for birth control were not available as birth control was not pushed at the time there.

During the Cultural Revolution, all birth control drives as well as other drives were in abeyance. Also during those years there was quite an increase in "young" marriages, although late marriage had already started being promoted in 1963.

It was in 1971 that the latest birth control movement began, as usual with a great many meetings and debates. "Every county was asked to discuss the matter." Based upon the large amount of fact accumulated, the trial testing of previous methods, the new birth control drive will be, I am told, far more efficient and will now truly reach the grassroots and the important reservoir of population growth, the rural communes.

The latest birth-control movement

The aim is total mass participation, with the greatest amount of propaganda conceivable. "Education in birth control is really the key." Thus, I was told, of all the provinces in China possibly Kwangtung Province is the most lagging, because there "propaganda was not well done". It is surprising to hear that Kwangtung, nearest to Hong Kong, with the largest number of overseas Chinese families, is still considered the more retrograde in this respect. To my mind, it is not only due to propaganda, but possibly also to the fact that overseas families are better off, and consequently have more children; that Kwangtung people are still "traditional" to a great degree; and also, last but not least, that Kwangtung is not an industrialized province, but a surplus agricultural province, where the soil is very fertile and hence grain rations proportionately large.

That industrialization, with a large proportion of men and women workers, does have an effect is obvious. Thus the Shanghai area (population round 11 million with rural areas) has achieved remarkable results. Last year 210,000 women were on oral pills, 80,000 abortions were performed; 1,200,000 women of child-bearing age had 70 per cent of them using contraceptives, and 400,000 had been sterilized. The birth-rate was right down, in some districts, to 0.6 per cent (therefore zero population increase).

It may be argued that workers would feel "economic pressure" and therefore be compelled to restrict children, which is not the case for peasants, but I investigated this and found it incorrect as well. "Socialist security for the working class actually encourages children." This is because everyone in a worker family is guaranteed an average of 12.00 *yuan* per month per member of family, and any difficulty is compensated by welfare and state supplies. Therefore it is not due to economic stringency that industrialization has as an effect a more successful birth-control achivement, but due to "the heightened political consciousness of the working class".

The raising of people's awareness, to promote birth control, is therefore a major factor, and in order to do this, a whole web of organization has been set up. Nowhere else in the world has such a network of "family planning committees" been set up. Every street committee, every neighbourhood committee, every commune, every brigade and production team, has its family planning staff. "At every level, in the administration, in every institute, organization, unit, department, ministry, workshop floor, production team, street, village" they operate. And since propaganda and example are the major assets, this method is used most intelligently, by utilizing the people themselves.

Thus in every street there are housewives, volunteers, who are recruited by the local neighbourhood committee and the street committee. This is unpaid work, but most effective, because it is based on "activism". The general picture in the cities is as follows: These family planners make house-to-house visits (each house in the city may contain four or five or even six or seven families; blocks of flats will house up to 40 families). In certain cities they circulate questionnaires, in others they do house-to-house surveys, to find out the number of children per family, the babies born during the year, etc. In Peking this has already been done and has resulted in many meetings among the housewives, in which they "plan", house by house and street by street, the number of women who are eligible for having a baby that year. This "giving birth in turn" is also followed in organizations and also is done by collective consent. The family planners bring contraceptives to every house if the housewives cannot come, or they arrange to take the housewives to the local doctor (every street is seen, twice a week, by an ambulant doctor from the hospital in the quarter).

In the Peking area already mentioned, 2,200,000 city workers and 3,700,000 rural workers are covered by this network: 70 per cent of the city workers and 60 per cent of the rural workers are now practising birth control.

In rural areas, it is not the barefoot doctor, surprisingly, who has been found adequate for birth control education. This is because most barefoot doctors are young and unmarried, and the village people do not take easily to being told about birth control by "unmarried young people". "The best people to do family planning in rural areas are the women cadres." These older women, on the management committees of the communes, brigades and production teams, themselves practise birth control and hence are also living examples. They now have the responsibility to bring every woman in the communes to understand contraception, and to practise it. This also means that there must be at least 30 to 40 per cent of women cadres at every level among the cadres and administrators of the communes, and hence the tendency for men to monopolize positions of leadership is lessened. With the re-emergence of the federation of women this year (April to July), another surge, through the voluntary activity of several million of women, will occur in the field of family planning. Since every commune already has its medical installations (clinics, midwives, health personnel staff, barefoot doctors) the addition of women cadres for propaganda will multiply the efficiency of the medical effort without costing more. That the whole thing is very serious is reflected in the fact that it is the Communist Party secretary of each branch committee, at every level, in the provinces, who is in charge of this "mass movement". This denotes intense concentration on this problem.

This kind of organization, all-pervading, all encompassing, it also to be found in each factory at the level of the shopfloor, and male "activists" will propagandize male workers as female propagandists do housewives, and street factory workers (female). In the textile industry, where 80 per cent of the workers are women, management committees, mostly female, propagandize their workers. This double approach is very necessary, I am told, as it is self-reinforcing. Thus workers and technicians who go home only from time to time (some are in jobs which temporarily require separation from their families) are given contraceptives and enjoined not to forget to use them when they return to their wives.

All operations (sterilization, vasectomies) and all contraceptives are free, as is all medical advice on the subject. Yet this intensive, personal, constant propaganda is done without a single poster appearing on the street. In India, there are posters in city streets urging people to have only three children, but in China, I was told, this would be of doubtful value. In Yunnan Province, for instance, I was definitely told by an obstetrician that this would still "shock" a great many people. "Women will talk among themselves and to a woman doctor about these things, and will practise contraception, but older women are still very reticent, and this would harm the movement." In the commune, however, the loudspeakers (which broadcast news, music, and weather reports twice a day) will also be used for family planning, but only in general terms. The main propaganda is house-to-house, person-to-person, meetings, example, a constant "climate" of persuasion, and above all the availability at every level of immediate medical care, of contraceptives of all kinds.

Besides this, the organization of young unmarried people into a state of mind which will accept birth control as part of their social duty is being "grasped strongly". Through the middle school organizations, the pioneers, the Young Communist League, throughout the unmarried years, the propaganda goes on. That is why, among the techniques which are considered most valuable, late marriage figures largely.

Late marriage, though not a contraceptive technique properly speaking, is certainly a most powerful instrument for lowering the birthrate. In India, where the marriageable age is 16, it has been found that retarding marriage to 18 would make no dent on population growth, but retarding it to 23 would do so. In China, there are emulation drives among the young people to make them consider retarding marriage a revolutionary, a noble action. Hence although there is the possibility to marry when 18 is reached, as in the Marriage Law, young people are enjoined to wait a few more years. "Although actually marriages at 18 and 19 still do occur in the communes, there is gradually a building of public opinion against such early marriages." The ideal age, as propagated today, is 25 for girls and 28 for men in the cities, and 23 for girls and 25 for men in the rural areas. But it is emphasized that there are cases when earlier marriage is allowed, for instance, if there is an only son, and a young woman is needed to look after his old parents.

Figures for percentages of "late marriage" are gathered in every factory and organization. In factories and workshops apprentices are not to marry until they become workers (this is a three-year term). In universities no student is eligible for higher study if he marries. In a certain commune (Kwatien Commune in Tunghsien county, Hopei), the population increase rate, which was 3.2 per cent in 1963, has fallen to 1.8 per cent in 1972, and late marriage has been instituted. In 1972 150 couples married in that commune (total population 19,711) of whom the average age was 24, and this year 80 couples in the first half of the year of whom the average age was 25.4. The commune has decided to have a population increase of only 1.6 per cent this year (1973) and has started doing "birth in turn" propaganda among the young just married couples.

This vast web of organization of family planning is under the control of the Family Planning Council, which is part of the Ministry of Health. But it is directly under the supervision of the Party.

Before going on to contraceptive techniques (apart from late marriage, which is really an organizational problem), we must first define "child-bearing age". How many, how much of the population, is really the target of this intensive birth-control education?

If there were no limits to the marriageable age, the percentage would be higher than it is; supposing, as in old China, girls married at 14 or 15, the problem would be much bigger. But because of the customs and mores of socialist China, where absolute monogamy and conjugal fidelity exist, where there are no concubines (and no prostitution), the problem has its own limits. Child-bearing age does not correspond therefore to biological capability, but is a term to define those men or women who are married and within the ages of child-bearing. This works out, according to statistics that I have individually acquired in several different areas and provinces, to 11 per cent to 13 per cent of the women, and therefore also of the men.

This kind of limitation is only possible in a country like China where extra-marital sex is unknown, or almost, and where a man is defined as "of child-bearing age" between his marriage and 50 years old, not after. The reason given for this is that by the time he is 50 his wife is also 50, and therefore past the child-bearing age. However, I was also told that in pre-Liberation days the menopause of Chinese women was stated to be 45 years; it is now between 50 and 52 years. This is said to be due to "better health and better food".

Actually the number of "child-bearers in potential" from 18 to 45 are 18 to 20 per cent of the total, but with late marriage this is cut down to 11 to 13 per cent. The years of puberty are therefore not taken into consideration, and the percentages of women "capable of pregnancy", as it is described, is 11 per cent of the population in the cities, and round about 12 to 14 per cent in the countryside (where there is earlier marriage).

It is these women, and their husbands, who form the object of education in contraceptive techniques. "The technique has to be different, each case is individual. Careful attention must be paid to each case."

The oral pill was introduced in 1964; it is mostly in use in the cities, but not so much in the countryside. In rural areas, it is very difficult to make the women take their pills regularly, and in some communes a volunteer in each production team in each work team is delegated to remind the women to take their pill *every day*. One can hear them in the fields early in the morning, just before work begins, shouting: "Have you taken your pill?" Supplies of pills are immediately available.

"In rural areas we have had some failures with the pill. Women who took it for a while then forgot had withdrawal bleeding and panicked and refused to touch it again. In another commune 70 per cent of the women got pregnant while taking the pill because they had not really taken it regularly. In another commune all women who gave up the pill got pregnant."

Hence in rural areas the introduction of a ring (stainless steel) *in utero* is much preferred. It can be left *in situ* for 5 years without changing and does not seem to incommode or cause any infection. Intra-uterine devices (nylon) are in use in certain areas such as the east coast, but there is an 8 per cent failure with these.

The use of male contraceptives is much preferred in other areas, and the reason for these individual and regional preferences is not known. In a city area of 17,000 people, of whom 5,200 women were "child-bearer potential", 4,900 of them used contraceptives, the men did not. In Kiangsu province in the county of Taichang 45 per cent of the potential child-bearers were taking the pill with success, although this is a rural area.

In a factory visited near Tientsin, 81.3 per cent of the couples (11,299 people) were using either pills, condoms, or i.u.d.'s.

The "emulation in birth control" movement which stimulates contraception is practised also street by street, or quarter by quarter, factory by factory, commune by commune. Thus the street of Kuang An Men in Peking (pop. 47,000) has resolved to bring its population increase down to 7.5 per thousand this year, or 360 babies total, by "common decision of all the children-bearers in the street".

The practice of sterilization of women is very common, and many women ask to be sterilized after two or three children (two is the ideal, but three is allowable). But here again there are many differences in region. The practice of vasectomy is being encouraged, and some surprising figures emerge.

In Szechwan province, once considered most retrograde, in the county of Hsingtou, which I visited, 12,000 vasectomies had been performed in a population of 500,000 people. If we take "women of child-bearing age" to be the corresponding 11 to 13 per cent of the population, and the number of men between 18 and 45 to be 20 per cent of the population, this means that in that county all the available 12 per cent were sterilized. When I asked how this had been performed, three reasons were given. The first was good propaganda. A medical team from Peking had been there for almost 18 months, and a vast amount of propaganda had been done. The second was "living example". All the members of the revolutionary committee of the county had had themselves vasectomized. The third was that all the men vasectomized had three children or more because people in that county married young. The youngest thus vasectomized was 29 years old. I saw him, and he was a leading cadre with three children. But there was another, and a curious reason. It is that in Szechwan province, quite contrary to expectation, the men prefer vasectomy. The same also obtains in Shantung province. Ninety per cent of the operations there are vasectomies; only 10 per cent are on women. The reverse figures are obtained in other areas. It is impossible to explain why this happens. "Good propaganda" is not quite the whole answer, but it may be a good part answer.

Abortion is practised on demand, and now the consent of the grandparents is no longer necessary, neither the consent of the husband, if there are already two or three children and if the wife demands abortion. "But abortion is not the way to do contraception. We want more prevention, and fewer abortions. This is our policy."

Some figures for Yunnan province, considered most backward, and with a real lack of adequate medical personnel still, are illuminating. There the vigour and activity of the health ministry officials, the doctors, and the health personnel is striking. The figures are revealing. In 1963, 1,788 intra-uterine devices were inserted, 6,000 abortions performed, 2,650 sterilizations (female) but no vasectomies. In 1972, 54,000 insertions were performed, 79,000 abortions, 15,000 sterilizations, and 8,500 vasectomies. The province has 23 million people of whom only 12 million are Han, and the target of contraception.

Where grain distribution is concerned, another system is now being devised. Instead of giving an adult portion to each baby born, in the communes, babies up to 3 will receive only one-third the ration, half till 12, and full ration after 12. In some areas only one-fifth is given from 0 to 3 years old. But my suggestion that after the third child all rations be cut off was met with the sentence: "It is not democratic." The idea is that this would be some kind of "economic coercion", which has to be avoided in the socialist system. The planners appear most confident that within the next ten years the drive will be successful, and an overall average of 1.2 per cent or 1.3 per cent will be achieved (with under 1 per cent in the cities, and round 1.4 to 1.5 per cent in the countryside). It may even be possible to beat this figure, and some are suggesting an overall rate of 1.1 per cent.

With the Cultural Revolution, with mass participation, with good propaganda, and with the methods outlined above, it does seem as if

China is launched on a tremendous social experiment, combining both humanity and conscious collective emulation.

All this applies to the Han population, 94 per cent of the total population of China. Where the national minorities are concerned (there are 54 national minority ethnic groups in China) there is no drive for family planning among them, because of consideration of their own feelings. "All national minorities want to increase, and we must let them ... but we do recommend late marriage, for the good of the women, their intellectual emancipation, and their health."

(1973)

How China Tackles Cancer

O N MY recent trip to China in the autumn of 1974 I
had a full morning at the Cancer Hospital and
Research Institute of Peking, where I met again my
friend from university days, now Director of the
Hospital, Dr Wu Huan-hsin, and also the Party
secretary and cancer specialist, Dr Li Ping, a charming, energetic
woman with three children, who had become a doctor in Yenan in
the early 1940s.

Cancer in China, they told me, was not considered a "priority
problem" before 1958. A survey in five main cities prior to 1949
placed it in ninth or tenth position as cause of death; and this appears
to have remained true until 1953–54. The prevalence of other
diseases, epidemics, and tuberculosis, relegated cancer to a category
of low importance. But immediately after Liberation there were
mass drives to eradicate epidemics; for instance, the vaccination
(against smallpox) of 185 million by 1952, the eradication of bubonic
plague, cholera and venereal disease. Mass line movements, involving the population, also brought schistosomiasis and tuberculosis
under control by the 1960s.

The net effect was the rise of cancer from ninth or tenth place to
second or third place as cause of death. Today round half a million
deaths a year are due to cancer. The lengthening of the life span is
also a factor in this rise.

"Our statistics are more accurate than previously," said Dr Wu.
"In old China there were no births or deaths certificates. In 1953–54
birth and death certificates became compulsory. This also helps us to
determine the pattern of the disease." In Shanghai cancer is the first
cause of death, and heart disease the second; in Peking, heart disease
ranks first, and cancer second.

But, the approach to the whole problem of cancer, at first, had
been heavily "conservative". Until 1958 it was only in the cities that
treatment was available. Very little was done in the rural areas;
although investigation teams sent out made surveys, they merely

went for a few weeks, collected some material, and rushed back to the cities.

The Great Leap Forward, in 1958, broke this élitist attitude. In that year Chairman Mao's call to "serve the countryside", with the advent of the communes in 1959, marked the beginning of rural medical care on a solid basis.

It was, however, the Cultural Revolution which really changed the whole approach and orientation of medical care, and also the orientation of investigation, research, and treatment of cancer. "We began to understand that (a) our research and investigations must be primarily oriented towards the rural areas and (b) that they could not be successful except by practising the mass line as in any other disease."

"And then we realized that until now our attitude had been: Let the patient come to us. Now we knew that we must go to the patient. We must go and find him *before* he has to come to us. In other words, early detection, the earliest possible, and if possible, *prevention*. This is the orientation upon which we are building now."

The first radium institute for cancer was founded in Shanghai in the 1930s; it was on a very small scale. In Peking a 100-bed hospital for cancer treatment was built in the early 1950s, equipped with a cobalt bomb, but it catered "only to higher personnel, diplomats, and so on". In 1958, 230 beds were added to the cancer hospital, and that year five cancer hospitals were set up (2,000 beds) in five main cities.

Today, after the Cultural Revolution, and based on nationwide surveys and investigations of cancer, the plans are to build in Peking an up-to-date cancer research institute. "It will probably be the largest and the most modern in Asia, with the most comprehensive planning, the best equipment and facilities for research, study, clinical care and treatment, and for training." The time was ripe for such an endeavour. But fully equipped cancer hospitals cost five to six times more than ordinary hospitals, and "some of the equipment we cannot yet make ourselves". However, Premier Chou En-lai had given all encouragement to this project.

At the moment, however, there was still a scarcity of beds, and two-thirds of the patients were treated as ambulatory outpatients. "This is possible because through the network of street committees and nurses we can give care to the patients at their own homes." There was a 99 per cent rate of follow-up of cancer cases, even when they returned to distant provinces such as Sinkiang. This follow-up efficiency was possible through the services of local networks of committees; instead of waiting for the patient to come to report, the patient was visited by someone who took responsibility for bringing him for check-up.

So far, five research institutes for cancer are in existence; the Peking institute could coordinate all research and studies done by the branch institutes in other cities. Fourteen new cancer hospitals are being built; they will be completed within a year or two. The plan is that each province will have at least one cancer hospital with research facilities. "Some provinces are very active in this respect; they have even begun to build cancer hospitals in each country. Within the next five to ten years we shall have overall coverage for early detection and treatment of cancer at county level."

Both specialists stressed the link between the mass line and early detection of cancer. People were asked to report immediately when they suspected anything wrong, rather than wait. "In eight cases out of ten there is nothing wrong, but we much prefer it that way." Barefoot doctors in the communes were alerted to early detection and its importance. And since the cost of medical care is so low, peasants were responding very well. The cooperative medical service (one *yuan* to one *yuan* fifty per year) was a great help in getting people to come for investigation, since they paid nothing more.

The studies and surveys conducted during the last years, and especially in rural areas, were the basis upon which the research institutes and also the hospitals were being built. These studies and investigations had delineated areas in China where one form of cancer was more prevalent than others. "We have therefore operated a division of work among the research institutes, handing over to each as special study the most prevalent form of cancer in the area where they are located."

For Kiangsu and East China where liver neoplasms seem to be dominant, Shanghai Institute will be the centre for research. In South China, where nasopharyngeal carcinoma seems to prevail, the institute is in Canton. Breast cancer is tackled in Tientsin; "and here in Peking," said Dr Wu, "we are studying at the moment, in particular, cancer of the oesophagus."

Why cancer of the oesophagus? Dr Wu and Dr Li have been engaged in this particular study for the last five years. The reason is because of its prevalence in certain provinces in North China.

The story of this particular type of cancer begins in Linhsien, the county in Honan province made so famous recently by the construction of the Red Flag Canal. As everyone knows, the Red Flag Canal brings water from the Chang River, across the Taihang Mountains, to irrigate 80,000 hectares of once drought-ridden plains in Honan province. Linhsien became famous because of the Canal, which is 1,250 km long with its man-dug branches. It was completed during the Cultural Revolution, in 1969.

And Linhsien county, which is situated very close to the Taihang Mountains massif, has the highest incidence of oesophageal carcinoma in China, "almost 50 times the national average".

"It was due to the construction of the Red Flag Canal that our medical teams hit upon Linhsien and, from Linhsien, extended their study into other counties in pursuit of this type of cancer."

During the construction of the canal, the field work medical teams there lived, laboured, ate and integrated with the inhabitants. This was a totally different approach to the previous "come and see and go away again" attitude. "Our medical workers no longer wanted to go back to the cities; they want to stay and work and research on the spot."

"The teams also changed in composition. Due to the studies we undertook on carcinoma of the oesophagus, our teams became what we call 'complete'. They now consist not only of clinical personnel, of doctors, but also of laboratory men, biochemists, chemists, geologists. All stayed in peasant families, and really began to *understand* the local people. And this is the standard now. To study the cancer prevalent in the area, medical teams *live* with the local inhabitants for one year, two, or three...."

"Only thus shall we be able to understand cancer. Not only to treat it but to understand it, and perhaps find a means of preventing it."

Why is cancer of the oesophagus so prevalent in Linhsien? If we can find out why, can we not alter this cancer-causing factor and thus prevent it from occurring?

"Linhsien is a county which early formed part of a liberated Red base, in 1940-41. From 1941 to 1970, our medical personnel in the base had already carried out investigations in 76 districts of this area, and we had found an enormous amount of people with cancer of the oesophagus in this particular region."

These 76 districts are now brigades, part of communes. Since 1949 the standard of living has risen considerably, this being an extremely poor district before then. In the last four or five years, due to the water from the Red Flag Canal, there has been a great leap in living standards; and also a vast improvement in diet.

"Yet the mortality from cancer of the oesophagus remains the same as before."

Dr Wu and Dr Li then showed me a chart, which showed

mortality per 100,000 in certain districts of this area. The chart showed no variation over the years.

"For the last 30 years, the graph we have traced has shown no abatement; cancer of the oesophagus occurs in men and women alike; in spite of the raised standard of living in the last 25 years it has remained the same as before.

"Why is this? Our research team had to delve into every aspect of the lives of the people to try to find out the cancer-producing factors. To begin with, food. Before Liberation people ate only *k'ang* (chaff of sorghum). They were so poor they did not even use a toothbrush to clean their teeth. Now they are eating far less *k'ang*. They eat fine flour, wheat; but they have cultivated the habit of roughage, which they still mix with their food. Food habits are very difficult to change. But the amount is much smaller, and we cannot say that they eat the same food as before.

"Then we found that the chickens and sheep in that area also have a high incidence of cancer of the oesophagus.

"The people in these counties do not eat chicken. They keep them for eggs, which they do eat occasionally. There are, therefore, hens three, four or five years old in the area; and we found cancer of the oesophagus prevalent among these.

"Before 1969, we conducted a survey in the Anyang district. We found, in 14,000 people over 30, 300 cases cancer of the oesophagus. This is extremely high.

"Since then, we have done many more investigations. I think we have to date seen 88.4 per cent of the people in an area including the whole of the Taihang Mountains area. And we have charted the incidence of cancer of the oesophagus in the whole area, county by county."

The Taihang Mountains massif is shaped like a tennis racket or a saucepan, with a bulky body and a prolongation or handle. The tail of this handle reaches near Peking. The whole range crosses three provinces – Honan, Shansi and Hopei.

"We began our research in the area where the bulk of the massif lies. From there we carried investigations outwards. And we found that the nearer we got to the central core, or massif, or the Taihang Mountains, the higher was the incidence of carcinoma of the oesophagus.

"Between 1969 and 1972, we thus investigated for cancer 7,300,000 people, covering 14 counties and one county town (Anyang). We mapped out the incidence of cancer in each county. While it is only 8 per 100,000 in Peking, it rises to 139.8 per 100,000 as we get to the core of the Taihang Mountains. As we get away from the Taihang massif, it begins to drop, from 58 per 100,000 to 31, 27, 17....

There seem to be concentric belts of incidence, radiating from a core in the Taihang massif.

"Since 1971, in the last three years, we have done further investigations, covering the three provinces and one city (Peking) affected by the Taihang range. This means 181 counties and 49 million people. We are investigating everyone."

This study of oesophageal cancer is done through the mass line. It could not have been possible otherwise to cover so much ground and so many people. Dr Wu and Dr Li then showed me the areas mapped out and the incidence graphs; the relief maps to show the location of the counties vis à vis the mountain massif.

"This brings us to the geological factor for cancer inducement. We now realized that we had to study everything: the water, the earth, the vegetables, everything.... We had to investigate everything that could possibly be investigated. For instance, we investigated the fungus which is found in the pickles consumed in winter in these areas. There are no fresh vegetables available during the winter and the peasants have the habit of pickling cabbage."

These pickles contain nitrites, which turn into nitro-amines, conducive to cancer formation.

"We then realized that our teams must also have with them geologists, chemists, virologists. We had to study the rocks forming the Taihang massif, the metals in the soil, the plant content of nitrites ... everything.

"We also found something which confirms that the cancer is somehow related to the geological formation. The Taihang massif is split; this occurred probably 50 or 100 million years ago, when the Yellow River began to form; part of it is on the other side of a wide swathe of lower-lying land. In this lower-lying land, which was dredged from elsewhere, there is a low incidence of cancer of the oesophagus, but in the remnant of Taihang massif south of it, the incidence rises again."

Dr Wu then showed me a map of the world, with incidence of oesophageal cancer mapped out. A high prevalence is also found in some parts of the USSR, on the north side of the Caspian Sea.

"I believe that the cause of this is multifactorial," said Dr Wu. At least, he felt one should look for more than one factor causing this cancer. Heredity is also being investigated. In view of the fact that many villages are clan villages (starting as one family, or at most two), a high percentage of people in one village bear the same name. Eight such "family groups" (or rather clans) were investigated in the Anyang district. This also was done through the mass line. Meetings of "old ancestors", or the oldest people in the villages, were called. Over 300 cases were traced genealogically in this manner. People voluntarily came to "tell their family history", and trace their family trees. But no hereditary factor, until now, has come to light. Investigations, however, are continuing.

The investigations also covered people coming from other provinces to this area. With the opening of coal mines in Hepi, there has been an influx of workers in the new township, coming from other provinces. So far, they do not seem to get this cancer, but it may be too early to tell. Check-ups on them will be performed.

As for people from Linhsien and other Taihang massif counties who have left this area and settled elsewhere they still have a high incidence of cancer of the oesophagus among them. Recently, due to the construction of the Red Flag Canal, villages from the Taihang massif were moved to Hupeh province. The inhabitants of these villages show a high incidence of cancer, while the local Hupeh people do not.

"It may be that the factors conducive to carcinoma of oesophagus were already implanted in these people before they left the area to settle elsewhere. We are continuing studies; perhaps their children will show an altered pattern of incidence."

"So now you see," said Dr Wu, "what an immense amount of work remains for us to do . . . 'opening new roads ... travelling ways yet untravelled ...'* making new discoveries. From now on we rely heavily on this pattern of research, mass line movements in the countryside. We are applying the same pattern to research in liver cancer and other cancers. We are now reappraising all work previously done, all our study ... we did not know what a treasure house of knowledge and fascinating research we could find in the rural areas ... now we know, Chairman Mao was absolutely right."

This was not all. "We have now discovered a pre-cancerous hyperplasia of the mucosa of the oesophagus," said Dr Li Ping. "This condition we are studying with great care. We have followed up many of these cases – several hundreds of thousands at the moment, but more are coming up all the time. We have found that some do develop cancer, but in others there is a reversion to normal. In certain counties close to the Taihang Mountains 50 per cent of the

* A quotation from Chairman Mao.

people over 50 years old have this hyperplasia of the oesophageal mucosa, whereas people of the same age in Shanghai, Chengchow or Peking do not have it. There must be certain factors which predispose to this condition and if we can master this pre-cancerous condition, then preventive work can be done among those not yet affected. At the moment we are treating this hyperplasia preventively, with vitamins (C and A) and with Chinese medicinal herbs.

"We are also doing animal experiments; we find that animals coming from Linhsien also have hyperplasia of the mucosa in a good many cases, and revert to normal under the same treatment. (It takes 4-5 years to 'revert'.)

"We have developed a method of doing periodical cyto-smears (smears of the mucosa cells) for check-ups on the state of the oesophagus. We invented a very small plastic instrument, like a small sponge, which is easy to swallow and to regurgitate. It does not cause pain, only slight discomfort, and the whole process takes 40 seconds. Barefoot doctors can do this test easily and in 18 days we collected 14,000 smears. People cooperated with us, of course. The mass line. The peasant associations were the most active in promoting the test, in organizing people to come to be tested. Reluctant people were persuaded by other members of their production teams or brigades. All this helped tremendously. We could never have done it in any other way.

"Last year we did an experiment on people. We do not believe in making deliberately experiments using people as controls, but it did happen that eight people in one village refused any kind of preventive treatment, while twenty-five accepted. Since then, in two years, two out of the eight who absolutely refused treatment of any kind have developed cancer; of the twenty-five under 'preventive' vitamins, etc., none has developed cancer in two years. But they may still get it and we are continuing."

The peasants of Linhsien county have a ditty about all this now. Previously, they said, Linhsien was the "three cannot pass": no water passes here, no road crosses here, and no food goes through the gullet. Now "two passes" have been achieved; water and roads; and soon the third will be conquered. So they come.

Up to date, in China, 150 million individual investigations for cancer have been done (this does not include obvious cancer cases). All through the mass line. "We cannot wait for good buildings, or adequate equipment, to conduct these studies. We are now thinking in terms of prevention as well; and a lot more studies are necessary."

Dr Wu showed me photographs of experimental chicken farms

run by the institute. A total of 30,000 chickens are being investigated for cancer of the oesophagus. They are of course Taihang Mountains chickens. "In this, too, we practise the mass line," said Dr Wu laughingly. "Any chicken which looks unwell, or vomits, is given to the postman to bring to us. Any sheep off its food is also sent in. Five years ago, a sheep in a small herd was brought to the county hospital. The doctors did duly open it up, and found carcinoma of the oesophagus....

"And now we are investigating field mice. There is an old peasant in the county who knows the language of field mice, and he is helping us to catch them. School children are being mobilized to bring in field mice to us."

Teams in the field include also geologists, chemists. "Medical work cannot be separated from other disciplines. The battle against cancer means bringing in *all* the various sciences to do research together.

"We are also studying old Chinese medical books, for clues to the diagnosis of cancer, and for anti-cancerous herbal remedies of the past. One never knows. The theories behind the Chinese views on cancer in the past may also help ... cancer was known, and treated.

"Drugs in the Chinese pharmacopeia which prevent or restrict tumour growth have been described; we must also investigate them."

Finally, we spoke of the impact of this work upon the doctors, researchers, geologists who went down in "complete teams" to investigate. "They are changed. When they see the people coming, when they see how they grasp the mass line ... they are shaken. They want to stay for ever, never to return to the city...." Now they understand that we cannot "wait for the patient to come to us. We must go out and look for the patient. The importance of screening *everybody*, whether there are clinical signs or symptoms of disease or not, is a great lesson to them."

As we shook hands Dr Li told me that my own province of Szechwan also had one site of high incidence of oesophageal cancer, also related to a mountain area. A "complete team" was also in the area. "Hope you will come with one of our teams, and do some writing on the spot," said Dr Wu as I left.

(1974)

Mao Tsetung, Chou En-lai, and the Chinese People

A WEEK after the first anniversary of Premier Chou En-lai's death last 8 January 1976, the big square of Tienanmen in Peking was still aswarm with milling crowds bringing marvellous paper wreaths and garlands and baskets filled with blossoms. The kilometre-long stands on both sides of the old Ming palaces were covered in these confections, and from every lamp-post and tree hung white bouquets and sprays. All of these were hand-made and none of these offerings government-directed: nor were the millions who came to place them, the hundreds of thousands who trudged, often 20 miles or more in the bitter cold, to bring these fragile and wonderful tokens of their love to the beloved Premier. Poems by workers, schoolchildren, university students, commune peasants and housewives hang or are pasted on every available wall. "Your ashes are all over our land; we breathe your courage in our air; in the ripple of our rivers we hear your laughter...."

Never was there such intense, immense emotion. Far from repressing it (there is a total absence of control, Chinese crowds seem naturally well-behaved), the government installed floodlights so that wall-posters and poems could be read by night, and rows of toilets for the convenience of travellers with children.

Above this homage to Chou En-lai hangs the portrait of Mao Tsetung, from the centre gate of the Ming palace. "To Chairman Mao's most loyal, most devoted companion-in-arms, the great revolutionary, and our best model, Chou En-lai." Thus the thousands of mottoes, slung from each offering.

Reading the wall-posters, one is impressed by the fact that they are very different from the orchestrated platitudes I saw in Peking a year ago. Now they reflect a massive expression of the people's will, demands for a return to revolutionary legality, which the "Gang of Four", Chiang Ching and her acolytes, destroyed. "My name is so and so, my address thus, and I ask the authorities to look into...." Thus begin many wall-posters. And this new fearlessness, the clear articulation of demands for an end to injustices committed, to the ease with which a person could be labelled and then condemned without any evidence, is very exciting.

Nor is the government anything but aware of this, and apparently very much in touch with the people. "The leadership now does things even before we ask for them," I am told. And so it grows in popularity and esteem. "Our new Chairman – Hua Kuo-feng – he truly listens to us."

This new awareness is not confined to one level, the intelligentsia. The latter, harassed and persecuted by the "Gang of Four", is blossoming out in a massive renaissance. Scientists, poets, writers, singers, painters, burst into new activity, emerge from hospitals where understanding doctors helped them to nurse "weak hearts" or other ailments while the terror which the four unleashed was on the rampage. "The hospitals are empty now. My heart? Nothing was ever wrong with it, but my doctor thought I needed a rest...." Of course, not all the intelligentsia were so lucky, and an appraisal of those who did not withstand the tyranny unleashed must be made.

It is among the workers, who come in massive squads to honour Chou En-lai, that the hatred for the four is extremely vocal. "The gang made us fight each other; they put hooligans in control of our factory ... told us we must not produce, must stop work.... We protected our machines from their destruction and they beat us up...."

I have just returned from a tour of four provinces inland, looking at factories, investigating the harm done to industry by the Gang of Four. Everywhere the same story, of deliberate sabotage, incited strikes, beating up workers who insisted on working.... "They thought that by sabotaging production there would be discontent, demoralization, uprisings.... then they would come in, claiming the government was incompetent ..." Meanwhile, there will be shortages this winter, of coal, and light consumer goods, because it will take some months to make good the losses in production.

Among the peasantry, too, Chou En-lai is cherished and remembered as the man who wanted to fulfil Mao's great plan for agricultural mechanization, an end to gruelling hand labour, a rising living standard. The strangest paradox of all is that wherever the Gang of Four penetrated, with its ultra-Left slogans, and managed to disorder the communes, there arose not socialism but, on the contrary, a return to feudal landlordism and to peasant exploitation.

The arrest of the four was the most popular thing ever done by a

Chinese government since Liberation. "It is our second liberation," I hear everyone say. "If Chiang Ching and her three monsters had come to power, there would be civil war ... there would be fascism, for they were fascists ... they hated Chou En-lai, because he fought for the people. ..." The deafening silence of the people in the last two or three years with regard to the Gang of Four (and the whispered execration of Chiang Ching, Mao's wife) is not hard to understand within the Chinese context.

The four controlled the Ministries of Culture and Education, the mass media, liaison with "friendly" groups abroad, the Health Ministry, and were beginning to penetrate the Foreign Ministry. Their big drive was to capture the youth. They stirred up children against their schoolteachers, so that in some schools adolescents beat up the teachers. They recruited bands of young people, the less educated the better, and turned them into hooligans who assaulted older officials, and under cover of revolutionary slogans attacked the administrators of factories. They distributed Party membership cards indiscriminately to gangsters; thus a notorious pickpocket, jailed several times, became a member of the Central Committee; a ruffian of 29 almost seized control of the administration in a city; a band of young people took over a security bureau in one town; a 14-year-old girl became secretary of a Communist youth organization ... "Anyone over 35 is a capitalist-roader and should be replaced" was one of the slogans launched by them in my province (Szechwan). It produced a good deal of disorder.

So an atmosphere of uneasy terror reigned. People began to feel unsafe. They feared a recrudescence of violence, as in the Cultural Revolution. "The Gang of Four had spies everywhere, reporting directly to them. ..."

Documents in the handwriting of the four circulate among the people. In the Politburo, the four formed a cohesive, active block. They seized documents addressed to other members (three of whom were to die between December 1975 and June 1976, and who, previous to their demise, did not attend for months the meetings of the Politburo) and answered them in their own names. Thus they were a real majority at the highest level and could do as they pleased, circulating condemnations against the other members of the Politburo and Central Committee, calling meetings and holding briefings, in the name of Mao, and ignoring all Party rules. Very swiftly, anyone who defied them or refused to obey their orders found themselves labelled "counter-revolutionary" and in jail - or worse.

The death of Chou En-lai in January 1976 seemed, to the four, herald of their accession to power.

But here, as so often during the Chinese revolution, Mao, though failing in health, intervened and neatly turned the tables upon them.

The way it was done is so typically Chinese that Westerners find it hard to be convinced. If, they contend, Mao so often criticized them and upbraided them (as the documents do show), warning that "Chiang Ching is madly ambitious ... she will make trouble when I'm dead," and telling the four: "Don't make a gang ... he who does will fall," why did he not, far more simply, remove them two years ago, before they could do more evil?

The answer is that far from solving the problem, this action on Mao's part might have created *more* problems after his demise. Even three years ago, the four still had, particularly among youth, a "revolutionary" image, and a following. "Never act until a situation is ripe" is Mao's dictum. The gang had not completely revealed their fascism to the people; despite their persecution of artists, scientists, and older cadres and especially their hostility to Chou En-lai, they had not yet engaged in the criminal conspiracy, the planning of a military *putsch*, which would be their downfall.

But Mao acted by nominating in April 1976 Hua Kuo-feng, whom he had known for 20 years, and trusted, as Premier and *First* Vice-Chairman of the Party. Emphasis is on the word *First*, written in Mao's own hand, giving Hua, automatically, precedence over all others in the Party. This was subsequently confirmed by Mao's letter to Hua Kuo-feng: "With you in charge, I am at ease." And his specific direction for "solving the problem" of the Gang of Four.

"The final act in this drama," says a knowledgeable friend to me, "was not an unpremeditated move. Believe me, the script had been carefully, quietly prepared, months and months ahead." Which goes to show that, contrary to outside appearances, the Gang of Four would *never* have been able to come to power.

But, very foolishly, they now proceeded, by a single act, to lose *all* support, even among the naïve young. This was when they forbade people to wear mourning for Chou En-lai; closed the universities to stop the young from coming to Tienanmen Square to place wreaths; and finally, because they could not stop the people, created a "riot" by sending in armed hooligans. Twenty young students are said to have been killed by these armed gangs. And now the hatred of the people was intense, universal.

The death of Mao Tsetung himself, on 9 September 1976, saw the four hasten to their own undoing. They went to Shanghai, armed

million-strong militia, drew up plans to seize strategic posts;
quartered the only army group they controlled in Paoting, an
important railway junction, drew up lists of important leaders to kill
off, lists of their followers to nominate in place of the dead....

This bloody *putsch* was planned for 8–13 October. On 6 October,
in the evening, they were arrested "without a drop of blood being
shed". "You can't arrest me, I am Chairman Mao's widow," shrieked
Chiang Ching. But she was. "We tried to give her one whole month
of mourning, but she herself hastened her own arrest," says someone
to me. So the month was short by two days. And, as photographs
show, she was not mourning for her husband....

The militia in Shanghai did not rise, but immediately joined the
deliriously happy millions in a three-day festival to celebrate the end
of the "Gang of Four". The army group in Paoting surrendered,
around twenty ringleaders being court-martialled. "The four did not
have righteousness on their side, so they lost." They did not have the
people, the Party, nor the Army on their side either. Even old
officials are surprised at the unequivocal, enthusiastic response by
the people. "We've been hoping for this to happen...."

The happy outcome is not only a popular administration, but a
restored unity, willingness to work, and a new maturity and
sophistication, coupled with outspokenness among the people. If the
word democracy means anything, then what Mao Tsetung fought
and worked for throughout his life, what the well-beloved Chou
En-lai fought and worked for, may yet come to pass. "Without
democracy, there cannot be socialism," said Mao. The fact that the
four, so swiftly, could destroy the constitutional rights of the
individual has been a great lesson; hence the new administration's
priority is to provide safeguards and guarantees against repetition of
such tyranny. And at last the Chinese people, who have a long past
of tyranny, have grasped the point: there must be the right, legally,
to dissent, so as to promote a real, human socialism.

(1977)

China's New Hundred Flowers – a Turning Point

THE SHOPS in China's cities are crowded with buyers, as suddenly a blossoming of folk art, prints, ceramics, porcelain, beautiful things which the "Gang of Four" suppressed have again come out, and shoppers queue to acquire them as gifts, together with food and wine, in order to celebrate Lunar New Year, also known as the Spring Festival, on 18 February.

"After great disorder through the land comes great order," said the new Chairman Hua Kuo-feng, quoting his illustrious predecessor Mao Tsetung. Hua is becoming increasingly popular. "He seems to know what we want, and everything is done," say the people. A feeling of security, ease of mind, is current among the population instead of the previous fear and anxiety. Everyone looks forward to "the great healing and stability" of the new year.

1976 indeed saw catastrophe: the passing of the well-beloved Chou En-lai, of Mao Tsetung himself; the frightful earthquakes which ravaged North China and caused nearly 600,000 deaths, floods over twenty counties ... above all, the disruption, sabotage, factional fighting, havoc deliberately introduced by Chiang Ching, Yao Wen-yuan, Chang Chun-chiao and Wang Hung-wen, who strove to paralyse the administration and thus wrest power by inciting civil war everywhere. On the happy side came their arrest, to the immense joy and relief of fully 99 per cent of the population.

Today, in a China where family reunion at New Year fills the trains with youths returning from the countryside, the new year opens under the auspices of Mao's policy, launched in 1957, of the Hundred Flowers. "Let a hundred flowers bloom, a hundred schools of thought contend." This policy, which Mao said must be a "long-term one, not temporary", corresponds to the new atmosphere of happiness and freedom in China.

This new "hundred flowers" is very different from the first experiment launched by Mao in 1956. Mao Tsetung and Chou En-lai (the latter throughout the years protected and educated the intelligentsia into what socialism really should be) were trying at the time to mobilize the intellectuals, in an effort to speed up China's modernization along socialist lines. For, contrary to what some people in the West believe, the modernization of China in all sectors has always been Mao's long-term aim, and Chou En-lai was the man who knew best how to translate Mao's grand, overall vision into practical planning.

But in 1956 the intelligentsia was only seven years away from the habits of old China; they were intellectually arrogant; despised and ignored the workers and peasants. The latter were still mostly illiterate, and politically ignorant. Although many intellectuals did realize that the new system was good, not all did; and so the first attempt was not an overall success.

But today, twenty years later, things are very different. "Today the Chinese population is not illiterate. The workers and peasants read, write, think; they attend night schools and discuss politics. The many twists and turns of the revolution, and above all the Cultural Revolution, has given them political understanding, an acumen and a wisdom, unequalled by any other peoples in the world." The person who says this to me is not a Party man, but an old intellectual, a gentle poet. And some Western diplomats in China, too, are commenting on "the astounding political sophistication, responsible behaviour, of the Chinese people".

"The people are ahead of us, far ahead of us in understanding," says to me a veteran Party cadre. "We, the leaders, must learn from them." Today, it is the people, the workers and peasants, who are supporting the government in a wave of popularity in condemning the "Gang of Four", and rebuilding socialist legality, which the four so utterly ignored and violated. The people clamour for a speed-up in all sectors. Through the Cultural Revolution, which was an immense education in mass involvement and participation by the people, the most profound change in China is that every worker and peasant feels involved in China's continuing revolution and the construction of a humane, democratic, socialist state. "Socialism does not mean want, hunger, poverty, but exactly the contrary," everyone says. This does *not* mean a return to "capitalism", to material incentives, to élitism, but on the contrary the "supervision by the masses of the Party members; their right to criticize leaders who, like the Gang of Four, abuse their position to acquire privilege and exercise tyranny; the safeguards of the constitutional rights of assembly, wall-posters, the right to strike, and to speak out."

Of course, these rights are to be exercised in the direction of building a better socialism, a better Party leadership. The intelligentsia of China, far from wanting a return of the past, is wholeheartedly devoted to this common objective. What is happening in China today is *not* similar to the "dissidents" of Eastern Europe and the Soviet Union, where because of the people's discontent with the tyranny and arbitrariness of what they think is "socialism", protesters are in favour of a return to capitalism. There will be no Solzhenitsyn in China; because in China not only the intellectuals, but the masses of the people, understand that the attempts at imposing fascism by Lin Piao, and after him by Chiang Ching and her group, were not socialist, but precisely the contrary.

This is the enlightenment which the Cultural Revolution has brought about. "True, we suffered a good deal during the Cultural Revolution," many of my friends, artists, writers and painters, say to me as I sit in their houses for long hours of heart-to-heart talk. "But we all know that the violence and ill-treatment of people was *not* the Cultural Revolution. It was not what Chairman Mao wanted and indeed he had forbidden any violence at all. It was the work of Lin Piao, and also of Chiang Ching and her adherents, who, under cover of extremely revolutionary speeches, practised the most ruthless oppression."

"In such a tremendous mass upheaval, everything comes up, good things and bad," says a seasoned official, who himself suffered greatly during the Cultural Revolution. "But the people now all know about the two-line struggle; they have seen so many high leaders toppled: Liu Shao-chi, who attempted a return to a bureaucratic arbitrary élite, ignoring the peasants and workers; Lin Piao, who attempted a military fascist coup; and now the 'Gang of Four'. Their understanding has grown by leaps and bounds."

"This is the turning point in China's revolution," says another veteran official. "The recent tyranny exercised by the four was itself a factor in catalysing, accelerating, the process of mass understanding of events. After all, the whole idea of socialism is total participation in *all* affairs of state by the people themselves. Now we have reached this point."

Today, the Chinese intelligentsia, old and middle-aged and young, are not alienated from the people. Mao's policies to diminish the gap between mental and manual labour have now borne fruit. Not only are there schools and cultural centres in every commune and factory, but all cadres, officials, intellectuals, whatever their rank, have also done spells of manual labour, integrating with the workers and peasants. The sons and daughters of ambassadors, high officials, and intellectuals, have become educated workers and peasants, workers and peasants have become Ministers and Vice-Ministers.

The demonstrations of love and affection for Chou En-lai were also a political manifestation. "Actually, the Gang of Four caused their own downfall when they ordered that there should be no mourning for Premier Chou En-lai; no memorial meetings; nothing even in the newspapers about him."

Although Chiang Ching was unpopular, and unease prevailed over her and her doings, it was only in January 1976, at Chou En-lai's death, and because of her clique's overt hostility to the Premier, that the masses began to understand the political significance of their actions. "Why do they hate so much our beloved Premier? Why do they organize disruption everywhere?" And very swiftly, all over China, hatred of them grew; this is when they lost *any support among the people* which they might have acquired through sounding very "revolutionary". "We saw that their own scandalous private lives, full of luxury, did not correspond to what they said." Then on 4 and 5 April 1976, the people on their own, spontaneously, organized huge demonstrations of love for Chou En-lai. Not only in Peking's Tienanmen Square but in almost all cities of China, and despite the orders of the four: "No mourning for Chou!" In Peking they filled the square with wreaths and flowers; all the trees were covered in small white flowers by the children, each one inscribed: "To our well-beloved Premier, your child." April 4 and 5 was the Chingming festival of mourning for the dead; instead of going to the graves of their ancestors, people crowded into Peking to honour Chou. This was a political demonstration of enormous significance, against the Gang of Four, as innumerable poems and wall-posters affixed to the wreaths and flowers testify. People stood and sang, recited poetry: "However devils rage, you cannot tear our beloved from our hearts...." "We don't want empresses" (Chiang Ching had been for three years extolling Chinese empresses of old, claiming that "even under communism, there will be empresses....")

When they saw the determined, million-strong demonstrations, the Gang of Four sent in hooligans to shout: "Chou En-lai was a capitalist roader." This infuriated the people. The four ordered their own trained gangs to kill: about 30 to 40 people died, and many hundreds were arrested. The people are (now released) asking for a full investigation (which is being carried out) and punishment of the culprits. "After that, everyone, including the young (they were especially trying to capture the young, telling them: All the old officials are no good, they must be killed off.... We haven't killed

enough in China ... then you can have their jobs), execrated them,"
say my friends. "We used to mutter every day: boil them alive, boil
them alive," some housewives told me. "We hated them so much."

"We were forbidden to leave the universities, but many of us
jumped the wall and went to mourn Chou En-lai ... afterwards they
arrested many of us," say to me some university students.

No wonder their arrest, done so neatly, and without any
bloodshed, was so popular. And immediately, within a month, all
factional strife stopped, all fighting stopped. "No one rose for them."
Thousands of protests, of wall-posters put up against them by
fearless men and women throughout the land in the last three years
are now made known (previously all the mass media were under the
four). The immediate release with honour of those who resisted the
four was proclaimed three months ago. The idea that the people did
not participate in their overthrow, and were merely "passive", is
derided in China. "Had there not been the massive support by the
people, the Party, and the Army, their arrest could not have taken
place so easily."

It is not "de-Maoization" but true "Maoization", following Chairman Mao's policies as they should be practised with the methods of
Chou En-lai, which is the basis of China's new advance, and of the
new Hundred Flowers.

It is, as a vast mass movement, not confined to an intelligentsia,
but involving all the people, that the new Hundred Flowers will
unfold. It is the mobilization of all enthusiasm, energy, creativity,
talent, ingenuity, in the consolidation of a democratic type of
socialism; in Mao's word, freedom with discipline, unity of will and of
action together with personal ease and liveliness. And the people are
already practising it. Never have they been so outspoken. They show
a tremendous power of self-organization and this is *not* repressed, it
is actively encouraged. Without the political maturity acquired
during the upheavals of the last ten years, such a level of
consciousness could not have been reached.

At the moment, everything is being taken in hand. There are an
enormous number of meetings, at all levels. The mechanization of
agriculture; streamlining of industry, transport, commerce, communications; every day in one or other sector swift and popular reorganization. In the realm of art and literature, also, there is a large
activity. Painters, writers, musicians, publishers, are all debating,
discussing: "The Gang of Four tried to kill all art and literature. They
said: Nothing good was done between 1880 and Chiang Ching's new
operas." This absurdity is of course now condemned; but it does not

mean that the new operas will be banned; "Chiang Ching did not invent them; she used them to promote herself; they were a creation of the people." So we shall see more and better books, music, plays, as well as the return of many works of art created during the 1949 to 1966 period which Chiang Ching had banned as "counter-revolutionary".

Magazines, radio, television, the press agencies are disentangling themselves from hackneyed, mindless jargon. A good many young people have been fed for years on this singular pap and are unable to write in any other way than by a continuous string of clichés. They have to be retrained into clear writing; and for this the works of Lu Hsun are an excellent model. The Foreign Languages Press is also making a great effort to tailor its articles to the needs of the readers, instead of employing a mangled idiom of no known language on earth – being merely literal, word-for-word translation from the Chinese.

There is not going to be in China a massive purge, certainly not in the way it was practised in the Soviet Union. "Re-education" comes first; everyone has a chance to amend, to recognize their errors and mistakes, and to be rehabilitated. But this will certainly not apply to the four themselves. "The people are too angry with them." "The Gang of Four used violence, coercion, physical duress; we must not use these vile, illegal means."

"We take Premier Chou En-lai as our model," say the people. "We have a great and noble culture; but we must also learn the good things from other cultures and nations," say the intelligentsia. "We have a great responsibility towards our own people towards the peoples of the world." The old qualities of integrity and steadfastness, the resilience of the people, their grasp of the wider aspects of the history they are in the process of making are evident now. "An enlightened, responsible people, their destiny in their own hands," say my friends, as together we toast the new Hundred Flowers.

(1977)

Looking Forward

NOW, MORE than ever, the future of humankind is being shaped by our present activity, both physical and mental. Yet despite our abilities to build a better world, and the means at our disposal for doing so, never have so many people on our globe entertained such emotions of powerlessness, confusion and gloom. Economists link this state of mind to financial crises, to depression, recession, stagflation. It is, I think, a persistent feeling of devalorization of the self which haunts a great many of us both in the Western world – now called the North – or the affluent world, and the South, also called the Third, or developing world. It is brought about by a realization that something is very wrong in a world where economic crises recur, indebtedness mounts, famine stalks many countries and millions die of hunger, where the threat of nuclear war seems more menacing than ever. The North, with the greatest power to change the world for the better, is unwilling or unable to do so; men of talent shirk from visioning a future with promise of good for all; and men of power are reluctant to abandon outmoded prejudices and actions which perpetuate inequality and injustice.

Yet the world has changed; and is changing all the time. Situations reverse themselves, so that yesterday's boon is today's problem. Public health measures have provoked demographic increase now considered economically catastrophic. 1.7 billion people will be added to the world's population in the next two decades, 92 per cent of this increase occurring in the South. New knowledge, liberating humankind as never before, increasing our control of the universe, also increases the ease with which bondage and constraints, a total invasion of privacy, can be imposed upon us. High-grade technology and its uses has created this fear of new domination since it is, at present, a monopoly of power in the hands of the few.

Pessimism and gloom may be logic, but I believe in a more dispassionate, more optimistic view. I am sanguine that the saving grace of the quirky human being, forever thinking our formless, disreputably contradictory thoughts, forever impassioned and unpredictable, will bring us back to a new coherence. True, we are at the moment outstripped in our emotional and social consciousness by the technological advances of the last 30 years. We seem unable to fully grasp the meaning of the knowledge revolution that we have created, to envision it shaping our future. But I think this confusion is temporary. Awareness is growing, everywhere, in every country of the world. Humankind is reaching a stage of self-cognition never attained before.

The knowledge revolution before us (also known as the computer or information revolution, or the third wave) is feared because we fear the purposes to which it may be applied, not the techniques themselves. And it is in the choice of *purpose* that our future resides. This is the crux, the heart of the matter: how shall we use the tremendous advances which high-grade technology (HGT) has put at our disposal? To what end?

Humanity is the miracle in our universe. The great enigma is our human consciousness, spanning time and space, perpetuating its own accumulated experience. And consciousness implies *choice*, which is the unique, godlike attribute of the human being. We, not God, create our own heaven or hell.

Consciousness is the universe within us, capable of indefinite expansion. It is all that makes us human: love and courage, self-sacrifice and vision. Cognitive scientists tell us that we are using but a fraction of our total brain potential; billions of untapped neurone connections remain; and one of the tasks of our future evolution – for we have not done evolving – will be to reshape our thinking, our actions and emotions, to use our brains "better" than we are doing now – the word "better" implying not "smartness" but true intelligence, wisdom, acknowledgement of ourselves as part of a total humanity, fraternity in its full meaning. What is the purpose of the human being on earth? Whatever philosophy, religion or scientific discipline pursued, the question has haunted and will continue to haunt all thinking human beings. It is the main thrust of all cultures and civilizations to legitimize for us our presence, thoughts and actions. Our achievements are inseparable from a belief in their worth, therefore in a certain purpose, which is goodness, happiness, for all. And as our self-cognition becomes clearer, as magnificent opportunities to create the future or to destroy it become ever more tangible, so do the yearnings for new ways out of injustice, poverty and war become more conscious and clamorous.

The knowledge revolution, like the sudden coalescence of a galaxy out of nebulous gas, is transforming all existing societies with overwhelming speed, producing incoherence and confusion. Today's technology puts every kind of knowledge at the disposal of the common citizen at the touch of a button. Children of seven or nine are programming their own home mini-computers; and in the affluent North it will be common for each home to own a computer. 1983 has been proclaimed *World Communications Year* by the United Nations. Communications is knowledge, is education, is power, resources, and wealth.

The rhythm at which we are being carried forwards is such that the volume of information/knowledge handled by machines doubles every two years. The sum of social technical industrial transformations in the next two decades will be equivalent to that from the beginning of humankind's time on earth. Within our own generation, we are entering a brave new world of our own making; all humankind will be affected, in diverse ways; even distant rural areas will have their barefoot microchip.

The knowledge revolution brings hope to the developing world, the poor, the rural 80 per cent of the world. For these new machines, though requiring trained personnel, are cheap, extraordinarily cheap, and getting cheaper. "If the auto industry had done what the computer industry has done in the last 30 years, a Rolls-Royce would cost US$2.50 instead of 25,000 dollars, and get two million miles to a gallon of oil," says one expert. What hope this brings to the poor of this world, to be able to effect great changes at affordable cost? For example, education through the video cassette and the television screen (already practised in China) will enable enormous savings to be made in education budgets. True, the requirements of training or retraining technicians to deal with the programming needed will entail much effort; but it can be done. True, the investments in research which have led to this high-grade technology have been prodigious, but the non-affluent hope that with the cheaper and cheaper trend in the cost of the equipment turned out they will be favoured in the long run.

The knowledge revolution would go a long way towards solving most of the South's pressing problems, enabling it to produce the surpluses which would fuel development. And yet, and yet, accessibility to this knowledge appears difficult to achieve. And there is a growing feeling that there is a lack of *common purpose* to solve the problems of the South, as if what is good for the South would be a loss for the North, when all facts point to the absurdity of such thinking. The knowledge revolution offers the possibility of industrializing swiftly and at low cost many regions now deprived of industry. As for agriculture, a sector which has proved the one needing most input in toil and capital investment, the sector employing most of the South's people, input from the knowledge revolution would mean abundance; production doubled, or tripled, or more.The manufacture of synthetic proteins at low cost could totally abolish malnutrition - if such was the aim of such production. In most countries of the South there have been supreme efforts at development. Some have been successful, others not. Today, gloom prevails in a world faced with crises; contraction of financial flow, of economic growth, precisely at a time when new discoveries multiply the potential for abundance. The "accuse and demand" stance of the South, that it should be helped to the HGT to make up for past iniquities, has proved useless because power is master. Yet the unequal terms of trade, which emphatically and undeniably strangle development; protectionism, which aggravates the difficulties of the Third World, are still being used, as if these measures could save the North from its crises and mounting unemployment. In return the North cites the fact that many governments in the Third World have mismanaged their economies. Deepening poverty, massive debts and payment deficits, collapsed commodity prices - how can the South, then, deal with the new knowledge revolution?

The reality, however, is *interdependence*, a fact which is being slowly recognized by all. Interdependence between North and South, have and have nots, is here, has come to stay. It forces an overhaul of all political and economic thinking and policies as they are practised today. The shattering of the economies of the poor leads to the crisis of the rich, and all governments pay lip service to commitment for *world* recovery, yet continue to withhold the knowledge and skills which would make this possible.

The division of the world into socialist and capitalist is now no longer tenable either; it is a hoax and a delusion, for the socialist countries are as involved in interdependence as others. The poverty of the Third World also bogs down the affluent. And yet we are still caught in a dilemma of commercial exploitation, of petty manipulation, of sordid greed, where new technologies are being used as a monopoly of power and their accessibility denied. And yet, the potential in certain areas to build their own pool of high-grade technology (in India, in China) is already present. And there is percolation, even if not complete accessibility. The stalemate in the North–South dialogue, due to obstinacy, leads the South once again to call for a new, overall examination of the international trade and payment systems – in short, a new economic order. This hegemonism on the part of the North – for hegemonism is not confined to superiority in the arms race, or territorial domination – is the real danger. The pessimistic report of the North–South Round Table Forum at Oiso, Japan, reveals some of the shortsighted, greedy, unscrupulous and out-of-date mechanisms of exploitation which still prevail.

Awareness is present in the Third World that self-reliance, the reshaping of national policies of development, is the only possible way to strengthen themselves in the "confrontation" necessary to negotiate a new international economic order. Such negotiations will not, it seems, be successful, even though there may be apparent conciliation on certain points. The reason is this clinging to outmoded structures and ways of economic thought, in some instances a growing search for control of the South through propagation of weaponry and the incitation of local wars. We hear much, in this connection, of the activities of the TNC, or transnational corporations. The TNC are a product but also a creator of the high-technology revolution. Among many of them, it is said, prevails still the shortsighted view that dissemination of such HGT as they possess and market is unfavourable for them; that if everyone got free access to what they own and possess, there would be no monopoly of wealth, power and knowledge, and they would be the losers. But is this quite true? The picture is more complex. Far more powerful than governments today, the TNC richly repay the brains set up to do the research which produces new inventions. And HGT, not only the machines but also the know-how and the skilled personnel, is becoming an important article in the trade and commerce of the TNC.

Excluding certain areas of the world such as the USSR and China, in the last 25 years, 85 to 90 per cent of world trade has passed in the hands of the TNC, and 40 per cent of international trade is transacted through TNC intra-firm transfers. But this exchange is not without its dangers..In the last 15 years the hold of TNC on the South has grown, until it can really be said to govern certain states. This should not lead us to condemn, it is the very nature of "big business" to run things. The present trend among TNC themselves is concentration, centralization of capital, merger and conglomerates, also internationalization of capital, tending towards a global economic system of gigantic corporations. According to certain projections, of 30 dominating corporations with sales of

US$200 billion, 10 will have disappeared by the year 2,000 and another 10 merged; leaving only 10 in power. As to the famous seven sisters of oil, we are told they will be reduced to four within the next two decades.

Microprocessors are dominated by an oligopoly of 5 corporations in the USA, 4 Japanese and 3 European; and there will be mergers too. Antitrust laws are illusory, or inoperative in many areas.

But this very pyramidalism carries its own potential for ruin. The crises in the financial markets are an evidence. It is not a question of the non-adaptation of society in the North to this monopoly of power and wealth. Recession and unemployment are due to the trend towards more and more concentration by the TNC; technological changes are pushed as part of the strategies of corporate profit maximization and aggrandizement; many companies must close down because their production has now become obsolete. In the race for power between corporations and companies, everything depends on a very small margin of profit or loss; on the decision of a very few men at the top. There is very little, or no planning, in terms of the human element which is involved in these complex operations. The enormousness and power of the TNC are accompanied by an inbuilt vulnerability; a loss of vision as to the purpose of wealth and power, the purpose of humankind.

What profits profit? What if we gain the whole world and lose ourselves? This question is as vital today as it ever was. All over the world a new consciousness of the issues at stake is present; no amount of Keynesian or post-Keynesian monetarism can give an answer. The need is for better management of the world economy in a sane way, with, as its purpose, not profit for the few, but economic prosperity for all.

We must recognize that the thrust and scope of the TNC is *the* most dynamic force in today's economics, working towards a global economy *beyond the control* of nation-states. Yet because of the policies of the TNC a parasitic relationship between them and the national economies has evolved; especially towards the Third World countries whose economies are most subject to their pressure. These countries have no viable substitute for the capital, technology, knowhow and skilled personnel offered by the TNC and essential for their development. And these are available at terms and in conditions both degrading and defeating, quite often, any attempt at enrichment by the receiving nation.

And yet, and yet ... a world which cannot afford what the TNC has to offer is a danger to the TNC themselves. For robots cannot consume, cannot provide the market for the flow of goods of all kinds which is the very essence of consumerism and the viability of the TNC. This is most obvious today, when so many Third World countries – almost half of them, if not more – are falling behind in debt repayments, and have to be bailed out. Indeed, so linked are lender and borrower, debtor and creditor, that debt rescheduling is preferable to hounding the debtor; money is loaned to hopeless cases to avert a crash among the affluent, so fragile has our imbalanced interdependence become.

It seems, therefore, that the wisest course would be a new spirit of economic internationalism. Sustained growth in the developing world *must* be promoted, maintained by the very ones who are now denying it the ability to grow well and freely. Protectionism to conserve outmoded industries, contraction rather than expansion, spell disaster for the TNC and their affluent sites; because they only maintain at high cost what has become obsolete and unproductive. Because the danger is visible now, even in the great corporations (for there are people of great worth and ability who direct these enormous states-within-states), a theory of *compound involvement* is now being enunciated. It presupposes a code of moral conduct for the TNC, to improve their relations with developing countries; a new style of resources transfer, with guaranteed return-prominent business; an undertaking that the TNC will comply with the host country's laws and development plan.

Without any illusion (the very enunciation of compound involvement leaves one with a feeling of sad hilarity), it is quite certain that the TNC's code of conduct must change, for their own good and their own survival. And change will come, though not easily, for it is not the nature of the human being to change willingly, and between pelf and good sense, pelf often comes first.

The day will come, however, I believe, when socialist countries, and Third World ones, will become effective joint-venture partners with the TNC, and perhaps compound involvement will also involve the TNC in respecting the host country's development plans.

The connection between the mighty TNC and the military industrial complexes is total. This is probably the worst facet of TNC involvement; we see a continued flooding of the countries who can least afford sophisticated weaponry with weaponry so sophisticated as to fall quickly into disuse and non-use. Alas, alas, I say, for the foolish, the improvident, the unshrewd of the Third World! The conflicts among them threaten their very existence. The non-aligned movement of 101 nations is sadly frayed. The politics of the arms race, displaced towards proxy protagonists, encourage and utilize the nations of the South in their suicidal squabbles, so costly and detrimental to themselves.

It is all this: the unequal terms of trade, the oppressive and manipulative strategies, the lack, on the other hand, of adequate development policies, of trained and dedicated national administrations, which bedevil an *interdependent* world; which make dialogue so onerous, but which necessitate a thorough overhaul of *all* structures. In New Delhi, the non-aligned have called for awareness that the poverty and lack of purchasing power of the South also prolong and worsen the financial crises bedevilling the North; this is a call for moderation and compromise.

The TNC can be a powerful force for progress in the countries of the South: where and when each side recognizes the interests of the other; when the plans for national development and the operations for maximal profit do not conflict; when the TNC recognize the forces of change, and change their planning and policy making from maximal short-term profit to long-term friendly and profitable cooperation. The word profit should no longer be ugly; it should be the natural epithet for surplus created to benefit the people of the host country. This view is realistic. It neither condemns nor accuses. The great wave of social revolution which began in the eighteenth century in Europe and culminated with the Chinese revolution of the twentieth century is at the moment at ebb. Future revolutions – and there will be revolutions, like it or not – will assume different formulations from those which have governed the industrial revolution, now being replaced by the knowledge revolution.

I would now like to speak of strategies of development evolved recently, to cope with this interdependent/confrontation situation, in Asia. Because the subject is so enormously vast and complex, I have to leave out, regretfully, India, a nation-state with an important pool of technology experts and industrial know-how, now in the throes of entering its knowledge revolution, and in fact accused, or suspected, of creating its own South–South TNC. I shall confine myself to some remarks on China, the way in which China is entering the modern age, the mapping of a development strategy in China.

The Chinese Revolution is not altogether understood in the West, for observers are swayed by inbuilt assumptions about Communism. The main thrust of the Chinese Revolution, I think, has always been an intense nationalism; it was at once a revolution for national independence, and a change of system; the doctrine of Marxism serving to propel the notion of liberation from colonial and feudal domination. The Chinese Revolution was supposed to be a Marxist revolution but it certainly fulfilled none of the Marxist tenets. Overwhelming a peasant revolution (there were 400 million peasants and 4 million workers in China in 1949) yet conducted in the name of the working class, its course in the 30 years since has been the result of this dichotomy. Only now has it finally come to an understanding of its own dynamics and the obstacles to its progress.

Several attempts by China to go it alone, to refuse the Soviet model (anyway inapplicable) and devise its own model, failed under the overwhelming impact of China's peasant *feudal* society. This strong, basic feudalism still exists, and is an obstacle to modernization. It is based in village society, as is the anti-intellectualism exhibited during the Cultural Revolution, a revival of the old peasant hostility to the literocracy, the professional mandarin. For 2,500 years, China's intellectuals have been the officials of the government, the establishment, the power-holders. And the shifts in social classes, in the intelligentsia's status and role, are only now being recognized. China's intelligentsia is no longer the ruling officialdom, a new generation of intelligentsia has been reared, whose mentality is totally different; who are geared to modernization; and who are, now, proclaimed part of the working class; workers in the full Marxist sense, hence they qualify as leaders of the new revolution, the four modernizations. Perhaps this astonishing flexibility in dealing or modifying Marxist concepts will surprise; but Chinese culture has always been able to operate such syntheses, and to comfortably marry opposites.

It was Premier Chou En-lai who saw the crux of the matter, the confrontation situation between the intellectual and the peasant, and who already in 1956 formulated means of protecting the intelligentsia. At the same time, the intelligentsia also had to be taken out of the world of Confucianism, and become technocrats rather than literocrats, to organize a pool of scientists to serve the modernization plans. All these 32 years have been years of search, of experimentation for the methods and policies which would promote modernization and prosperity.

This ideal is not new; it was set forward in 1911, with China's first revolution which abolished the empire, by Dr Sun Yatsen. What has emerged after these 32 years, and many mistakes but also many achievements, is China's entry into the modern world. I do believe that the originality, the inventiveness deployed by China during these years, and also the new experiments for a strategy of development deployed today, are attention worthy. A strategy for development also implies an attitude, a vision, a purpose, the capacity to think and to envision, to plan and to analyse, in function of certain aims.

First, therefore, I would like to posit that China is *not* abandoning socialism, but tailoring the ideology – discarding what no longer applies – to Chinese concrete conditions. This was one of Mao's tenets, as his works on Contradiction and Practice, written in 1937, reveal. The present Chinese leadership comprise some of the keenest brains, such as Ma Hong (President of the Chinese Academy of Social Sciences), Hsueh Mu Chiao, Hu Chiaomu. They understand the present world and the gap between China's conditions and the high-grade technology world of the future. They are convinced that the foundation of socialism, which is the collective property of means of production, is not outmoded. They also argue that far from adopting capitalist modes of production, recent innovative experiments – the reform in economic management, in the structure of collective ownership – are a process of developing socialist modes of production.

The basic condition in China is land, land property and agriculture. Here all efforts at "modernization" hit against the immense capital investment required for 800 million peasants. And statistics show that all these 32 years much more has been taken than put into agriculture. Collectivization did abolish the stranglehold of feudal landlordism, open the way to collectives, but how to conduct collective agriculture remained a dilemma. The communes became a total insurance for the peasant not to starve, whatever effort he put in the land, and thus an incitement to a permanent go-slow. "Marx wrote very little about how to work the land once landlords and the capitalists were abolished," said to me the eminent theoretician, Hu Chiaomu, in a recent three-hour interview on the theoretical basis of the present economist experiments in China. "Stalin proceeded by the ruthless method of abolishing the rich peasant physically ... this was a mistake. Lenin thought: all must go to the co-operative, from which each individual then draws what he needs; but he did not envisage the methods of this suggested distribution. In China there is a very different situation from that of Russia. Our most striking difference is very little land for very many peasants. And a great diversity in the land. This must determine the structure and method of making Chinese agriculture productive and efficient. We cannot have blanket, overall rules; state farms or large farming areas are impossible except in certain regions, we must operate a workable system to get maximum efficiency from the peasant, on the land that is at his disposal. Enterprise, initiative and efficiency are ruined when the peasant has no personal interest in production. Again, to administer the communes, a three-tiered bureaucracy was set up, which did no work, produced an immense amount of useless commands and became finally parasitic upon the peasantry." There was progress, nevertheless, and advances of many kinds were possible, relying on the mobilization of manpower. But the fusion of political and economic leadership in one bureaucracy made for inefficiency, very few of the cadres had any knowledge of agricultural techniques; and political slogans never grew a blade of rice. What had been needed to break the old feudal bondages became in turn an obstacle to expansion of production, and to enrichment of peasants' lives.

The present job responsibility system, according to Hu Chiaomu, is a demand of the peasant. It defines clearly the division of labour and profit between the peasant family and the collective; and by leaving a margin of profit to the peasant, stimulates efficiency and productivity. At the present time, there are about 20 or 30 different systems of job responsibility in operation in China's countryside. "We are in a total experimental stage," say China's economists. "No two places can be alike. Each must tailor its economic aims and methods according to conditions." The basic factor is that no one can *own* land; nor can land be purchased or sold. The production team – which often is also the extended family unit – is also the basic accounting unit, entering into contracts with the collective for production, and keeping what is surplus as its own profit. To call this "a return to capitalism" implies that socialism cannot liberate initiative and efficiency; whereas precisely the opposite should obtain, and it seems the Chinese are embarked on an experiment to prove that well-understood socialism does work. Certainly a high degree of productivity has emerged in the past five years; peasant incomes have doubled, tripled, quadrupled; diversified economic pursuits for a variety of agricultural produce – including the processing of agricultural produce within rural communes – have grown so speedily that within five years, 100 million peasants out of 800 million have moved away from growing and planting and are engaged in semi-manufactures, in full-time side-line occupations, in industrial factories set up in rural areas. "From each according to his ability, to each according to the work he does" is socialism, says Hu Chiaomu. The inadequate, the inefficient, the lazy will no longer be carried on the shoulders of the community, as they have been for so long enjoying "all eating from the same big pot". Whereas welfare funds still remain in each locality for the truly needy, and each village cares for its less endowed families, it remains that total egalitarianism has disappeared. There is, because of increased income, no rush to the cities, as in other Third World countries. Life in the rural countryside is becoming increasingly better; to note the number of television sets, sewing-machines, radios, the watches on peasant wrists, the cameras and soon the washing machines. A vast consumer market is developing in rural areas. Bicycles, new clothes, new houses, the demand for better furniture and shoes and all the amenities of the city are creating shopping centres and small towns where semi-manufactured goods derived from agricultural produce concentrate. In a short five years, the purchasing power of China's peasantry has been liberated. One only has to go to Sichuan, and count the TV sets or the bicycles in the villages, to understand what is happening.

In industry, too, China is the scene of not one, but at least two dozen new experiments. These are carried out at pilot points, and care is taken not to dislocate the whole industrial setup by blanket or wholesale changes.

The USSR is watching with great care these experiments, the decentralization, the new managerial methods, the insistence on work-efficient staff and methods; the responsibility for profit and loss applied even in nationalized industries, etc., etc.

Where high-grade technology and industrial modernization are concerned: after some errors, such as the buying of whole plants, the Chinese have come to the strategy of replacing with better machines the existing plants, while they actively encourage the training of technological scientists and needed personnel. A technology policy has been formulated (as in India) for determined central and regional efforts to undertake serious technological forecasting, and technology assessment. For think-tanks and the upgrading of enterprises, for studying project feasibility, etc. There must be a total restructuring of education, and of the whole administrative structure.

China is bedevilled by bureaucracy and this is not new. The restructuring of industry, of agriculture, saw as its first bold step a division between the political and economic spheres; a very bold step for a Communist Party to take, deliberately withdrawing the inept heads of cadres whose only asset was political slogan from interfering with the due process of getting on with the work. The restructuring of the administration involves promoting young, technical minded people, in each sector; in short the advent of the technocrat instead of the bureaucrat. It is fascinating to go to China today and to watch this administrative and industrial and agricultural restructuring; to follow it in every office, bureau, corporation, even in publishing houses and artists' associations. The immensity of the work undertaken, and the relative smoothness and speed with which it is proceeding, are worthy of attention. The acquisition of HGT, and the necessary trade and business relations with the power-holders of technology, the TNC, form part of this four modernization revolution. The Chinese state corporations enter into joint ventures with TNC and Western companies. Power in all its forms (hydroelectric, nuclear, coal, oil, etc.) is a main sector for development, and so is transport and communication–computer and microprocessor. They do not see joint ventures as relinquishing socialism, but, on the contrary, as fulfilling Lenin's tenet that socialism has to learn how to operate the big trusts as well as or even better than the TNC do. The Chinese road to socialism does not lose sight of the heart of the matter, the crux of all this endeavour, its ultimate *purpose*, which is to bring prosperity and raise living standards of *all* the people, and to do this as swiftly as possible.

Besides agriculture, industry, science and technology, there must also be the creation of new ethics and a new morality. For the way of all performance is through the human being. And we need spiritual aims as well as material ones. Without ethics, without morality, the valorization of humanity, our sense of purpose and endeavour cannot be achieved.

Modernization, then, also becomes a cultural consciousness; spiritual values are essentially pragmatic, the practical application of morality in all relationships. Already the youth in China are demanding with a new hunger new ideas and ideals; merely material satisfaction has never been enough for the human being. How far will they go along that road? Pretty far, and not so slowly. The knowledge revolution will certainly have an impact there.

Great discoveries and advances also need the passing or reassessment of old dogmas, a renaissance of cultures and traditions. Can then an ideal of "sharing", of being a satisfied individual *also* working ardently within the spirit of collective benefit, become China's road to socialism?

Without ethics, without morality, we perish. My friend Alvin Toffler, whom I rejoice to have introduced to China and who has been there recently, speaks of the total changes in society due to the Third Wave of Technology. He, as I am, is optimistic that, if the monopoly of technology in the hands of the few is broken, and there is decentralization and diversification, then also will arise, from the human mind, many diverse ideas and ideals, formulating new ethics and principles for living. I think this can happen, is, in fact, already happening now.

I am not pinning hopes on China alone; although I do feel that it is the only Third World country so far which is going to any great length in evolving a new ethic and a new morality in line with the knowledge revolution.

Looking forward, I do not envisage cataclysm, but a world which is livable; where not all problems will be solved, but where increasingly the "isms" that today create such artificial great walls will be looked upon as systems which had their validity, and have either been outgrown, or remain viable. Where increasingly linkage, interdependence, will force a dialogue, and co-operation. All this, of course, will take time. It will, as Ma Hong says, take "protracted fighting". But the world's conscience is aroused, and it will not go back to sleep.

I am an optimist. Anyone who has lived in Old China and seen China today would naturally be an optimist. There is no other way but faith and trust in humanity, however frail, imperfect and fallible it is. For fraternity is a sustaining virtue, the heightening of the human being's discovery of ourself. And today we are bound to each other as never before.

(1983)

A Personal Memory of Zhou Enlai

TO WRITE with any validity about the man still called by many Chinese "our beloved Premier Zhou Enlai" would require a large book. This short memoir can only attempt to convey the undiminished reverence and affection with which I, as millions of others, remember him. Whatever I have done in the 30 years since 1954, when I first talked with him in Beijing, is due to the impact he had on me, and to my conviction that he had an overall vision of the world, of relations between nations, which far outstripped that of any other contemporary statesman.

Zhou Enlai was loved all over China, and admired and respected in every other country. Even his hostile critics conceded his charisma, his drive, his intellect. No one could question his total integrity in service to his country.

Zhou was not only a statesman, a man who understood politics. His acumen and intelligence were honed by seeking, through a most able staff whom he had trained, information in all its forms. He thrived on debate, for he knew that only by argument, by listening to contrary views, could he acquire real knowledge. "Why do you agree with me? You want to disagree, then disagree," he would say, with that impish grin upon his face which was quite irresistible.

His capacity for total recall was legendary. He would remark: "Two years ago you said . . ." remembering something which I had forgotten. From the length of Egyptian cotton fibres to the influence of Yellow River silt on turbine palings; from the history of the twelfth-century kingdoms of southeast Asia to the banking procedures of Switzerland, his mind would roam, implacable in its accuracy, seeking and clutching at facts. It was this quality of brain power which fascinated those who approached him. Yet never would he make anyone feel silly or inadequate. "Well, we must both study the problem a little more," he would say when someone (me, for instance) would foolishly blurt something inapposite. And this would fill me with an urge for finding out; a drive which has never left me.

Zhou's capacity for work was staggering. Unrelenting, meticulous hours and days and months of work, never losing sight of the essential, but going over every detail. "The small things matter as well as the big ones," he would say. And for decades he pushed himself without respite, working till 4 or 5 in the morning, back again at work by 9. Sometimes he would go without sleep, working round the clock. Those of us privileged enough to see him would be called in the middle of the night for a talk, and he so galvanized us with his own vibrant energy that we forgot everything, forgot tiredness or hunger, imbued by the same devouring passion for getting the work done.

Those of his staff who worked with him through the years are stamped with what I shall call the "Zhou Enlai spirit," knowing life meaningless unless one gives all of it, all one's energy, to what one believes in. For a great cause needs the evidence of ALL our life, and this he taught me. Always to seek more knowledge, to reappraise one's own ideas: that was Zhou Enlai's gift to me.

Zhou Enlai was not only a formidable intellect and a man of action, whose deeds have shaped and built New China to an extent as yet not fully recognized; he was also a human being full of care and affection for others. He always had time, however busy, to inquire about the comfort of those who worked with him. He would make sure that the drivers had had their meals; that the waiters who served in the big receptions, the security personnel, were not neglected. From all over China people who needed help wrote to him. He cared for years for the orphaned children of friends he had known, and he never forgot a friend.

Testimonies of this care and concern are innumerable; I recommend, as one of them, the excellent memoirs by President Wang Bingnan of the Association for Friendship with Foreign Countries, who details a part of Zhou Enlai's life when Wang served under him at some important conferences and also in Chongqing. During the distressful years 1966 to his death in 1976, it is well known that Zhou Enlai protected and saved many people, as well as art monuments and libraries. Numberless are those who still recall how much he did then; and it is this capacity for caring for others which keeps his memory alive in the hearts of millions.

Zhou Enlai was the most frugal of men. Material comfort meant little to him. He was thrifty, walking instead of taking the elevator during the Great Leap Forward when there was a shortage of electric power. It was common knowledge that he wore his clothes longer than any other leader, and this was not for show, it was because he was keenly aware of China's poverty, of the need to save. "Do you know how many meters of (rationed) cotton we give for each newborn baby?" he asked me one day. So he would save for others, for he believed in giving an example of thrift and integrity, even in the smallest things. Only thus could the country build itself up, build for prosperity by thrift, saving, a total absence of corrupting greed.

I first saw Zhou Enlai in Chongqing in February 1941, after the sanguinary attack by Chiang Kaishek's armies upon the Communist New Fourth Army, right in the middle of the war against the Japanese invaders. Zhou made a speech then* and a vast crowd listened to him. But it was in June 1956, in Beijing, that I had my first interview with him. I went to his residence at Zhongnanhai, and he was at the door of his residence, his wife Deng Yingchao by his side. We talked for about two hours, and those two hours changed my life. We talked as if we were one family: and at the end Deng held my hand gently. "I believe you will think more about all this," she said.

I never thought of Zhou Enlai without thinking of his wife, Deng Yingchao. They were *together*, not only as a married couple, not only lifelong partners in the great cause of China's Revolution, but also as two people whose harmony was total, whose love was total because it was also founded upon common dedication, upon unswerving sacrifice for a common goal.

In the following years, I was enormously privileged to meet Premier Zhou Enlai again and again, often at night, but also sometimes in the day. And now I know that he was teaching me, teaching me to think, and that these hours he gave to me so unselfishly were the most precious gifts that life would ever give me.

From thence onwards, it seemed to me that I would despise myself did I not try, in my own way, to make China's Revolution, and the importance of China's tremendous creativity, known to the rest of the world. During those 30 years I was to do around 1,500 lectures, seminars, conferences, radio and television appearances throughout the world. "We must unknot all the knots," said Premier Zhou Enlai, speaking of the tense situation which prevailed in the late 1950s and erly 1960s, and which would lead, ultimately, to the Vietnam war, and to the dangerous confrontations which still exist today.

* See *Birdless Summer* by Han Suyin, Triad Granada and Jonathan Cape, London, 1984 edition, pages 214-19.

In 1959, when the border dispute with India produced another wave of anti-Chinese hysteria, it was a talk with Premier Zhou which enboldened me to visit Prime Minister Nehru.* Although this might have been futile, yet I continued later to see Madame Indira Gandhi, for whom I grew to have respect and great affection. In 1970 my Indian husband came to China, and Premier Zhou received us and talked at length about the border problems. "Your Premier is extraordinary. He knows the name of every peak, valley, river in the contested area," said my husband afterwards. He, too, "caught fire" and would continue to work for better relations between India and China; we believe that this is most important for the future of Asia.

In Autumn 1965, Premier Zhou received me again in Zhongnanhai. He talked about the Vietnam war, for he knew that in January 1966 I would attend a seminar at the University of Chicago in the USA on US-China foreign policy. I would do more lecture tours in the USA in subsequent years, and in 1968, at the University of North Carolina. Edgar Snow and I were gratified to realize that some of the things that Zhou Enlai had predicted in 1965 were coming true. By then, a process of change in US policy towards China was already obvious.

During the most distressful decade 1966 to 1976, Zhou Enlai kept China together. One day historians will recognize this, although at the moment a strange silence about his role during the decade of the "cultural revolution" seems to infect sinologists. He kept China from civil war, from chaos. He was deprived of 80 per cent of his staff, and kept working on and on; keeping in mind a global policy and vision, which historians will have to analyse. I cannot speak of these times here, but I can only say that Zhou had an enormous burden upon his shoulders, a burden no one else carried. I hope that one day, all emotion spent, Zhou Enlai's actions during those harrowing times will be understood.

By 1973, it was evident that Zhou Enlai, already thin, was getting thinner; but he seemed as brisk as ever, leaping out of a small car at the airport carrying his own briefcase, smiling and shaking hands with my husband and myself. "He's like a burning flame ... but he's getting almost transparent, he works too hard," said Rewi Alley, who also happened to be at the airport that day. I think that Zhou was then already touched by the disease which brought about his death. But none of us knew it then.

* See *My House Has Two Doors* by Han Suyin, Triad Granada and Jonathan Cape, London, 1980, pages 254-62.

On 1 October 1974, Zhou Enlai spoke at the Great Hall of the People. When he rose, clapping broke out among all of us, an enormous ovation, lasting many long minutes. It was homage, born of love, admiration, respect, for this man who had done so much, so much, an unbelievable amount, to keep China going. That was the last time I would see him in person, and hear his voice. "Unity," he said. "Let us keep united." This was an appeal, for at the time the division within China's leadership was very great. But the Gang of Four, sitting there, were only concerned with power for themselves. . . .

In the next year and a half, it was impossible for me to see Zhou Enlai. He was in hospital and inaccessible. In January 1975, looking very gaunt, he would address the National People's Congress, and proclaim the four modernizations of China.

Then came January 1976; that bleak, freezing day, when the news of his death stunned us all. In the street, people walked, tears streaming down their cheeks. Silence. What could one say? The fullest heart has no words for grief. Zhou Enlai was dead, and we all feared, feared for China. We felt bereaved, desperate.

But Zhou Enlai was not dead. His spirit lived on, among the people of China. His spirit was there, and so there was 5 April 1976, and it was obvious that the people of China had no use for the Gang of Four. Zhou Enlai's spirit lived on in all those who had the great good luck of serving him; in all those who, like myself, had the enormous privilege of hearing him. Today his speeches, statements, directives, whether about fundamental research in science or education; whether about culture or foreign policy, are being published. I hope that a new generation will read him, will be inspired by him, will realize that he is immortal, because he served China and the Chinese people with every cell in his body.

Deng Yingchao – Elder Sister Deng, as I call her – will forgive me for writing so inadequately about one of the greatest men of history. She has always been so kind to me, to my errors, coming to see me with flowers and the blossoms of affection. The abiding love for both Zhou Enlai and Deng Yingchao which today exists among the Chinese people will go on. Young people today are confused, seeking for a role model. They could have no better model, no more satisfying, fulfilling endeavour, than to learn from Zhou Enlai and Deng Yingchao.

(1986)

Land and Water in China

D
ESERTS are a problem for the whole world. This is due to different factors – geographic, climatic, ecological and human. Here are a few statistics; at present 38,437,770 square km of the world are desert or threatened by desert; of this 32.5 per cent is in Asia, 27.9 per cent in Africa, 16.5 per cent in Australia, 11.6 per cent in North and Central America, 8.9 per cent in South America and 2.6 per cent in Europe. In the past 50 years, the Sahara has spread a further 650,000 square km and a further 50–70,000 square km threaten to become desert every year. By the year 2000 one-third of the arable lands of the earth will have been lost, and 14 per cent of the world's people will be living in arid or semi-arid zones.

Desertification can be due to changes in the planet: in China, desert areas arose due to the rise of the Qinghai Tibet Plateau in the Pliocene epoch, when the Himalayas were pushed upwards by India joining the continent. The north-western plateaux are thus cut off from the southern moisture-laden winds, and mainly receive the arctic siberian winds which cause shifting sand dunes and arid loess. The latter though not technically desert, is threatening to become so. In the Pleistocene epoch, a period of aridity coincided with a late glacial period from 18,000 to 12,000 years ago when loess, called "Yellow Earth", and deserts were formed.

The Taklamakan is China's largest desert, covering about 500,000 square km. Its name means "the place where even birds die", and it is indeed a true desert with no life or vegetation at its centre. Gurbantunggut is the second largest, followed by the Korqin, Gobi and Tangkuli deserts, and the Hexi corridor semi-desert area. The provinces of Xinjiang, Qinghai, Gansu, Ningxia and Inner Mongolia are the areas most severely affected by desertification. Sixty-five per cent of China's desert is made up of crescent-shaped sand dunes, of varying size and mobility, which are described in old maps. The fixation of these sand deserts to prevent their extension is an extremely important task in combating desertification. The movement of the desert is mainly eastwards and southwards, but some also move northwards.

What are the causes of desertification in the past and present? I have already mentioned climatic and geographic factors from an early time, several million years ago. Desertification in China can be classified as ancient – i.e. from before the Han Dynasty 2,000 years ago, and the extension of deserts since then. There were many well-inhabited oases in the north-west which are now covered by sand dunes. Formerly thriving towns have since been uncovered and excavated. The historical records show a noticeable quickening of the desertification process in the last 2,000 years.

But there are also other causes and one is the destruction of forests. I have rather horrifying statistics from press articles about the loss of forests and those which have been lost already in the world: over 40 per cent of forests destroyed. Non-rational utilization of resources has also played its part in the loss of lakes and streams through deforestation. In China tree coverage has greatly diminished because water has been utilized for the fields and also trees used for firewood. This still goes on today and is a very great problem in China, which has a very small amount of forest. The policy for protecting forests first started in 1955 but has not been followed up adequately for several reasons.

Something can be done by organizing human activity and here I should say a few words about the nature of Chinese society. Wittfogel called China a hydraulic society (like Egypt) because the control of water was vital. In China's case, this was especially true of the north where the Han people were already threatened with aridity. The response of the Han people was to create this "hydraulic society", with the mobilization of manpower to sink wells and to build canals and dikes to control the flooding of the rivers. So the story of China is the story of the control of water. Wittfogel links this type of society with despotism, because of the numbers needed for this work. The emperor had to have the power to mobilize the mass of the people to carry out great public works. This is why people often mistook what happened after 1949. They thought it was something specifically to do with Communism that so many people were working to rebuild canals and dikes. It was in effect a continuation of what had gone before – there was nothing specifically "revolutionary" about mobilizing people to undertake these works, but now they were fired with enthusiasm knowing it was to better themselves.

All over north-west China we find ancient towns with canal

systems; there are abandoned cultivated lands covered now by sand, blown in from the desert. Secondary salination of soil was caused by badly planned irrigation over a long period and whole areas of cultivated land turned into scrub and sand mounds and, finally, into desert. Desertification of oases in the Hexi corridor, Gansu Province and in Inner Mongolia was accelerated by wars and invasions. Consider the Great Wall: it was not built only to keep out invaders, but possibly also to keep off the wind and sand dunes. If city walls were destroyed in war, the cities became covered in sand. There was also the problem of the bed of the Huang He or Yellow River, which would rise because of the loess silt carried down, causing the river to swell and flood. Hence the river's other name: "China's Sorrow".

If you read certain records of the fourth and sixth centuries, some areas of Shaanxi province, which are now arid, were described as having fresh streams flowing unceasingly. By the ninth century, however, the town of Tongwan was surrounded by shifting sands, as high as the city wall. It was abandoned for military and political purposes in the tenth century and disappeared beneath the sands. Inside the Great Wall in the Ming Dynasty, the land was recorded as being "all land of rich herbs fenced inside the great wall", but again there was large-scale destruction due to warfare. During the thirteenth and fourteenth centuries, there were areas in Gansu Province which had been denuded because the Mongols used them to pasture their horses. Even today, the people there talk about these horses. Early in the Qing dynasty (1644–1911) there was a policy to close in and fence the Ordos Steppe for livestock grazing. The policy was successful; the vegetation in the arid land was renewed, but then the area was opened to cultivation in the eighteenth century which disturbed the ecological balance and it became desert. In Inner Mongolia, the desertification was caused by over-grazing, not cultivation. There had been a policy of renewing the grasslands and in the past there was not too much population pressure. By the tenth century, however, the area became agricultural. There was also the problem of fuel collection. This removed everything on the surface and reduced land to a barren and unproductive state and inhabitants began to starve. When we have understood this, we can understand the resulting shifts of population.

In the thirteenth century, people moved southwards because they could no longer live where there was no water. While the centre of political power stayed in the north, the south became the economic base and the source of food for the country, with massive amounts of rice being moved north. This, in fact, had already begun in the eighth century. You can understand the enormous pressure on the green areas in the south to feed the north, and from this, the importance of the Grand Canal. The history of China has thus indeed been fashioned by the problem of land and water. Of course with the shift in population, the pressure on the northern lands diminished and the area recovered. However, with the pressures of the population increase of the eighteenth century, the cycle began again. We find therefore a correlation between over-utilization of resources by humans and the extension of desertification, especially at the margins of already desertified areas. This helps to explain shifts of population in Chinese history.

But now to contemporary times. Very little was done from the late nineteenth century until 1949. This period was one of great misery, and China was brought to a wretched condition. In the early 1950s conferences were first held on the importance of "stopping the deserts" and of "greening the land". 1959, the year of the Great Leap Forward, saw the first programme to control the sand dunes. It involved 22 study teams from universities working under the Chinese Academy of Sciences (CS) in the affected provinces. The first problem the Academy of Sciences started studying was how to stop the sands shifting. This led to the fixing of sand dunes by the planting of a long line of trees to act as shelters and also to green the land on which, in the early years, an enormous amount of money and time was spent. Some of these tree belts were successful, others were failures. The death rate of the trees was high because often there was insufficient water available for these tree belts stretching for three to four hundred kilometres. What was the rationale behind this planting? It was to stop the wind and, having stopped the wind, stop the sand. Some were planted to protect the new canals and reservoirs and also to prevent the railway tracks from being buried under the sand. Reports from 1960 onwards refer to the enormous infrastructure being built for water and soil conservation. The rationale was good but, to be perfectly honest, those working on the schemes did not quite understand the problem. (In 1979 I went to Gansu where they said they had planted 900 million trees in the past five years. I guessed that 70 per cent did not survive.)

State farms were being developed in the north in the 1960s. In the Tarim Basin, a large settlement was established on the edge of the desert. It used water coming down from the Tianshun mountains, and had fields as well as belts of trees specially suited for the desert area. Some farms were successful, but some did more harm than good as they added to the over-cultivation and salinity of arid land.

There were campaigns for tree planting on mountain slopes but the young trees were soon cut down for firewood.

There were also contradictions with the demands of industry. Water was diverted for dams to generate electricity for industry and the cities, which meant the loss of water downstream where there was already little water. The cutting down of trees for the new towns compounded the existing problem. The Head of the Desert Institute at Lanzhou told me: "We did not understand the relationship between loess and the desert, nor the total ecobalance of the whole land. This has meant several years of study."

During the Cultural Revolution (1966–76) this work went on but, due to the push for more grain, the hillsides were denuded and areas fit for grazing were given over to maize, and pasture land was given over to cereal planting. Owing to the lack of qualified personnel many plans remained very localized and small scale – they still do. Often provision is not even on a district level, never mind a national one. When I discussed the damage done to trees by gathering firewood in Jiangxi province, the local Party Secretary said, "Where will we get coal instead?" So when you travel around you see that the problem is very difficult. There are so many people wanting so many things – how can everything be provided? Lowering of the water table has been serious in the last few years, both in the northeast and round Beijing. The level has dropped about 20 metres in 30 years.

There is also the increasing aridity and desertification of the loess land. What is loess? It is wind-blown dust of minute yellow-grey grains. The thickness of the unstratified deposit can be over 250 feet and the texture can be as fine as talcum powder. It is prone to vertical cleavage, creating the unique landscape of northern China, which is shown in the film *Yellow Earth*. In Shaanxi and Gansu, caves are scooped out of the loess, but given its easily-disturbed structure, a whole hill can collapse after a storm. Below the loess blanket lie great coal seams, but railways have to run through it and often tracks are washed away by rain. The Huang He's silt is made up of loess – that is why it is called the "Yellow River". Because of this silt, the bed constantly rises. Unless constant watch is kept on the river banks, there is danger of flooding. But the change of the loess to desert is proceeding, and ways have to be found to stop the process. In the last 50 years, 50,000 square km have deteriorated and there is another 150,000 square km threatened by the end of the century. Having said all this, which sounds pessimistic, I should say that in China no one is pessimistic because there is always another day and they have coped with the river for 2,000 years.

One problem is the Chinese intelligentsia and its élitism. When I went to see people at the Desert Institute in Gansu I found that it was only 1978 that they became a separate institute on their own – for so long they had been part of other bodies, not getting any recognition. There is also a lack of personnel. You would be surprised how few trained people want to go there to continue the work in the Institute or in forestry stations. They want to stay in the cities and are not prepared to take up the challenge. In some forests, there is still pressure to maintain the cutting rate and hence be profitable. So there has to be a comprehensive policy to preserve forests without demanding too much timber from them. Often the contradictory results are due, not to ill will, but to the fact that local cadres do not understand what they are doing.

The vicious circle of desertification must be stopped. The enlargement of cultivated land is bad because it increases wind erosion, which leads to decreased yields, requiring further enlargement of cultivated land and so on. The principal reason for vast areas of steppe being degraded is over-grazing, which should now be strictly controlled. This is a challenge for the reformers, as peasants are over-grazing as a result of the liberalization of the agricultural policy which allows them to produce more. Cultivation pressure is being relieved by other means as industry has drawn a lot of people away and these areas are not densely populated. But other problems remain: the constant need for firewood, and the misuse of water resources which comes with the growth of cities and industry. With modernization, everyone wants flush toilets – not only does this use up a great deal of water, but peasants are no longer clearing the waste to take off to the land as they used to because they now have chemical fertilizers. This is just one example of the use of water by a city and the differing demands on the supply of water.

Attempts are now being made to stop the loess area from deteriorating by re-greening this area. It has been realized that the loess has to be tackled and not the desert. You cannot grow trees easily, so it is done with grass and bushes. Extremely interesting work has been done to discover the most appropriate bush not only for binding the sand but also for use as fuel. I have been to see it and it looks excellent. I have visited 18 districts in Gansu. In one of them, the slopes of loess are terraced and varieties of grass are tested. This is done on a contract system by farmers, with a subsidy from the State. Incentives are given to the peasants – not only are they paid 7 yuan per hectare of grass, but they are given one ton of coal per year per family to plant forest grass. Educational work is carried on throughout the area. The *ningtiao*, which comes from the USSR, is the bush which does best, and has replaced several other experiments. The bush has a depth below around five times that of the growth above ground and it can be used for fuel, for sheep grazing and for making baskets.

In addition there needs to be population control. Agriculture should be centred in protected valleys and whole areas should be set aside to grow forage for animals to be fed in barns – the animals must not be allowed to graze. If these current measures are carried through, then in 30 years' time there will be quite a lot done. But the main problem is that there are not enough motivated people to do this important work. Those who are doing the work are isolated, with few direct contacts abroad and virtually no opportunity to travel outside. Foreign visitors go to lecture in Beijing and Shanghai, but not to these areas where they are really needed. The people working on this vital issue of desertification and its control are the ones who should be visited and be able to go abroad.

(1987)

Two weeks in Beijing

THERE were black Mercedes with red lettering indicating they were army vehicles; antiquated "Red Flags" conveying government officials in compliance with the new regulations that Chinese cars be used for all functions; and some Toyotas, including the one placed at my disposal. In procession we rolled to the Eight Talisman Hill, Babaoshan, where national heroes, revolutionary martyrs and high Party officials lie buried or rest in ash urns on shelves in the old-fashioned pavilions.

A ceremony was being held for the late Zhou Yang, once president of the Chinese Writers Association. Zhou Yang had been, in the 1950s, a hated man, responsible for sending many a "rightist" writer to the remote provinces in the wake of the Hundred Flowers repression of 1957. Yet today many of his erstwhile victims crowded the alleyway leading to the room where his embalmed body awaited our three bows. As in a family there is forgiveness, so had Zhou Yang been forgiven; he had apologized to those he had injured. I caught sight of Wang Meng, also a "rightist". Wang Meng, my good friend, was reported dismissed, arrested – yet here he was. "Wang Meng!" I called. He turned, we clasped each other. "The Western newspapers say...." He laughed: "I resigned in March. I want to go back to writing." The next day I saw him in his beautiful house and later invited him to dinner. He asked me about royalties and contracts with foreign publishers. "I've been translated in Italy, Greece, the USSR – one hundred thousand copies in Russian. But in China for the last three years publishers have refused to print more than five hundred copies of any book of mine. They prefer the porn from Hong Kong because it sells better. 'Who wants to read about the past?' they tell me."

I had come to Beijing to explode, to reprove, armed with fifty questions, collected from many scholars and universities abroad. The student demonstrations in Beijing had filled me, like millions of others, with joy. "I am so proud to be a Chinese now," many of my

234

overseas friends said. We shared an electric euphoria, a high hope. It came from the orderly, disciplined marches of the students, from the crowds that supported them. They were demonstrating against corruption, against nepotism, against inflation, for more "glasnost". "Never have the people in Beijing behaved so well. There is an ambiance of fraternity, of solidarity," friends in Beijing told me.

On 10 May 1989 I had sent a telegram of congratulations through the Association for Friendship, my usual host in China, praising both the students for their patriotism and discipline, and the authorities for their restraint. It seemed to me a great opportunity for the Party to rejuvenate itself, to incorporate the young students, through advisory bodies or councils and make them involved, participate in serving their country better. The "understanding gap" between the ageing leaders and what is called in China the fourth generation was very wide. It had to be bridged. I had already sent suggestions along those lines in 1987. There was urgent need for "dialogue", I had written. As I went from institute to university, lecturing, among other things, on "The History of Democracy in the World", I had become fully aware of the gap. Frustration and discontent among the young educated was obvious. There seemed no way for their feelings and views to be productively channelled or understood.

After 1985, the obvious economic difficulties disturbed me: corruption, hyper-consumerism, wasting of valuable foreign exchange to buy non-essential goods such as cosmetics, cars, beer, cigarettes, refrigerators, the stranglehold on essential raw materials by high-ranking (or even low-ranking) cadres. It was increasingly worrisome. China's national industries were *not* being modernized, but stagnated or even closed down. In a land with so little electric power, there were extravagances. Cookers and air-conditioners were the rage, while factories lacked electric power. I lectured against all this, citing the example of India. India had, for decades, restricted the entry of non-essential consumer goods. Indian officials rode in Indian cars, drank Indian beer, smoked Indian cigarettes. Indian women wore clothes made in India. Only after Indian industries were solidly established was a trickle of foreign products allowed.

I had sympathized with the student demonstrations of 1986; they were directed against the indiscriminate purchase of hundreds of thousands of Toyotas for use by the Party élite and for setting up taxi companies run by Party high-rankers. "Do you realize that within three years these cars will cost you exactly double in spare parts?" I had asked a Party cadre. He ignored me. I decline to criticize any single person; the fault lies in the total leadership, a lack of long-term and careful planning, absence of a holistic view of the process of modernization.

But the spiral of corruption, inflation, loss of foreign exchange, the greedy buying of non-essential luxuries, the deliquescence in integrity everywhere, the loss of idealism, the network of black-marketeers, carpet-baggers, ex-convicts now become millionaires and operating gangs of their own, all this was known. It grew so rapidly that one could scarcely believe it had happened.

In the countryside, the disbandment of communes, the return of land to the individual peasant, hailed as a major step forward, had indeed at first appeared to stimulate production, lead to an increase in peasant income. I, too, for a while believed in the agricultural miracle, the *monetarization* of the countryside, the hugest market in the world. But there was a limit, which fell as abruptly as a steel curtain on the blissful scene. The peasant no longer planted rice or wheat, which brought in very little money. He concentrated on cash crops. There was more money to be made by peddling, running to the cities to hire himself out in construction work, leaving his wife to cope with their patch of land. Arable land in China is less than 7 per cent of the world's total, on which 22 per cent of the world's peoples must be fed. The size of the average farm in south China is often diminutive, perhaps a fraction of an acre. How could agriculture be modernized in such conditions? And now seed, fertilizer, was being hoarded by unscrupulous new "companies" (run by Party cadres), which bought and sold them across provinces to raise the price, until the farmer found it difficult to get good seed or fertilizer except at exorbitant prices. Privatization of land also led to the return of male domination in the family. Women were no longer paid for their work and again became dependent on husbands and fathers. Child marriage, arranged marriages, the sale of women and children, female infanticide, returned in full force.

As for the laws, there was no structure, no apparatus to enforce them properly and the Party cadres circumvented them. Tax collecting proved a dangerous job; a good many were killed trying to collect taxes. Decentralization, without the installation of proper local controls, led to a confused situation. The state lacked money to pay the peasants for their grain or cotton, and promissory notes were issued, which were not redeemed for many months.

While this went on, the Western press, and "experts" as well as journalists, wallowed in praise of the "freedom" that came with privatization, jubilated over a "capitalist" change. But this was *savage* capitalism, what President Mitterrand called an "unacceptable" brand of capitalism, the country being ripped off by the new compradore bureaucrats, the Party cadres. No wonder the young were frustrated, cynical, losing the spirit of service to their country. With inflation, it was the intelligentsia, scholars, academics and civil servants who suffered most. A university professor earned half or one-third what a bicycle repair man could make.

In a major medical institute, 80 per cent of the students had applied for research jobs, which meant an opportunity to go abroad, since clinical work for foreign students is not allowed in many Western countries. Clinical work was demanding and less well paid than "research". Physicians in hospitals were overworked or simply did not attend to their jobs, preferring to go into private practice.

In October 1988 I told my friend Dr G. Oldham, director of the Science Policy Research Institute of Sussex University, that I felt there would be a "coup" in China. For China is a Third World country, and when economies go wrong, there is political trouble.

What took place at Tiananmen Square, the bungling, the overharsh and brutal reaction, the deplorable loss of life, has been written, dramatized, even embellished with lurid extravagance, throughout the world. I did not believe, and am still not convinced, that there was at the time a fully formed "counter-revolutionary plot". I felt the student movement represented genuine popular grievances. In my talks with some forty intellectuals, including renowned scholars such as Xia Yen, seasoned diplomats such as Huang Hua, there was not one who did not show distress at the heartrending episode, the killing of innocent people. Demonstrations, large or small, occurred in 70 cities. Millions of young people, as in the cultural revolution, crowded the trains without paying for tickets. The fact that the students were increasingly infiltrated by hooligans is also well known.

Fifty days is a very long time for any government to put up with such upheavals, as Henry Kissinger remarked. He said that "no government in the world" would have not reacted. Even so, the killing and wounding of innocent people in the avenue leading to Tiananmen Square *cannot be condoned*. It is said that the army was provoked by being attacked first. But the whole episode was so badly handled that it will take a long time to know exactly the sequence of events.

The aftermath is a situation where alienation of the young and of many urbanites, chiefly in Beijing but in other cities too, is hard to cope with. It will be an uphill task to restore trust between the intellectuals and the Party. Harassment of intellectuals, trying to "ferret out" all possible conspirators, the questioning of everyone, is the wrong way to set about restoring trust and confidence. It will prove counter-productive.

One of the purposes of my journey was to plead that there should be no repetition of the anti-intellectual political movements that had occurred in the past. Therefore, I drew up a list of questions for the new Party Secretary, whom I was to meet.

I arrived in Beijing on 29 August and saw Mr Jiang Zeming, the new Party Secretary, at 3 p.m. on 1 September. Our talk lasted three hours.

Jiang Zeming looks like a prosperous Shanghai businessman. He has a happy, roundish face behind thick glasses. He received me in his office at Zhungnanhai and at once established an easy informality. Two weeks before my arrival I had sent a 13-page memorandum of protests, criticisms and queries, incorporating not only my own views but those of several eminent personalities in England and the USA. "I have read your memorandum. I know you came to find out what happened. This was courageous." He gave a sketch of his own background. Trained as an electrical engineer, he too was an intellectual, from a family of intellectuals, his grandfather a painter. The family originated from Yangzhou, noted for its scholars and artists. "Tsinghua University, Chiaotung University – my family and myself were students at one or the other. Therefore I understand something about students and about intellectuals." He was also very aware of the impact and power of the "image", through the information media. He had made a study of the communication revolution and written about it.

Jiang referred briefly to the demonstrations in Shanghai in 1986, which, in some ways, were possibly "more difficult" to manage than those in 1989. He referred to an incident where the students had surrounded his – the mayor of Shanghai's – office and had been dispersed without bloodshed. The young were extremely vulnerable to outside propaganda, and the fault lay in China's organs of communication, "the pen". They were not only inadequate in "hardware", with faulty apparatus, slow transmission, lack of distribution to the outside world, but even more so in "software", with uninteresting, badly thought out programmes, which did not meet the demands and expectations of the viewers. He referred to a new instrument "like a small box" which could beam directly what was happening from Beijing to Tokyo, and had been installed by foreign TV media on Tiananmen Square. Everything that happened was immediately picked up by television networks in Tokyo. During the events, Voice of America had doubled, quadrupled, its output, broadcast 24 hours a day in Chinese and other languages, spreading rumours, inciting the students, while the Chinese media failed totally to come out, and there had also been a "total lack of direction" in their transmissions.

Jiang said the students had been well organized, and it was precisely this organization that showed there were people behind the movement. It was also strange how the slogans changed. There had been *direction* in all this; "some of us were aware of it early, but others only much later." There had been turbulent demonstrations in front of Zhung Nanhai for some days. The police restrained them, but after some days the police were exhausted. There were too few police, while the students came in relays. The students established checkposts and examined everyone who passed in or out. Jiang himself went through one of these checkposts "in disguise".

It was not true that there had been no attempts at dialogue. Many of the city leaders had spent hours trying to talk with the students. But the students kept escalating their demands. The slogans also changed, finally becoming anti-government. Jiang emphasized that the vast majority of the students did not know they were being used; of this the government was aware. But behind it all was a well-organized nucleus. And there was documentary evidence, television evidence, telephone evidence, that the students were receiving orders from such people as the wife of the astrophysicist Fang Lizhi, Madame Li Shuxian and others. Whenever agitation looked like flagging, a fresh flood of rumours, actively propagated by the Voice of America, started again.

Jiang now diverged into personal anecdote. He had been to San Francisco when the city was twinned with Shanghai. Asked by the Mayor to sing a song, he had recalled a few learned as a youth from "One Hundred Best Songs", in English. He had also sung some Chinese opera. President Bush's brother was his friend, and he was looking forward to seeing him. (Mr Bush came to China some days later.)

Most of the students were innocent, and patriotic, but the whole event made one think deeply. Deng Xiaoping had summed it up when he said what had occurred was the "micro-climate", reflecting the "macro-climate" abroad, the "big wind" sweeping Eastern Europe. But, Jiang hinted – without actually saying so – there might have to be second thoughts on the matter. In fact this was a "first attack" on China's socialist system, seeking to destabilize it, utilizing objective factors, discontent, inflation, corruption. He knew I did not believe in a plot, I did not believe that the students wanted to overthrow the government. This was true for the immense majority of students and intellectuals who had taken part. But it would become clear one day that they had been used. (The foundation in Paris of the Democracy Front, the declarations of Mr Wuerkaise, made quite openly, that the purpose was to overthrow the government, statements of Front leaders that they wanted to restore capitalism and a market economy, appear to bear out the Chinese government's contention that there was a "plot".)

Jiang Zeming spoke of the visit of the economist Friedmann to Beijing some months ago, when he had talked with him. Some of Friedmann's theories were worthy of study, but others were totally inappropriate. Jiang had discussed agriculture with him and pointed out that the USA made large investments in its own agriculture and heavily subsidized it. "America, in fact, does a great deal of planning in her economy, while preaching laissez-faire to others." In China, agriculture was a problem; there would have to be much larger investments in that sector, part of the total rethinking of how reforms should be conducted. Of course the open-door policy, economic reforms, would continue. There would be even wider opening.

Freud and Sartre had taken the place of Marx and Mao in the minds of young people in China, who did not know their own history. His father's generation, his generation, had loved their country and returned to serve it, but today's 20-year-olds had lost the notion of patriotism and service to the country. Their minds were swamped with illusions, with dreams, like colour-TV sets. They hankered for a life which did not correspond to reality but which they thought was theirs by right, a life preferably to be spent in the Western countries. Yet students were so much better off today than their fathers had been. In the university canteens they wasted a prodigious amount of food. "They have lost touch with the reality of their own country."

Jiang knew I was extremely concerned that the intellectuals who had participated should not be treated harshly. "We must, and we will, be very careful to differentiate between those really involved in a plot against the government and those who merely demonstrated, or gave money, but did not plot." The hunger strikers would not be punished. The whole problem must be studied in depth, seriously, carefully.

He, everyone in the government, was saddened by the loss of life. The army had had most strict instructions not to fire, but they had been attacked, violence had erupted; soldiers had at first fired in the air, but later they had to defend themselves against the thousands of hooligans. Very few students had been on the streets where the killing occurred. As for Tiananmen Square itself, everyone now knew that it had been evacuated, and no one had died on the square.

There was the testimony of Taiwan artist Hou Dejian, and there were others. No government in the world, after 50 days of turbulence, would have not reacted. There were thousands of hooligans in Beijing, and at the end they had done a lot of harm. There were many problems. Unequal, irrational income distribution. Corruption and nepotism. I said that I had read of his "seven proposals" to curb inflation, stop the sons and daughters of high cadres from doing business, etc., and that this was a good beginning. Jiang said there was much more to do. More money must go into fundamental research. China must develop her own capabilities, practise *self-reliance*, not reliance on the West.

Although I had been only two days in Beijing I had begun my investigations among the intelligentsia and had found a few cases of false accusations and arrests. Jiang said yes, this did happen, but he reiterated that there would be "very few" who would be punished.

I concluded by talking of the study sessions going on among the intelligentsia "to understand the true nature" of the events. Was not this harassment? It was humiliating for the intelligentsia. Jiang again assured me that "all due care" would be taken. Our talk ended at 6 p.m. Obviously Jiang Zeming, having just come into his job, was still trying to find his feet. I felt that I should see him again, in a few months time, when the rethinking would have taken hold.

I have known vice-premier Yao Yilin for some years. There is an affinity, since he was a student at Tsinghua in the 1930s when I was at Yenching University. His English is excellent. He is a forthright, at times charming, individual. It was the afternoon of 9 September and he received me at No. 17 Fisherman's Terrace. The interview was followed by dinner, altogether three and a half hours.

In our last three meetings I had told him I was worried about the economy. "We are building five-star hotels but the schools in the countryside are crumbling." He was now called a "hardliner", in that specious way in which the media make up our minds for us without letting us really grasp a man's personality. If he was a hardliner, then so had I been, since early 1986.

"Economics indeed has been one of the motor forces in the recent turmoil," said Yao. He divided the last ten years into two periods, "before and after 1984". "Everything became different after 1984." Before, agriculture was thriving. It was in the passage that year from rural to urban reform that troubles emerged. How to handle the link between theory and the practice of economic reforms was a very difficult thing.

Yao Yilin said the return of land to the peasants and the abolition of communes had been very popular, and at first all had gone well. But this was because of the enormous amount of long-term investment in agriculture that had taken place over the decades since 1958. (In the much maligned Great Leap Forward, as some American economists admit, hydraulic infrastructural works had permitted more than 40 per cent of China to become drought-free at all times.) Wells and reservoirs and canals, land improvement and the setting up of fertilizer plants had contributed to increased productivity.

It was through the communes, the mobilization of peasant labour – which represented a considerable investment – that China's advance had been fuelled. China was able to live, and even progress, without outside aid. But the peasants' lot had remained static, and so land liberalization with its accompanying hike in individual income had been enthusiastically received and a great boost. (Here I wondered whether this popularity helped to stabilize the government, but Yao went on talking and I did not interrupt him.)

Excellent results in agriculture lasted until 1984, but there had been no new agricultural investment, no new hydraulic infrastructure. On the contrary, there was neglect, no upkeep of dykes and reservoirs. Land to the individual family made mobilization of peasants for public works almost impossible. Material stimulus was present, increased income for the individual, but these were short-term increments; long-term improvement plans were *not* devised. The contract and responsibility system of the rural sector was now applied to industry in urban areas. A dangerous slide towards decentralization, out of control, with only material stimulus in view. "Everything now became short-term: make money today and to hell with tomorrow." No long-term planning. "Some economists," said Yao, "operated on the simplistic idea that hyper-consumerism was good for the economy." There were now enormous demands and expectations, and inability to fulfil them. Whose economy was benefited by hyper-consumerism? Certainly not China's. Everything now veered to a "get rich quick" basis. As a result, *look to the*

West; buy from the West. "This has sapped China's own industries, which have been grievously harmed," said Yao.

There was the problem of oil and coal. China's Tach'ing oilfield had operated successfully for many years, but now the wells were getting exhausted, oil extraction was more difficult and far more expensive while the need for oil had multiplied twenty times or more. Coal was also a problem. Villagers had been encouraged to dig their own coal using primitive methods, but China's large mines had not been modernized. This was another example of short-sighted, short-term practices. There was a lack of raw materials in many essential industries, but non-essential goods were turned out to make more money. "For a while we wore the face of a false prosperity."

There were a lot of low-productivity fields. A strategy must be devised to ensure high yields, Yao said. (I think this means we shall see some measure of return to state farms with mechanization in certain areas.) Grain was a problem. The price paid to the peasant for cereal production must be raised. Because of "false prosperity", the peasants had built houses on good arable land. This had to be checked. The system of new townships and rural-town enterprises were, obviously, not favoured by Yao Yilin. Although I would hear many contrary arguments from other sources, Yao said that these were inefficient, produced poor-quality goods, wasted needed raw material and resources, and were the foundation of a vast network of bribery and corruption, "including prostitution of women". It was "one large black market". It did not add any material benefit to the country's productivity.

Because of the economic changes, a floating population had been created, due to unemployment in the countryside. These people now came into the towns (some 40 million of them, according to other sources). There was delinquency, theft, "vandalism on the railways" with bands of peasants assaulting the trains. (According to another source, some of the bands had crude, home-manufactured guns.) The peasant, once he had tasted city life, did not wish to return to rural areas. This situation could not be quickly resolved; it would take at least three years.

Concerning the June events and the student demonstrations, Yao was terse. There had been a "strategic victory" but "tactical defeat". Victory because the socialist state had been maintained, but defeat because the aftermath was serious. In the minds of young people there was much confusion. Many intellectuals were not clear about the issues involved. Yao blamed Zhao Zeyang. Because of Zhao, "nothing was done for a long time". The turbulence in front of

Zhungnanhai had been quite severe. "At one time we were afraid of being kidnapped by the students." I felt that, for men like Yao, the Cultural Revolution and the Red Guards were still a vivid memory and possibly had conditioned their reaction to the student demonstrations.

There had been outside intervention, some "foreign personages" as well as Fang Lizhi. The latter had said that he wanted China to be run by "foreigners", said Yao. (I have heard this allegation six months earlier, in March 1989, when Fang had lectured in Beijing University and reportedly said that Americans should be asked to run China.) Fang and these other unspecified foreigners had all been lecturing at the "democracy salon" in Beijing University, a salon organized by Wang Dan, a student leader now arrested.

We ended talking specifics, again concerning several intellectuals. I stressed that there should be no over-reaction. The word "counter-revolutionary" was a vague but dangerous one, full of threat, a portmanteau word which might mean anything. Yao Yilin by then was looking tired and I told him I would write to him, with more questions, later in the year.

What is the prognosis? Will the present government be able to take matters in hand, to abolish or curb corruption and inflation, nepotism, to avoid further tumult and eruptions of discontent, especially potential ones in a countryside that is going to feel the brunt of many millions of unemployed being thrown out of the cities and returned to the rural areas?

Will the economic sanctions announced, the level of present indebtedness, the pressures to repay in 1991 a substantial amount of the money borrowed, not precipitate another crisis of confidence and hence of ability to manoeuvre?

There are other questions. The statement that "the open door will be maintained, opened even more" may possibly be seen as a contradiction to the statement that "measures against bourgeois liberalization" must be firmly applied....

Some intellectuals in China were extremely blunt in their talk. There had been "too much negation of Mao Zedong and what he had done," they told me. Though Mao had failed, we must see his work in perspective. Some American economists have objectively analysed the ideas of an *alternate* model of development which was behind the Leap. In the same way, the Cultural Revolution, so much abominated, was an attempt at vast, populist "democratization". Though a failure, its impact on the young in China persists today, and in some respects can be found in the events of 1989. It must be studied more carefully and with less emotionalism and partiality than hitherto. This trend is already seen among certain scholars in China.

I was impressed at the frankness, the critical spirit that I found in many of the intellectuals I interviewed, some of them well known throughout China. They were seasoned men, veterans of many political movements. The consensus, a consensus shared by some of the leaders themselves, is that the fault lay in the Party itself, in its way of conducting the government. There is a great deal of heart-searching undoubtedly going on.

Many – almost all – of the intelligentsia felt that the armed response to the protest movement was "possibly" over hasty, ill thought out, "an over-reaction", and that other ways might have been devised, with more caution, less dramatic and as effective.

The events did introduce an element into politics that so far had been ignored, though constantly present throughout the rule of the Communist Party since 1949. That is the PLA, the army. The army was the factor that brought the Communist Party to power. It was the army which, in 1959, decided against Peng Dehuai, and gave its support to Mao at the famous Lushan meeting. Through the Cultural Revolution, Mao was forced to call in the army to quell the anarchy that took place when he gave the young, in the name of "vast democracy", almost total licence against his own party bureaucracy. But, as Yen Jiachi, now the head of the "Democratic Front" recently inaugurated in Paris, says himself – and he is a historian – during the Cultural Revolution the army was a protective element, protective of the vast masses of the people. The comment today is that "never did the people in the streets expect the army to fire upon them". But that army elements fired in self-protection is also acknowledged by some eye witnesses. However, the response was exaggerated and uncontrolled. One can only say that any soldiers, when attacked and when not properly guided, respond by firing around them. One source told me that the troops employed were convinced they were facing vast crowds of "counter-revolutionary hooligans" and something went wrong with their radio apparatus so orders from higher officials were cut off. Whether this is rumour or truth, the government should investigate what really happened to cause some indiscriminate firing during that June night.

This in no way should be laid as a responsibility upon individual soldiers. Soldiers always react by firing, and there are many cases where this happened in other countries, including France, where "bavures" among policemen and other security forces are a common feature. However, this army reaction has created much bitterness and resentment among the people. And much must be done to palliate these wounds, which so far has not been done.

In order to enforce the restructuring, the curbing of corruption, at local and provincial level as well as generally, the army, or para-military forces, will have to be used. For this delicate task, total discipline is necessary. This brings the question: how good is the army? It is far more united than Western reports say, but it also has its sources of corruption, as was revealed in a book published by a young author in China. What is the competence of the younger officers? What will happen when the veteran top leaders still in charge disappear?

What is the threat to the present government of the "Democratic Front" abroad? Certainly, the Front will almost automatically be financed – indirectly, if not directly – by Taiwan.

According to some of the intellectuals both abroad and in China, the threat is "inside China, not from outside". If the Party regains control, and is successful in enforcing economic reforms, there should be little impact. In December 1988, in Hong Kong, I had already hinted – hinted only, since it sounded so outrageous – that "sooner or later", when and if Taiwan reunites with the mother country, China would have to operate something similar to a "two-party" system, or at least expand and encourage a "loyal opposition".

In order to progress in the restructuring announced today, it is essential, I think, that structures be set up to engage the Chinese people, the eight non-Communist parties among them, in *more* participation, involvement and discussion with the ruling party. These structures *must* be devised, and swiftly in the next three years.

Can this be done? Will it be done?

Within the Party today, there are some men who have *not* seen the necessity for more participation, and who still think in terms of pre-1949. "Even Mao Dzedong could accept criticism ... but now we have people who cannot stand a word of criticism," said one embittered person to me. Other Party high-rankers do realize there must be change in the Party itself. The publication of Deng Xiaoping's article, "Party members *must accept* supervision", may be a sign in that direction.

Finally, because the Chinese people are essentially a moral people, they need a model, combining "correct ideology" with pragmatic, down-to-earth implementation. Combining patriotism with a world-wide outlook, clarity of vision with meticulous, well-thought-out planning.

Such a model – in fact the only person who can stand the test of time and the zigzags of change – is Zhou Enlai, the late regretted Prime Minister of China. He should be studied in depth. This seems to have already begun, at least in the Ministry of Foreign Affairs, where his way of conducting negotiations, his diplomatic subtlety, his wide-ranging knowledge, his thirst for information beyond the rigid views of professional Marxists – and I am well-placed to know, having had contacts with him from 1956 until 1972 – is now set up for intensive study.

There is more to Zhou Enlai than foreign affairs. His defence of the intellectuals; his ideas on a "common united front", which he thought should persist for many decades and involve also the Guomindang, the party now ruling in Taiwan; his numerous articles and speeches and his actions to promote education, to promote fundamental research, to expand scientific training; all this, which has stood the test of time, should be studied again. This could serve as a *beginning* to clarify thinking in a party which, at the moment, exhibits ideological confusion, and where opaqueness in many vital areas persists.

(September 1989)